DUSTOFF

NO COMPROMISE
NO RATIONALIZATION
NO HESITATION

FLY THE MISSION!

i

Although the author and publisher have made every effort to ensure the accuracy and completeness of information contained in this book, we assume no responsibility for errors, inaccuracies, omissions, or any inconsistency herein. The author challenged the organizational leadership when he served with that unit in Vietnam. All efforts have been made to conceal the identity of those people he disagreed with regarding leadership style. Any slights to other people, places, organizations or units are unintentional.

First printing 2003

ISBN   0-9741256-0-1

LCCN   2003111913

ATTENTION CORPORATIONS, UNIVERSITIES, COLLEGES, AND PROFESSIONAL ORGANIZATIONS: Quantity discounts are available on bulk purchases of this book for educational or gift purposes. Book excerpts, 'Guys in the Back' and an electronic format can be obtained by request. For more information contact Wild 'n Woolly Publishing PO Box 731452 Puyallup, Washington 98373 telephone (253-906-2938) or through www.dustoff40.com

Foreward by A.J. Bergeron (COL, Ret) and coached by his bride, Judy.
Initial edits by Ann Ryan and Larry Kipp, PhD
Proof reading by Carolyn Perkins
Final edit by Lori Vermillion
Cover Design by Dan Campos, www.luminary1.com
Back Cover Design by Lori Vermillion
Printed by Print NW, Puyallup, Washington

'GUYS in the BACK'

All to often in Army aviation, pilots feel the world revolves around them. If the truth could be known, the "guys in the back" were really the ones who made it happen.

An unarmed medical evacuation helicopter in Vietnam was crewed by four people, generally in their late teens or very early twenties. The "guys in the back" were our crewchief and medic. Both were integral members of the team—commonly known as DUSTOFF.

We entrusted the crewchief with our lives everyday we flew, for he is the one that performed the never-ending daily maintenance on the helicopter. He ensured the myriads of components were maintained within prescribed tolerances. Daylight, darkness, the blazing heat of 'summer' or the monsoon rains that could chill a person to the bone were his operating environments. Pilots often left him with a helicopter damaged either by combat or through their own mistakes. In either case, we always knew that the "guys in the back" could get us flying again!

"Doc", as our medics were affectionately known, rode in the "back" with the other guy—the crewchief. With wounded on board, "doc" became "god." Pilots listened intently to him! The wounded entrusted life and limb to the medic who they prayed had the skill to keep them alive long enough to reach the hospital. Time and time again, doc brought the dead back to life through the magic healing powers he seemingly possessed. There were times, even with all of his wisdom and skill, he could not coach life back into a damaged and war beaten body. More wounded lay on the floor of his helicopter—crying out

in anguish from the wounds that had been inflicted upon them—
he had to tend to the living, the Chaplin would tend to the dead.
The "guys in the back" could do no more.

Medics were cross-trained to do basic helicopter maintenance.
Crewchiefs learned basic emergency medical care. As a team,
they ensured the helicopter was mission ready. As a team, they
cared for the wounded during the fast trip from the LZ to the
medical facility. No stronger team or bond between two people
can ever be found than that formed between the "guys in the
back."

In tight LZs, it was the "guys in the back" who kept the chopper
clear. On the ground, they were the ones who jumped out in
harm's way to load the wounded. A hoist mission in a hot LZ
often found one of the "guys in back" receiving a "free ride"
down on the jungle penetrator to help load the wounded. The
"guys in the back" made it all come together.

The heat of day, darkness of night, marginal weather or withering
enemy fire could not prevent this dedicated team from
accomplishing their mission. It was truly my pleasure, as one
of the "guys up front" to fly with the "guys in the back."

Steve Vermillion
Dustoff 40
1969

Acknowledgments

Those that I flew with as pilots and crewmembers made this book a reality since we served together under the most difficult of circumstances. A special thanks to Armond "Si" Simmons, Rob Spitzer, Mike Casper, Larry Kipp, Del Williams and Richard Dean for sharing recollections of missions from long ago. Through their assistance, the stories are as accurate as our feeble minds can assemble. A thanks to the men of the Black Lions 1st Battalion, 28th Infantry who helped piece the mission of Fire Support Base Oran together—sharing the ground soldiers perspective.

A Big Thumbs Up to John Cook, author of *Rescue Under Fire*, for providing his insights, encouragement and assistance with this project. My editors, Ann Ryan and Larry Kipp, who volunteered their expertise, insights, and who diligently read through my ramblings from the beginning to the end. Dan Campos, www.luminary1.com, deserves the credit for a simple but yet very dramatic design for the front cover page. Their assistance is greatly appreciated.

And no thanks big enough can be extended to my wife who allowed me to lock myself away in my den for over two years in order to put my fingers to the keyboard. With both of us working full time and my spending every free moment I could wrangle free to work on this project meant time that I could not spend with my wife. I hope this venture will have allowed our love for each other to grow to greater heights. Lori also completed the final edit on the manuscript.

The majority of the quotes contained at the end of the chapter's or stories came from the collection of Dr. Gabriel Robins at www.cs.virginia.edu.robins. My other source for quotes was located at www.quoteland.com.

And to those of you who have purchased a copy of this book—thanks for spending your hard earned money to read a piece of history from one pilot's perspective.   v

 **Photo Credits**

Armond "Si" Simmons-page 11, 20, 38

Author-pages 26, 27, 29, 31, 32, 49, 55, 61, 75, 79, 87, 90, 94, 98, 101, 102, 126, 131, 154, 164, 166, 173, 174, 176, 197, 204, 229, 233, 234, 247, 248, 249, 250, 251, 252, 253, 254, 259, 260, 261, Front Cover and Back Cover Photographs

Bell Helicopter-pages 227, 228,

Bob Bixby-page 255(T)

Gerry Baldwin-pages 70, 72, 78

John Sabanosh-page 200

Microsoft Clip Art-pages 221, Acknowledgements, Photo Credits

Mike Casper-pages 91, 245, 256, 257, 258

Richard Dean-pages 92, 169, 244

Rob Spitzer-pages 118, 135, 255(B)

www.theaviationzone.com-pages 76, 125

www.dustoff.org-page 9, 246

www.farfromglory.com-page 7

www.globalsecurity.com-page 99

www.history.amedd.army.mil-pages 5, 6

www.lazengrave.com-pages 45, 64

www.Vhdaonline.org (Dennis Herrick)-page 171

Foreward

DUSTOFF is a definitive, precise and incredibly well documented book about a key portion of the history of the Vietnam War. It is a compelling and hard hitting novel. Its candor and pace are superb and mirror the personality and experiences of the author. It brilliantly describes in graphic terms how the men of the 45th persisted through great and awful leadership. It captures the essence of dangers to all involved in a "Dustoff." It shows how that magnificent creation we call the US Soldier persists, perseveres, and penetrates the minutiae to get the job done. They do what they must because they know the life and welfare of their brothers-in-arms is on the line.

Steve Vermillion is the real deal and he has written a book that is a must read for anyone who wants to know what really happened with "Dustoff" in Vietnam. It comes from the author's soul. This book is compelling prose that explains why the "Dustoff's" credo was "No Compromise, No Rationalization, No Hesitation," and most importantly "Fly the Damn Mission" because America's finest were wounded and deserved the right to timely emergency medical evacuation and services.

Time has diluted the clarity of a lot of details of my experience in Vietnam, but the radio frequency and the call sign, "Dustoff," the evacuation of wounded soldiers, is as clear as the names of my family. This incredibly positive impact of the availability and responsiveness of "Dustoff" to the troopers under my command cannot be overstated.

DUSTOFF by Steve Vermillion is a notable and wonderful depiction of my experience with aerial medical evacuation units in Vietnam. You know it is written by an officer who consistently did the deed for the right reason. You know it is real. Literally hundreds of graying veterans like me are enjoying the rights of citizens of this country because of pilots like "Dustoff 40", the medics and the crewchiefs that flew these hazardous missions. We are eternally grateful!

A.J. (Beau) Bergeron
Colonel, US Army (Ret)

This book is dedicated to all of the pilots and crew members who flew unarmed aeromedical evacuation helicopters in Vietnam. They flew against all odds in order to give the wounded soldiers the best chance of survival. These crew members are the unsung heroes of a long and bitter war. They should be held in the highest esteem.

SECTION I   *Basics of Dustoff*

SECTION II   *Leadership*

SECTION III *War Stories*

SECTION IV *REMF Tales*

SECTION V *Closure*

Appendix:

.

Prologue

Why did I write this book—memoirs, if you might, about my tour as a pilot of an unarmed medical evacuation helicopter—Dustoff? Why not? Very little has been written from an individual helicopter pilot's perspective regarding combat experiences in Vietnam. And I am not sure why. Over the ten year period encompassing the war, there were over 40,000 helicopter pilots who were trained from all services and flew missions in Vietnam.

This book began as an effort to place into print my experiences as a Dustoff Pilot so that my children would have some insight about my role in Vietnam. Kind of in response to the age old question of "Daddy, what did you do during the war?"

In the 1980's before the proliferation of user friendly and reasonably priced computers entered our lives, I was unsuccessful in producing any type of meaningful manuscript. There was more paper in the trashcan than in story form. My thoughts were all in place but nothing flowed easily from my brain that resulted in a product a person would be interested in reading. To retain these thoughts, I did a lot of mind mapping—linking ideas together. My thoughts were recorded on a crude diagram looking much like a PERT chart. I read stories, books and performed a great deal of research to ensure my facts were as accurate as possible. From that point, my only hurdle was overcoming the mental block that seemed to thwart my attempts at effectively putting pen to paper. Rather than dealing with the frustration of not being able to write my story, I set everything aside for a later time.

While penning a personal story for the Northwest Chapter of the Distinguished Flying Cross Society's web page, thoughts and words flowed unimpeded. Not wanting to lose the creative edge, I pulled out my mind mapping work from years earlier and sat down at the computer. Putting fingers to the computer keyboard, memories easily downloaded from my mental hard drive to the one in my computer. The "delete key" became my close personal friend along with the cut and paste features of MS Word. Neil Diamond songs playing in the background accompanied by a few brewskies always helped with the process. With too many brewskies though, the thoughts flowed freely but the physical process of typing on the keyboard was impeded making the resulting text fairly nonsensical. With the right commitment of time, music and brewskies, the missions, stories and events began to take shape, chapter by chapter. Those who read my first drafted ramblings enjoyed what I had to say. They encouraged me to continue refining and adding to what had already been written. And now you have the end product in hand.

For people who have never experienced combat, flown a helicopter on the 'edge' or lived on adrenaline for twelve months, I hope what I have written provides the insight as to what it was like to do so. I hope that you are able to strap into the co-pilot's seat and envision the missions as we experienced them. Likewise, I want you to think about the decisions I made in the various stories that I have shared with you. If you agree with the decisions, ask yourself why and if you disagree, ask the same question. There are many lessons to learn—some I have pointed out directly, others are more subtle. They are there for you to explore and learn from. I learned a tremendous amount about myself as a person during my combat tour. I found traits that I truly believed were strengths and some traits that needed further development and maturation. Life is an evolutionary process and we should all continue to learn and grow until the day the Lord calls us for other purposes. It is also my desire for you to appreciate what Dustoff pilots and crew members were able to contribute on the battlefield. War has very few aspects that can be viewed as being positive. Our role in the medical evacuation of the wounded soldiers from the battlefield was one of those exceptions. You hear and read about the two Medal of Honor holders that served as Dustoff Pilots. Both Mike Novosel and Pat Brady helped bring prominence to the role of Dustoff in combat. Both are humble in referring to their awards. Pat Brady says he was doing what other Dustoff crew members do—the difference was that someone noticed. Many of the other 1398 pilots and crewmembers remain unnoticed to this date. I would like readers to reflect on the achievements of all of these crewmen whether they were "decorated" or not. They certainly flew into harm's way—quite possibly to bring back one of your loved ones from death's doorstep.

As the reader, I hope you approach this book with the understanding that I do not profess to be any greater or lesser of a pilot than my contemporaries. But every time I strapped the helicopter on to my butt, I became an integral part of the machine—as if we were one. Integrated together in thought, anticipation and movement. As an introvert though, I did have a quiet confidence in my abilities that others may not have enjoyed. And I carried the majority of my emotions inside, being careful not to expose any 'weaknesses.'

All of the pilots and crew members did the best job that they could--without any doubt or hesitation.

I have tried to share stories where I thought as a crew we "done good." Other stories demonstrate my lack of appreciation for incompetence and bureaucracy. These are my recollections of war that will never be erased from my memory.

I hope you enjoy reading what I have written!

> "The credit belongs to the man who is actually in the arena; whose face is marred by dust and sweat and blood; who strives valiantly; who errs and comes short again and again; who knows the great enthusiasms, the great devotions, and spends himself in a worthy cause; who at the best knows in the end the triumph of high achievement; and who at the worst, if he fails, at least fails while daring greatly."
>
> Theodore Roosevelt

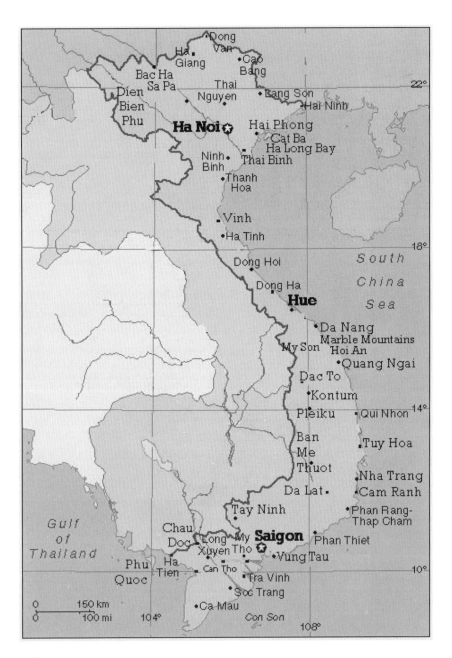

SECTION

The Basics of Dustoff

Dustoff: Its Origin

The Call-sign

Priorities

Lord! Why Me?

Fear This!

No Compromise!
Do not make a shameful or disreputable concession

No Rationalization!
Do not provide plausible but untrue reasons for conduct

No Hesitation!
Do not hold back in doubt or indecision

Dustoff—"Its Origins"

Chapter 1

This introductory chapter to the origins of Dustoff is not intended to be an in depth history on medical evacuation. Some insight to the history and background of medical evacuation is important so that you can derive a better understanding of how Dustoff evolved and what our role was in the overall scheme of the Vietnam War.

The helicopter's technological advancements allowed medical evacuation from the battlefield to transform itself from a fledgling concept into a highly capable resource in support of modern warfare. Every day that passed saw a spurt of growth in the maturation of the medical evacuation capability. If the military is again involved in combat on a nonlinear battlefield, I am not sure how the role of Dustoff will unfold. Sure, there is doctrine on how the battlefield will be supported and I would like to believe that the helicopters will be flown with the same fearlessness, cunning and skill that we did. But I do not think that will be the case. Young Vietnam era pilots were not trained in rules, regulations, and power charts that told the pilot they could not fly unless certain parameters were met. Vietnam was an era of and to itself and the way in which we flew will not be seen in future aviation units.

The evacuation of an army's wounded has always occurred in one form or another. The expediency of the evacuation depended on how much the soldier was valued by the army as well as the organic capabilities to evacuate the wounded. In 1776, soldiers remained where they were wounded. There was no corpsman coming forward to provide interim treatment nor was there any evacuation of the wounded to the rear echelon until a "time out" was called. The break in fighting was honored by both opposing forces so that the wounded could be evacuated without being impeded by the heat of battle. "Medical personnel" used to evacuate the wounded were not necessarily the best or the brightest soldiers and contributed very little to the life saving process other than patient transport to where medical assistance was available.[1]

During the Civil War, Doctor Jonathan Letterman, Medical Director, Army of the Potomac, believed that if wounded soldiers received prompt treatment not only could their lives be saved but a high percentage could be returned to combat duty. The Civil War saw the establishment of the three tier medical system which is still used today. The first tier was where the field dressings were first applied to the wounds while the soldier was on the battlefield. Typically this was the aid station either at company or battalion level. The second tier involved evacuating the wounded away from the front lines to the field hospital for further treatment. In the Civil War, the field hospital was often a barn or house that was commandeered. Today they would be the "MASH" type units. The third tier is the "formal" hospital system where the patients are retained for prolonged treatment and/or rehabilitation. For battles conducted on foreign soil, these hospitals are typically located out of country such as in Germany, Japan and the United States.[2]

The life of the wounded soldier depended on the skill of the person who first applied the dressing. This was a statement bearing truth and providing guidance for further development and refinement of the medical evacuation system. In World War I, military tactics had not kept pace with technology. The airplane, machine gun, chemical agents and very high explosives were introduced onto the battlefield for the first time. Battles did not stop so that the wounded could be evacuated from the battlefield. For the first time in history, medics joined the troops on the front line. More akin to today's paramedics, their job was to find the wounded, stop the bleeding and evacuate the wounded soldier back to the aid station. Medics were no longer viewed as being expendable as they were in previous wars. Medics were highly trained soldiers and earned the respect of their comrades because of their skills and bravery.[1]

Between the wars, greater emphasis was placed on the training of medics. They were trained in how to start and administer plasma, lifesaving drugs,

4

open airway passages and how to stop the bleeding through the use of pressure bandages. Along with advanced medical training, medics received more emphasis on their tactical skills. Tactical training allowed the medics to learn skills such as map reading, terrain usage and the general flow of tactical operations. Medical personnel followed suit with their predecessors of WWI by wearing red cross armbands. Additionally, red crosses were generally painted on all four quadrants of their helmets. In both the European and Pacific theaters, the enemy realized the importance of the medic on the battlefield. As such, the red crosses became a target for enemy snipers. No

"time outs" for the extraction of the wounded. No free pass to soldiers wearing the red cross. Medics now possessed one of the most dangerous jobs on the battlefield. And, by the way, medics were not armed. Wounded soldiers in World War II had an 87% chance of survival if a medic reached them within an hour and provided medical treatment. Very limited use was

made of fixed wing aircraft to evacuate wounded. This occurred primarily at the hospital level for the evacuation of the more critically wounded to a theater level hospital—tier three in the evacuation level.[4]

The Korean War saw the first use of the helicopter in the medical evacuation role. Helicopter evacuation commenced in January 1951 with the arrival of three helicopter detachments. Each detachment consisted of four helicopters, four pilots and four crewchiefs. Two of the detachments were equipped with OH-13's and the other detachment had OH-23's. The helicopter detachments were placed under operational control of the IX Corps Surgeon. Where the helicopters were physically located in the corps sector evolved through experimentation. They were initially located at corps headquarters. Ultimately they found that by placing them at the division clearing stations, they were closer to the front lines and minimized the time required to extract the wounded soldier and get him back to medical care.[5]

High density altitude, night time, reduced visibility and winds limited the helicopter's utility. Because there were so few helicopters in the combat theater, limitations were placed on their deployment. Helicopters of the OH-13 and OH-23 versions could sustain little or no damage inflicted by enemy ground fire. Helicopter pilots and ground commanders were discouraged from making extractions where the helicopter would be in direct firing range of the enemy. Helicopters were restricted to only extracting

OH-13 landing at a medical facility in Korea.

wounded soldiers that had injuries to the head, chest, abdomen, multiple fractures of the limb(s) and/or a great loss of blood. Even for these injuries, a helicopter was used only if the wounded could not be reached by ground ambulance, or the travel over rough roads would cause the soldier's wounds to worsen, or the soldier needed to get to a medical treatment facility in a faster time than a ground ambulance could get him there.[6] Medical treatment of the wounded while in flight was nearly nonexistent. Wounded soldiers were placed on stretchers affixed to the upper cross members of the skids (landing gear). Initially, the ride for the wounded soldier was pretty breezy and one could imagine a bit scary. The motion of the helicopter was probably a new sensation for a soldier. The helicopter took off from a hover in a slightly nose down attitude. With the soldier's head facing in the direction of flight, the sensation of sliding off of the stretcher head first was probably a bit overwhelming. Here again, trial and error lead to more improvements for transporting the wounded soldier. A plastic shield was developed that protected the wounded soldier's head and upper torso from the air stream. Not being subjected to the airflow eliminated major concerns with chill factor for the patient. Being located outside the fuselage of the helicopter restricted

OH-23

the soldier from receiving medical attention in flight. But as the war progressed, medical personnel devised a method by which an IV could be administered during flight.

The lessons learned in Korea set the stage for the early beginnings of Dustoff in Vietnam.

The Vietnam War presented commanders with a new type of battlefield. The typical battlefield up until this time contained forward and rear echelon areas enabling the companies, battalions, brigades and divisions to extend from front to rear in a linear manner. Other similar sized units were located on the flanks so there was an array of force spread both laterally and longitudinally throughout the operational sector. Logistical operations could be conducted in each sector without significant fear of major disruption from enemy operations. Supply lines existed to carry materials from the rear echelons to the forward combat units. Wounded were evacuated in a reverse process—from the combat area rearward to the first medical level capable of treating the respective type of wounds. Lightly wounded were first treated at the company and battalion aid stations. The more seriously wounded were treated as far forward as possible but were eventually evacuated to the major treatment facilities located in the rear areas. With the nonlinear battlefield of Vietnam, rear areas consisted of fire support bases or major supply bases which were separated geographically. The turf between the fire support or supply bases was essentially no-man's land. It could be either enemy or friendly with ownership changing hands frequently. The battlefield was very

7

fluid. Ground supply lines, with rare exception, did not exist from the rear support bases to the forward deployed units. The helicopter was used in every conceivable role possible--and some that go beyond reasonable imagination. It quickly became the tactical units' life line. One of the most critical roles performed by the helicopter was the medical evacuation of the wounded.

In February 1962, the 57th Medical Detachment (HA) was alerted at Fort Meade, Maryland of its projected deployment to Vietnam in April of that year. The detachment commander, Captain John Temperelli, Jr., set about his difficult task of preparing the unit for an overseas combat deployment. The combat TO&E allowances didn't provide for the essentials like cooks and other equipment absolutely necessary to operationally support his detachment. Likewise, he was going to deploy with the Army's latest and most technologically advanced helicopter, the UH-1A. Even a novice at military planning could forecast the problems this unit would encounter prior to it ever being deployed—primarily the lack of spare helicopter parts in country. The UH-1 from its inception was an excellent helicopter and each subsequent model increased performance and capability over its predecessor. But as with any machine, more so a helicopter, maintenance is a very high priority. Without spare parts, an aviation unit will be quickly brought to its knees rendering it incapable of performing its mission.[7]

Captain Temperelli, as all of us who served as military leaders did, gallantly faced the bureaucracy and ineptness found in large organizations. The 57th Med was initially located in Nha Trang with the 8th Surgical Hospital, more than 300 kilometers away from the battlefield where they were needed the most. The UH-1 at that time used JP-4 aviation fuel. The aircraft and other helicopters involved in Vietnam combat operations typically had reciprocating engines requiring a different type of fuel that was incompatible with the UH-1's turbine engine. JP-4 was not readily available within the supply system.[8] As a means to increase his operational range that would enable greater battlefield coverage, Captain Temperelli requested authorization to remove his cockpit heaters and to install auxiliary fuel tanks. Higher headquarters did not acknowledge his request.[9] Without the authorization to install auxiliary fuel tanks, Captain Temperelli had to establish contractual agreements with civilian fuel contractors at specific locations. As one might imagine, these contracts were tenuous at best. When the helicopter arrived expecting fuel, it may or may not have been available.

In August 1962, the 57th Medical Detachment was down to three of five aircraft flyable. Two helicopters were cannibalized of their rotor blades in order to keep the other three aircraft flying. I can surely empathize with Captain Temperelli. Even with "controlled cannibalization" the likelihood of the donor aircraft becoming a "hangar queen" and being picked to the bone is inevitable unless spare parts are forthcoming. His spare parts requests had to go to Okinawa in order to be filled. That time and distance factor alone would hamper any attempt at maintaining five aircraft on any

Colonel John Temperelli

reasonable maintenance schedule. By this time, other combat aviation units had received UH-1s which further strained the spare parts supply system. To support a major ARVN offensive into the Iron Triangle northwest of Saigon, combat aviation companies with UH-1s were tasked to escort CH-21 helicopters being used to lift the airmobile assault force. Facing their own maintenance problems, the combat aviation commanders raised their concerns to the Commander of the Army Support Group, Brigadier General (BG) Joseph Stilwell. Stilwell in turn tasked the 57th Medical Detachment in November 1962 for the necessary parts from their helicopters As a result of BG Stilwell's command directive, the 57th Medical Detachment was totally non-mission capable. For one thirty- day period, there was no helicopter medical evacuation provided in Vietnam. Eventually, one starter/generator was returned to the 57th Medical Detachment allowing for one helicopter to be brought up to a flyable status. The men of the 57th Medical Detachment did their best to provide medical evacuation coverage with just this one helicopter.[10]

Captain Temperelli's legacy to Dustoff was bringing the first helicopter air ambulance unit into combat in Vietnam and forging ahead against all bureaucratic roadblocks. He established liaison with and supported ARVN forces. He fought the battle with higher level commanders in an effort to convince them of the helicopter's viability in the medical evacuation system. Captain Temperelli returned to Vietnam for a second combat tour and was the executive officer of the 45th Medical Company (AA) during the first part of my Vietnam tour. Captain Temperelli relinquished the responsibility of command to Major Lloyd Spencer in February 1963. On March 11, 1963, the 57th Medical Detachment received the first five new UH-1B models to arrive in country. Three crews and helicopters from the 57th Medical Detachment were reassigned to Saigon to provide helicopter air ambulance coverage to the military units in the III and IV Corps areas. The other two helicopters and crews were reassigned from Nha Trang with one going to Pleiku and the other to Qui Nhon. Albeit, coverage over the entire country was spread very thin, Major Spencer kept his promise to BG Stillwell that he and the 57th Medical Detachment would provide coverage throughout the entire combat zone.[11] Major Spencer is credited with originating the call-sign of Dustoff. Chapter two, entitled the Dustoff Call Sign, provides more discussion on the origins of the call-sign. Spencer's contributions to Dustoff include being the "father" of the call sign, continuing to develop the evacuation model while providing coverage throughout Vietnam, thwarting the attempts of ground commanders to use Dustoff helicopters for administrative purposes and generating more positive support from higher levels of command. The role of Dustoff was expanding and even though ground commanders felt threatened by the evolution of the helicopter for this role, they developed respect for the pilots and crews who flew the dangerous missions to extract their wounded from the battlefield.

In January 1964, the mystique of Dustoff was kicked up a notch—a significant notch by all standards of measurement. Major Charles Kelly accepted the reins of command for the 57th on January 11, 1964. Kelly seemed to be more adept at cutting through the bureaucratic bull feces than his predecessors and was able to convince the command group of the importance of relocating his helicopters into the III and IV Corps areas.

In March 1964, Kelly, with authorization from his commander, moved each of his helicopters from Qui Nhon and Pleiku to Soc Trang. He formed a subset of the 57th Med by calling the group at Soc Trang, Detachment A. He coordinated with the 121st Aviation Group to provide the maintenance support for the two helicopters.12 The relocation of the two helicopters proved to be the correct decision. The evacuee numbers increased from 193 in February 1964 to 416 in March 1964.13 In addition to the increase in general patient loads, Major Kelly began to expand the name and mission role by flying a nightly circuit throughout the IV Corps area "looking for business."

Major Charles Kelly
Vietnam 1964

11

When he implemented his routine of flying a nightly route in the IV Corps area of operations, the evacuation of the wounded was his primary goal. Secondarily, was the establishment of rapport and relationships with the ground commanders and other facilities. His efforts served to make Dustoff a household name in both III and IV Corps. Commanders came to value the Dustoff knowing that if they had a wounded soldier, a Dustoff crew would be there to evacuate him. [14]

My research into the early beginnings of Dustoff as well as Major Kelly's contributions to evolutionary development of extracting the wounded from the battlefield provided conflicting information. Two authors state that the Commander of the 57th Medical Detachment, Major Howard Huntsman and the Commander of the 82d Medical Detachment, Major Henry Capozzi put an end to the routine of flying a nightly circuit in the IV Corps area of operations. They concluded that such a practice was a waste of time and resources.[15 & 16] The increased numbers of wounded that were evacuated due to a higher operational tempo of fighting indicated three aircraft and crews would not be able to maintain the operational pace that Kelly found himself dealing with. Pilots were flying nearly 140 hours per month—a change needed to occur. Armond "Si" Simmons, who was a pilot in the 57th Medical Detachment during Major Kelly's tour, states that the regular night routes that Major Kelly initially implemented were terminated by Major Kelly after a fairly brief period and long before he was killed, as the increasingly heavy workload had deemed "night routes" impractical.[17] The reputation of Dustoff established not only by Major Kelly but by his predecessors caused the Dustoff mystique to grow and take on a life of its own.

Senior commanders, most notably ground commanders, were concerned about Major Kelly's helicopter unit. With Kelly being a medical service corps officer, senior commanders tended to view both Kelly and his organization as a threat to their command and control authority. BG Stilwell, even though somewhat supportive of Major Kelly, showed himself to be a nemesis in regard to the role of Dustoff. Stilwell was an advocate of being able to use any aircraft for medical evacuation simply by adding removable red crosses to the helicopter. From his perspective, the helicopter could be used for troop transport on one day and then next day perform in a medical evacuation role by adding a red cross to the helicopter. One would assume they would also include a medic as a crew member and remove the mounted door guns to remain in compliance with the Geneva Accords. To the best of my knowledge, this dual use of the helicopters with removable red crosses never occurred. Later in the war, the Marine Corps operated their CH-46 assets in this same manner with the exception of affixing the red crosses to the helicopter and not removing the door guns.[18]

Soc Trang provided a superb training ground for Major Kelly. Unlike other commanders, he flew missions on a daily basis. Not only did the missions serve to evacuate the wounded soldiers, they also provided a training forum for Major Kelly to imbue his pilots with his skills and dedication in furthering the role of Dustoff. Captain Temperelli and Major Spencer nurtured Dustoff in its womb of infancy. Major Kelly gave birth to the concept and the tradition that set the tone for how Dustoff units operated throughout the remainder of the war.

On July 1, 1964, Major Kelly's life was taken while performing a medical evacuation mission in a hot landing zone. He died— while serving as a role model for all of his pilots and for those who he served with his Dustoff missions. From this point forward, there was no way Dustoff would ever be eliminated from employment during combat operations. Major Kelly served in the military well before my time and I never had the opportunity to meet or serve with him. Everyone that I have talked to that served with Major Kelly has stated, without hesitation, that they are better people today for having served with him in Vietnam. If there were ever a visionary leader that was well ahead of his time, Major Kelly was that person. He was a leader among leaders. He set the tone for how his pilots flew their missions. He trained them in his ideals. He valued his pilots' abilities to think for themselves and he supported them when they needed to develop policy on the spot or to ignore a regulation because it didn't pass the "makes sense test", for he viewed each and every action as a separate and distinct event and did what was in the patient's best interest.[19] He flew combat missions in keeping with his motto: No Compromise! No Rationalization! No Hesitation! Fly the Mission![20] Captain Paul Bloomquist assumed command of the 57th Medical Detachment on July 2, 1964.

In August of that year, the Southeast Asia Resolution became the turning point for the United States to increase its commitment in repelling the communist forces from South Vietnam. This brought about the need to begin deploying newly formed helicopter air ambulance detachments to Vietnam in order to provide greater medical evacuation coverage throughout the entire country. The helicopter had proven itself in Vietnam and the demand for its services had increased exponentially. Demand had outstripped Bell Helicopter's production capabilities for the newer generation helicopters as well as the military's capability to provide the pilots and crew members to operate them. Forces deployed to Vietnam by mid-1967 exceeded 450,000.[21] There was a growing need for increased aeromedical evacuation from the battlefield. General Westmoreland, in a communiqué to the Commander in Chief, U. S. Army Pacific, stated that he needed to have a total of 120 air ambulance helicopters in the theater of operations. There were 64 airframes dedicated to medical evacuation but the theater "allowable allocation" was 113 airframes.[22]

The 45th Medical Company Air Ambulance (AA), based at Fort Bragg, North Carolina, was alerted for deployment to Vietnam in May 1967. Under command of LTC Joe Martin, the 45th Medical Company assimilated twenty-five brand new UH-1Hs and was combat ready in September 1967.[23] Having flown the D model Huey in flight school and later the H model in Vietnam as well as after my tour, the addition of the H model to the theater of operations was a real plus for the flight crews and the ground units they supported. Not only did the III Corps area gain twenty-five additional airframes dedicated to medical evacuation, these particular airframes enhanced operational performance—saving fuel with an increased payload capacity. LTC Arlie Price followed LTC Martin as the commander of the 45th Medical Company (AA). He assumed command in June 1968 and relinquished command in June 1969 to LTC Warren Roler.

Commanders of the air ambulance companies and detachments that served in Vietnam varied in their leadership capabilities and their commitment to the role of Dustoff. Some commanders elected to lead a more conservative organization by restricting missions flown at night and during periods of bad weather to only those classified as "urgent." Others placed more requirements on the ground commanders to provide greater security in the landing zone intending to reduce the danger for their flight crews. There were also commanders who never lost sight of the Dustoff "tradition." The "Originals" that served in the 57th Medical Detachment for the years prior to other air ambulance detachments arriving in Vietnam established the procedures for the medical evacuation of the wounded from the battlefield. They ensured their pilots and crew members upheld the standards that Major Kelly had established in 1964.

There was a mix of leadership and crew member commitment throughout the era of Dustoff. From wild and wooly to conservative. From low-keyed to outlandish. Peter Dorland and James Nanney in their book entitled *Dust Off: Army Aeromedical Evacuation in Vietnam* state: "Most of the pilots, while not quite measuring up to the Kelly tradition, acted bravely and honorably enough to win widespread respect and gratitude from those who served in Vietnam."[24] They also state that; "a few pilots like Major Kelly, Major Brady and Mr. Novosel, would even fly into the teeth of enemy bullets to get to [the] wounded."[25]

From my experience in 1969 and limited to those with whom I flew and observed, I would have to disagree with Dorland's and Nanney's assessment of Dustoff pilots. Their use of the term "most of the pilots" does a terrible injustice to the other pilots plus enlisted crew members that diligently followed in Kelly's footsteps. Brady's and Novosel's efforts and commitment to the mission of rescuing wounded under extremely adverse conditions were recognized with their being awarded the Medal of Honor. And those awards were justly deserved. I am opinionated and informed enough to believe there are more pilots and crew members who "earned" awards but were never recognized for their efforts. Major Kelly certainly, and without challenge, led the way. Others following behind Major Kelly continued to innovate in an effort to build on his foundation. In 1966, the hoist was introduced as a new tool to extract the wounded from areas where no landing zone existed. The hoist mission considerably upped the ante in the risk factor category. Likewise the weapons the enemy employed changed from simple rifles and crossbows to very robust anti-aircraft systems.

Obviously there were some pilots and commanders who used regulations or fear to justify not flying a mission or not making an extraction after they arrived over the landing zone. Steve Huntley, who was a crewchief in the fourth platoon before I arrived in our unit, shared a story with me that caused him to leave Dustoff and to fly with another unit. The fourth platoon had a solid reputation of never turning down a mission regardless of the circumstances. Everyone was upholding the Kelly tradition. He stated that on one mission, the aircraft commander he was flying with was in contact with a ground unit who had sustained casualties from recent enemy contact. The aircraft commander wanted the unit to move to a more secure location. The unit was unable to move the wounded to another location due to enemy contact. The ground unit commander stated that if the wounded were not extracted, they would die. The aircraft commander refused to land because of his concerns over the security of the landing zone. The helicopter departed the area and returned to their home base. One would assume the soldiers died or were possibly extracted by a non-medical helicopter. Steve felt so ashamed of his unit's actions that he no longer wanted to be a member of the organization. From my experience, these incidents did occur but again were the rare exception rather than the norm. But for those soldiers who prided themselves in accomplishing the mission—regardless of the odds, not flying a mission and allowing others to possibly die without making an attempt to rescue them is an intolerable pill to swallow.[26]

The heroes in Dustoff encompassed a vast number of officers and enlisted personnel that remain unrecognized and unknown. I feel that anyone who flew their helicopter into a hot landing zone, hoisted from a non-secure site, or exposed themselves to enemy fire to rescue another soldier, have all lived up to the expectations of Major Kelly whether they flew Dustoff, Medevac, 'slicks', 'scouts' or 'guns.'

> "Wars may be fought with weapons, but they are won by men. It is the spirit of the men who follow and of the man who leads that gains the victory."
>
> General George S. Patton

The Call Sign—Dustoff

Chapter 2

A military tactical call sign is synonymous with a person's identity. In today's modern age of secure radio networks, call signs that are alphanumeric and change a minimum of every 24 hours along with the radio frequencies, each unit still strives to have an internal identity through the use of special call signs. In lieu of being known as A6E14 today and C9Z50 tomorrow, a person's inter-organizational call sign might be Saber 3. Everyone on the secure internal communications frequency knows precisely who Saber 3 is. As a Dustoff pilot, the word Dustoff represented what we did in the past and what our counterparts are doing in the present. Dustoff is the organization and the mission. The numerical identifier at the end of the call sign, as in "40", pronounced "four zero," is the individual—in this case, me.

Where did the call sign originate from? There are several stories around purporting to be the correct origin of the call sign. Two such stories have general sustenance and are shared within this chapter. For me, it really didn't make a difference where the call sign originated as its origin was before my time and I don't have a dog in the ownership fight. But the two credible scenarios are interesting and both show why the call sign came about and its importance. The first explanation is described in both John Cook's book[1] and that of Dorland and Nanney.[2] They say that the origins of the Dustoff call sign are attributed to the 57th Medical Detachment's second commander, Major Lloyd Spencer. Prior to June 1963, call sign identity over the radio was preceded by the word Army followed by the last five digits of the helicopter's tail number. There was no tactical call sign or set radio frequency assigned to the Dustoff unit. It is said that Major Spencer was exasperated due to a lack of unit identity via a designated call sign along with having no prescribed radio frequency for internal unit coordination.

Deciding a good offense was better than dealing with his situation on an on-going basis, Major Spencer paid a visit to the controlling agency in charge of all radio frequencies in Vietnam, the Navy Support Activity (NSA). The NSA had the responsibility of publishing the Signal Operations Instructions (SOI). The SOI listed all of the units, call signs, assigned frequencies and established a regular schedule for the change over of tactical call signs and frequencies. NSA essentially allowed Major Spencer to choose a spare or unassigned call sign. Looking through the list of those that were available, his eye caught the unused call sign of Dustoff. Having flown in the Delta during the dry season, he recalled that when the helicopter landed or departed from the tactical landing zone, the rotor wash from the helicopter blew dust all over the place. So he chose Dustoff as the 57th Medical Detachment's call sign.[3 & 4]

The other story comes from Armond "Si" Simmons and is posted on his web page as well. Si was the detachment's officer tasked to manage the accountability for the SOI's assigned to the 57th Med at the time the Dustoff call sign came to fruition. Si explains that the call sign came about in January 1964. In early January, the 57th Med was involved in providing medical support during a bloody two-day operation west of Saigon near the Cambodian border. As was the practice, units were randomly assigned call signs and frequencies by the NSA. As prescribed by the NSA, at specific points in time, the units changed call signs and frequencies. Since the radio network at the time was not secure, anyone with a FM radio operating in the tactical bandwidth could monitor voice traffic over any frequency. Obviously, once the enemy determined the friendly force's frequency and call sign, they could gain valuable tactical intelligence about the unit they were monitoring. By changing frequencies and call signs, the enemy was denied valuable intelligence information. At the same time, if a battle was ongoing and the established time to change frequencies arrived, chaos ensued as everyone changed frequencies and tried to re-establish communications with one another and sort out who was who on the radio network. During this specific two-day battle, the prescribed time arrived for all units to change call signs and frequencies. The 57th Medical Detachment had been assigned, on a random basis, the Dustoff call sign. The ground commanders and aircrews performing the medical evacuation mission agreed the chaos that would come with the change of frequencies at that critical point would jeopardize the evacuation of the wounded soldiers. Major Spencer agreed and coordination was effected with NSA to retain the Dustoff call sign until the end of the ongoing battle—presumably 24 hours or less. At the conclusion of the tactical operation, Major Spencer and the new incoming commander, Major Charles Kelly, discussed the call sign dilemma and decided that a permanent call sign would facilitate better medical evacuation for all people involved. Within a couple of days, Major Spencer submitted his request for the 57th Medical Detachment to be permanently assigned the call sign of Dustoff. His request was subsequently approved and the Dustoff call sign became permanent for the duration of the Vietnam War. Conflict in the usage of the call sign of Dustoff arose when other helicopter medical evacuation units began arriving in country. The 82d Medical Detachment was the second helicopter medical evacuation unit to arrive in country. They too faced a similar dilemma of not having an appropriate tactical call sign. Regardless of what call sign they were assigned and using, ground unit commanders began to refer to the 82d's crews as Dustoff. There was initially some friction among the older hands of the 57th Med not wanting anyone else to use 'their' call sign. Within a very short period of time, logic overcame emotion and the 82d Medical Detachment was also allowed to use the Dustoff call sign. Thereafter, each helicopter air ambulance unit arriving in country was assigned Dustoff as a call sign. Platoons then assimilated the ten numerical call sign numbers for their call sign suffix. As an example, fourth platoon used numbers from 40 through 49.[5] The 1st Cavalry Division's organic helicopter medical detachment chose to use the call sign of "Medevac." To the best of my knowledge, there were no other prefix call signs other than Dustoff or Medevac that were used to denote U. S. Army medical evacuation helicopters during the Vietnam War.

You have read two viable accounts of how the call sign originated. I'll let you decide which account is the correct one. With either choice, you end up at the same destination—the call-sign of Dustoff being used by each medical helicopter air ambulance unit that was assigned to the medical command.

Priorities

Chapter 3

When flying out of Long Binh, the first mission of the day typically came through operations who in turn alerted the flight crew. The three other crew members headed to the helicopter and had it running and ready for departure when the Aircraft Commander arrived. As the Aircraft Commander, I went directly to flight operations, grabbed the mission sheet, took a quick glance at the coordinates to determine where we were headed, and then sprinted to the helicopter. At times, the other three crew members were so fast that we would be airborne before I had my shoulder harness and seat belt connected. I merely pointed the direction for the pilot to head until I got my flight helmet on and could communicate with him.

The mission sheet contained the coordinates for: the landing zone; the number and types of patients (litter or ambulatory); the nature and seriousness of the wounds or illness; the tactical radio frequency and call sign of the ground unit to contact; any special equipment needed; nationality of the patients; marking for the LZ (smoke, strobe light, flares, etc.); tactical security of the landing zone; and any weather or terrain hazards. John Cook[1] as well as Dorland and Nanney[2] in their respective books say that the first four elements contained in the mission sheet were critical. Without them, there was no guarantee that a Dustoff crew would fly the mission. Based on my experience, the only two absolutely critical pieces of information were the location accompanied by a call sign and frequency for the unit in contact. A four digit grid zone location rather than the typical six or eight digit locations would get us into the neighborhood. Everything else could be sorted out enroute to the pickup location. Obviously, if the ground unit neglected to include the need for a hoist and we departed our base without one, the mission would be in jeopardy of not being completed. I believe my contemporaries would improvise as necessary to accomplish the mission so again these mission requirements were guidelines but not etched into stone. Dorland's and Nanney's example also contains "oxygen and whole blood" as special equipment items.[3] In our air ambulance company, we didn't have access to whole blood for use in flight and we didn't carry oxygen. For as many enemy bullets that passed through our helicopters, the last thing we needed onboard was a pressurized cylinder of oxygen. Whether enemy fire was the basis for the decision not to carry oxygen, who ever made the decision, made a good one.

In the latter half of my tour, the company commander confiscated every item of medical equipment not authorized under an outdated Table of Equipment and Allowances (TO&E). As my tour progressed, many of our medics didn't even have ambu-bags with which to provide resuscitation to those soldiers requiring it. The table of allowances is the authorization for what an organization can have on hand. This allowance table was designed more for a peace time unit than it was for a tactical unit since the Army had little or no experience in aeromedical evacuation during combat. The 1960s, especially in the aviation environment, saw technology and the use of helicopters in combat advancing by leaps and bounds. The TO&E document defining standard equipment allowances tends to lag behind the needs of the unit and is generally inflexible. With the ever changing battlefield and the rapid increase in the application of technology, commanders at all levels should have been more proactive in implementing changes or allowing deviations. Pretty good example in this case of the tail wagging the dog.

The intensity of the day determined how many "paper" mission sheets we had in hand. After the initial mission request, the remainder would typically be given to us while we were airborne. Thank God for a grease pencil and Plexiglas. Crewchiefs were proactive by installing a 6" x 12" Plexiglas panel in the radio console for us to write on. Once we filled that panel up, we reverted to writing on the inside of the windshield. After we shutdown after that sequence of missions, it was possible for us to sit in the cockpit for an extra 30 minutes or so transcribing all of the missions onto the formatted mission sheets. Then we would erase all of our grease pencil markings and be ready for the next set of missions.

The two components of the mission request that were the most inaccurate were the landing zone security and the urgency of the patients. After making radio contact with the ground unit who had the patients for extraction, I was able to paint a more accurate picture of the tactical situation and how secure or insecure the landing zone would be. Also the type of wounds described by the ground unit in the initial mission request gave some insight as to what we would potentially face. Fragmentation wounds from a booby-trap might mean to me there was more potential for the landing zone being relatively secure versus non-secure. If the wounds were from gunshots, then I treated the landing zone as if it were non-secure regardless of how the ground unit described LZ security. A non-secure landing zone did not deter me from flying the mission. It did influence the tactics that I employed to fly the helicopter into and out of the landing zone. My only true test for landing zone security was when we were on final approach to the landing zone and there was one or more soldiers standing upright providing hand signals to us for landing. And then it was still suspect.

On several night missions when we made contact with the ground unit, the RTO or commander talking on the radio to us would be whispering. When we queried them on why they were whispering, the operator would respond with "we don't want to give our position away." Such a comment would always call for a joke or two over our intercom system. We didn't have a silent operating mode for the helicopter. The noise from the turbine engine and the characteristic 'whopping' sound of the rotor blades would certainly mark the unit's location when we came in for the landing.

Patient priority was the other area that was questionable. If we had multiple missions stacked up, we would have to talk with the ground units that had submitted the mission requests to determine the type of wound and the part of the body affected. For a gunshot wound to the leg, a patient would probably be classified as urgent. Likewise, a soldier with a sucking chest wound would also be classified as urgent. But if we had to establish a priority for sequencing the patient pickups, I would probably place the soldier with the sucking chest wound ahead of the leg injury as the chest wound would tend to be more life threatening than the leg wound. That was not always the case, but without additional information, it was a good rule of thumb to go by. The Army employed three classifications for determining patient evacuation priorities. The highest level was urgent which meant the patient was in imminent danger of losing his life or a limb. Priority was the second classification meaning that the patients' wounds were serious but not critical. A unit with a "priority patient" could expect the medical evacuation to occur within a window of four hours after submitting the evacuation request. The last patient classification was called routine. Routine missions were flown or sequenced after the urgent and priority patients had been evacuated. Off the top of my head, I do not recall having evacuated any U.S. soldier from the field that was classified as "routine." Hospital to hospital transfers were typically classified as routine as the patients had been stabilized and not scheduled for movement until they were ready for treatment or rehabilitation at a different location.

Urgent and Priority classifications meshed with one another. The medic on the ground along with the ground commander generally determined whether their soldier, civilian or whomever was in an urgent or priority status. Patients tended to be over classified causing the priority system to be somewhat meaningless. A more meaningful priority system may have been to have just two classifications, urgent and non-urgent. Here again, there would be room for over classification of the patient. As an aircraft commander, I treated both urgent and priority classification with the same sense of urgency and responsiveness. If there was conflict between more than one mission that was in the queue for pickup, we established an internal priority by basing our decision on the patient's wounds and talking with the ground unit to get a more updated picture of what we had to work with. Also we had access to the medical control officer by calling "Wide Minnow" and a professional opinion was readily available if needed. Our sister service, the Marine Corps, had three classifications as well: Routine, Priority and Emergency. In brief, their Emergency classification implied that evacuation should occur within twenty minutes of mission receipt and the mission should be flown day or night. Priority for the Marine Corps meant that a soldier's wounds were not life threatening and that the soldier should be evacuated within an hour—but never at night. And their Routine classification called for evacuation within a couple of hours but never at night. If a Marine was injured at night, it would be fair to assume the soldier's medevac classification escalated to emergency status otherwise they would not be evac'd until the next morning.

It was not uncommon to get to an LZ to find the soldier that had been classified as Urgent was, by definition, really a priority classification. For me, this happened mainly at night. It might have been attributed to the fact the tactical situation had quieted for the evening and the unit had the time in which to coordinate the medical evacuation. The only abuse of the system I came across was when we had a night mission, in marginal weather conditions only to find that our patient was a soldier who was going on R&R the next day. During the day the unit couldn't get their resupply bird in due to weather so they thought the Dustoff guys could get in and get this guy out so he could make his R&R flight. Nice to be of help, but I was not impressed with having to risk our asses getting through the weather so this guy could get laid in Thailand.

During my tour, we medically evacuated a very diverse population. Our evacuees included men from the forces of the United States, Korea, Thailand, Australia, South Vietnam and North Vietnam to include the Viet Cong. Scout dogs supporting US forces had a priority for evacuation and were also among those that I evacuated out of harm's way. Vietnamese civilians were often the innocent bystanders to combat action whether injured by booby trap, land mines or other types of weapons. We responded to traffic accidents involving both civilians and military personnel. After giving birth to babies for centuries in their grass huts without any type of hospital care, pregnant Vietnamese women who had been examined by a medic attached to a US advisory team often received a trip to the hospital in our helicopter when medical complications were evident. No births onboard--but some were pretty close.

My average time from launch to the pickup point and then to the nearest medical facility was about fifty minutes. Some were shorter and some were longer depending on where we were based in relation to the pickup location and the tactical situation at the landing zone. The motto on the New York City General Post Office building, and attributed to Herodotus in the war between the Greeks and the Persians, closely parallels our mission. **Neither snow nor rain nor heat nor gloom of night stays these couriers from the swift completion of their appointed rounds.** [4]

Viet Cong soldier brought into Tan An. In the dispensery, a South Vietnamese Intelligence Agent intervened on the medical treatment that was being adminstered. The Intelligence Agent attempted to gain information through torture. The VC subsequently died from his wounds.

"Argue for limitations, and sure enough they're yours."

Richard Bach

Lord! Why Me?

Chapter 4

ROCKETS LOSE FOUR BY GRADUATION; MANY BACK

By MARVIN ROGERS
E-O Sports Writer

PILOT ROCK — Pilot Rock's baseball season is closed and even though the loss to Regis in the state class B finals last Saturday left them as the second best in the state it must be considered a tremendously successful season for first year Coach Ken Kramer and the players who made it possible.

Four of the Rockets played their final contest in high school ball as graduation removes them from the Rockets' ranks. They are Steve Vermillion, team captain at second base and a .380 hitter; Ken Stanton, right fielder and a .400 hitter; Jack Miller, shortstop and a .174 hitter and Paul Ellis, first sacker who carried a .178 average into the championship game.

Although all four seniors were regulars and two of them hitting nearly .400, Pilot Rock has a strong nucleus from which Kramer may build next season.

Donning Pilot Rock baseball duds again next spring will be Duke Chapman, top pitcher with a 6-1 record, the one loss coming in the championship game; Ron Bond, top hitter with a .456 average and 25 RBI prior to the final game as well as being the second pitcher with a 6-4 record. Both Bond and Chapman are sophomores as is Jim Jobes, a .354 slugging center fielder, and Dave White, a .333 sticker at third. The only junior regular who is returning is Rich Rasmussen, left fielder and catcher and a .326 hitter.

Also returning next spring will be three sophomores who have proven they could fill in capably: John Standley, called by Kramer, "the team's most dependable pinch hitter," Doug Coon a dependable outfielder, and Dave Wright, the teams utility infielder this year. Also back will be Mel Carrothers, the squads third pitcher at 2-0, plus freshman Tim McMahon, outfielder, and other good prospects.

The main problem for Kramer's forces seems to be in finding replacements down the middle to fill the smooth keystone combo of Miller and Vermillion, a first sacker and a third outfielder.

Where do I start my life's calling? Coming out of high school, my greatest desire was to become a professional baseball player. I thought my talent was good enough to make the trip to the "show." Even at age 55 years old, I still joke about waiting for the call to come from a major league team offering an opportunity to play in the big time. I suspect at this point, the only offer I might get is to sell beer—which wouldn't be all that bad.

Finishing one year of college in 1967, no job prospects in site and the draft board hot on the trail of anyone not in school, I began to look at the options available to me. Staying at home was not an option. My stepfather created a home environment akin to a mini-combat zone. School? Really not ready to choose a career path. Attending Blue Mountain Community College in Pendleton, Oregon (1966-67), I was enrolled in a pre-law course track. Since I was going to school on my father's GI bill benefits, I had to be tested and interviewed by the Veteran's Administration. The VA representatives I met with in Portland, Oregon said I didn't have the mental moxy to become a lawyer. Whew! I'm glad they were right! But what direction do I head off in now.

Reading an article in what I recall to be *Newsweek Magazine*, I became intrigued by a story that described the heroic deeds of Army Dustoff helicopter pilots. The more I thought about it, the more intrigued and excited I became. When I first walked into the recruiter's office in 1967, I was focused on two things— being accepted into the Warrant Officer Flight Program and becoming a Dustoff Pilot. The recruiter was very accommodating and met all my requests—just as you would expect a recruiter to do in 1967. With all of the testing and basic training behind me, my first stopping point was Fort Wolters, Texas.

In primary flight school, I built a plastic model of a UH-1 helicopter and painted red crosses on the nose and cargo doors. Under the small helicopter, I placed a 3" x 5" card with "DUSTOFF" written on it. Each day the TAC Officer would come by and give me demerits for a "dusty" helicopter. If I removed the card from underneath the helicopter, I didn't receive demerits for having a "dusty" helicopter. When I put the card back underneath the model, the demerits returned. From that early point forward, the helicopter

The author with an OH-23 at Fort Sill, OK. One stop on a cross country leg from Fort Wolters--circa 1968.

and the card remained—and so did my demerits. The TAC Officer understood the symbology and it became a friendly game between the two of us. The helicopter also served as a daily reminder of my near term goal.

When we advanced to our final phase of flight training at Hunter AAF, Georgia, I was notified that I had been selected to attend the AMEDD Aviators course enroute to Vietnam. Other classmates were headed to Cobra transition (AH-1G Attack Helicopter) or had been earmarked for assignment to specific tactical units. First Cavalry Division patches along with others were now appearing on the left sleeves of the dress green uniform jackets in preparation for graduation day. I wanted my *esprit* to show before our graduation date, so I mixed aircraft model paints together and hand painted a replica of the 44th Medical Brigade patch on the back of my flight helmet. The only time "trouble" visited me as a result of having the painted patch on my flight helmet was during our aerial gunnery range firing. The aerial gunnery instructor pilot that I was assigned to for that training period was not in any way, fashion or form, impressed with the fact that I was going to be a Dustoff Pilot. Gun drivers, in his view, were God's gift to women and the world. Depends on a person's perspective I guess. Bitching and moaning all through the aircraft preflight and engine run-up, the instructor felt obligated to at least demonstrate the finer techniques of aerial gunnery. The student or the person firing the weapons system does so from the left seat using a gun sight with the firing reticle mounted on a flexible control arm. The instructor made the first gunnery pass firing the weapons from the fixed mode. He laced the target with a stream of M-60 machine gun bullets from the dual mounted armament systems. It was my turn next. The instructor initiated the start of the low-level pass over the gunnery range, indicating targets for me to engage. On the first target, I sort of got reasonable "target coverage" with my machine gun burst. Since it was my first-ever aerial gunnery pass, I was happy to have placed lead on the target. Bringing the second target into my gun sights, I squeezed off a short burst from the machine guns. But that engagement found my rounds falling short of the target impacting into a grassy area. The high temperatures of the Georgia summer created conditions for a fine tinder just awaiting the application of the right amount of spark. We didn't have to wait long! The tracers from my rounds landing short of the target provided the necessary spark. As we turned downwind for another pass, a cloud of blackish gray smoke was rising from the burning range fire. Oops! Over the intercom came a verbal tongue lashing on my inability to ever be a gun driver. "Damn good thing you're gonna be a Dustoff puke. You can't hit shit with a machine gun." Ruined the instructor's day—and mine. The rest of my hour and thirty minute gunnery period was spent sitting in the left seat, quietly, I might add, watching him demonstrate for my edification, the superb attributes of a macho gunship pilot. Life could be worse—but not by much. He gave me a "C" for my flight period grade—which was like receiving a grade of "D" in an academic class. Says I showed up but didn't accomplish much.

The remaining two weeks of flight school were devoted to learning tactical operations. Hauling sling loads, low level flying and formation flying. Didn't much care for formation flights into a LZ to drop off or pickup ground troops. Formation flying is similar to playing follow the leader as a kid. You replicate what the aircraft does in front of you with your main job being to hold your exact position in the flight. If one of the flight crews in front of you deviates somehow from the actions of the aircraft to their front, the reactions of the flight crews behind him become magnified. The formation from that point can become one big goat roping exercise. I much preferred to operate as a single ship making my own decisions as a single crew and being able to influence the outcome of our flight rather than relying on some dumb ass that might get me and my crew killed for no logical reason.

Trail formation over Fort
Stewart, Georgia 1968

Flying a Dustoff helicopter was an honor for me—and I think it was something I was destined to do. When I reflect back on the events within my life,
there was an early pathway that seemed to be established that pointed me in
the direction of becoming a Dustoff pilot. Every time opportunity knocked
on the door, I answered the knock. Unknowingly, these opportunities were
taking me in a pre-destined direction. I fully subscribe to the belief that we
are put here on earth for a given purpose. As many people do at a young
age, I was certainly searching for my purpose in life. What roll would I play
in furthering the growth of humanity? Going to war didn't seem to create
growth for the human race but it seemed to be the place where I could, at
the time, give the most using the innate abilities that I possessed.

In my era, helicopter pilots had several common traits. We flew helicopters
into situations that I do not think the designer had ever envisioned. We were
young and invincible! We were able to do dumb shit and live to tell about it.
We all flew hard, tried to do the job we were trained to do and return home
in one piece. Dustoff crews experienced the horrors of battle on a daily
basis. Horrors that are beyond the belief of the human imagination! The
vast majority of us have been able to keep life and our combat experiences
in proper perspective. Most of us went into Vietnam as young men and
came home matured and saged well beyond our years. From the period of
Major Charles Kelly to the last day of the war, commanders and Dustoff

The senior man of a LRRP patrol clasps his hands together just as we touch down to indicate we are right where he wants us.

pilots varied in their commitment to the mission. The majority chose the path of high risk and danger, turning down no missions and flying against all odds to save other soldiers. A few leaders and pilots who were among us chose a less than honorable path preferring self-preservation and gratification over risking their life to save another soldier. If any of us lived up to the standards set forth by Major Charles Kelly, this small minority totally missed the mark. And may God rest their lame souls.

"He is most free from danger who, even when safe, is on his guard."

Publilius Syrus

Fear This!

Chapter 5

Driving down the highway, I often see a decal on a vehicle's back window reading "No Fear!" or "Fear This!" and have to chuckle. Either the driver of the vehicle is the world's bravest person who could conquer anything or he just doesn't have a clue about life. When I pass them and look into their vehicle while chuckling, you can see them looking back and lip syncing "What the fuck you laughing at duuuude?"

The old tale of there being no atheists in combat is probably very close to being one-hundred percent accurate. Any person who has been in combat knows what fear is all about. How they cope with it determines whether they conquer the adversity or the adversity conquers them. If someone purports being a combat veteran and tells you they were never afraid, ask them what unit they were assigned to as an administrative clerk. Beyond their fantasies, they have never been in actual combat.

Webster's Dictionary defines fear as: "being an unpleasant often strong emotion caused by anticipation or awareness of danger." Webster's goes on to say that fear "implies anxiety and usually loss of courage." An element of fear inside us prevents us from doing stupid stuff. Higher levels of fear inhibit our ability to function.

Where was I on the spectrum of fear? My first night in Vietnam was spent at the 90th Replacement Battalion in Long Binh awaiting assignment to the 45th Medical Company (AA). Lying in the bunk at night, I could see the flares in the distance and hear the outgoing artillery fire heading to distant targets.

I have to be totally honest and say that I didn't know if I was going to puke, or shit my pants first. Halfway through the night, there was a sudden realization that in all my eagerness to put on my spurs and ride off into combat, I had really done something stupid. As invincible as I felt I was, I didn't know for sure whether some bad guy out in the jungle had a bullet with my name on it. None of us ever know that answer until it happens.

The difference between meeting danger head-on or succumbing to cowardice is determined by how each of us handles the fear factor. I found that early on in my tour, anxiety was present each time I flew a combat mission. As time progressed, fear was less prevalent and flying missions became routine, whether they were intense or not. But I was glad there was some level of fear circulating in my mind each time I flew. Fear kept a little twinge of paranoia alive inside of me. This small amount of paranoia allowed me to suspect the mundane and not fall victim to doing stupid shit that would cause the loss of lives. Helicopter pilots are often referred to as being slightly paranoid anyway so I was probably in the right vocation.

Outside of scheduled time off, Dustoff crew members were either waiting for a mission or were flying one. The alert signal for crews flying out of Long Binh was a Klaxon. When the horn went off, the standby crew dropped what they were doing. The optimal time from receipt of mission to lift-off was three minutes. Regardless of what I was doing when that horn went off, a small knot formed in my gut. Hustling to the Operations Room and then to the aircraft normally dissipated the anxiety. When the turbine spooled up to operating speed, the heart rate followed accordingly. With the engine instruments and adrenaline flow all in the normal operating range, we were on our way. Once over the site, the level of anxiety would fluctuate depending on what we saw and what we were being told about the tactical situation. Generally there was little loiter time in the evacuation area so other than concentrating on flying the helicopter, fear didn't enter into the equation. Even when the situation turned to shit, things happened too fast for fear to be a factor. That doesn't imply that in critical times we were just sitting back, sipping our mint juleps and taking everything in stride. I do mean that the adrenaline flow was pushing us into the flee or fight mode and we opted for the fight rather than the flee mode. "Fleas" cause you to itch, anyway.

Enroute to the hospital, we were confronted with the human carnage that we had onboard the helicopter. Soldiers missing limbs, sucking chest wounds, exposed brains, blood all over the place and the cry of men in severe pain. For the wounded, they had a fear of their own. In some cases, it was their impending death which was just moments away. The soldier's fear and anguish was absorbed by the crew members as we became part of their life's scenario.

Back on the ground, coming off the adrenaline high could leave you feeling very drained. If intense missions came back to back, as they often did, my autonomic response to the stress and strain would seemingly tighten the cheeks of my ass to the point where you couldn't slide a slick dime between them. A few times, the carnage was so severe that after I created some distance between myself and the other crew members, I would stop and puke my guts out. After the guts were empty, those experiences were locked away in a mental compartment so they would not produce a stumbling block in the future.

When the next mission came in over the radio or if the Klaxon sounded, I was back at it. As I have described, we all dealt with fear. During my twelve months of flying in combat, I witnessed only two incidents where fear became overwhelming. The pilot who was flying with me in Chapter 13 was overcome by fear and it debilitated him for the remainder of our mission. A short time after we returned to Long Binh, he somehow found himself on top of the company's small water tower and fell off, injuring his back. He was still grounded when I left country. In the words of a friend of mine who was there when that pilot departed country; "He was a mess when he left."

The mission in Chapter 11 talks about the crewchief we medically evacuated from Xuan Loc for a suspected self-inflicted gunshot wound. I use the term "suspected" because there is no way to prove or disprove his action, as there were no witnesses to the incident. Self-inflicted gunshot wounds, especially to the foot, were the most common "ticket" used to avoid the rigors of combat.

Flying in Vietnam was strictly voluntary—especially in Dustoff. Crewchiefs and medics found that in some cases they couldn't handle the human carnage that confronted them on a daily basis. Pilots at times found the airspace too small and the bullets too many (exact opposite of the big sky little bullet theory) and couldn't cope with the fear. Crewchiefs went back to the maintenance platoon and medics went to work in the hospitals. Each person had to cope, survive and in turn live with their decisions.

"Without courage, all other virtues lose their meaning."

Winston Churchill

SECTION

Leadership

Where Were the Leaders?

Poof! The "AC" Orders Disappear

Busted!

No Stinkin' Badges

Major Charles Kelly

Where Were the Leaders?

Chapter 6

"Leadership is a combination of strategy and character.
If you must be without one, be without strategy."
General H. Norman Schwarzkopf

The mystique of Major Charles Kelly was something I knew before I ever joined the military. An article in what I recall to be *Newsweek Magazine* in 1967 portrayed the heroism of Dustoff pilots and the missions they flew. Since I was being pressed to join the military, the role of the Dustoff pilot intrigued me and became my focus until January 1969 when I officially became one. As I approached January 1969, I learned more about Charles Kelly and the men that followed him. He set the standards: **"No compromise! No rationalization! No hesitation! Fly the mission!"**[1]

Stephen Covey says there are essentially four roles of leadership. In his terms, he defines them as Pathfinding, Aligning, Empowering and Modeling. Pathfinding is the ability to link what a leader is passionate in providing to what others are passionate in receiving.[2] LTC John Temperelli, as a young captain, was the first commander of the 57th Medical Company (HA) when it arrived in Vietnam in 1962. He was passionate about providing medical evacuation to wounded soldiers and establishing Dustoff as a meaningful organization.[3] Those who succeeded him, continued the passion. He fought the battle against bureaucracy to establish a foothold for the fledgling Dustoff concept.

Covey's second role of leadership is Aligning. How does the whole system work together, what are the parts and how do we align these parts to achieve both a vision and a strategy?[4] Major Kelly, along with his passion, understood all of the parts and how they should join together. His vision far exceeded that of the senior military commanders in that era. It was his passion in life. He trained pilots to fly in accordance with his vision. He brought all of the parts into harmony. He was a champion for the cause, often at personal risk of limiting his career by challenging the sacred cows of an ingrained bureaucracy.

Empowerment is the third role of leadership——the releasing of the talent, energy and contribution of people. Cultivating or creating an environment where people learn and grow making greater contributions in turn. Empowerment leads to commitment and commitment ensures alignment with the vision and the passion for the mission at hand. Empowerment embodies trust making it the foundation of the organization. A leader's job is to develop the talent and focus its energy in the right direction. Modern terminology is to think win-win.

The nucleus of the leader and that which binds the other three roles together is modeling.[5] When the 57th Medical Company (HA) assumed a split role, Major Kelly took part of the unit to Soc Trang. It was his intent to remain there long enough to make that portion of the unit mission ready. Captain Brady was promised that he could assume the leadership role for that portion of the company once Kelly was satisfied it was mission capable.[6] In current vernacular, Major Kelly walked the talk. He didn't tell his people to "go do it." He showed them the way. Kelly built trust among those who either needed or would need the services of a Dustoff crew. Major Kelly gave his life while modeling the mission and commitment to Dustoff in combat operations.

When I arrived in Long Binh at the 45th Medical Company (AA) in January 1969, WO Van T. Barfoot and I were assigned to Lai Khe with the 4th Platoon. Our platoon was commanded by Major Basil Smith. We had two additional commissioned officers in the platoon. Captain Jerry Forester (Infantry Branch) was a former Long Range Reconnaissance Patrol (LRRP) Staff Sergeant of whom we were in awe. When we arrived, Lieutenant Dan Weaver, the other commissioned officer, had just returned from Japan after recovering from being wounded. I flew my first combat hoist mission with Jerry Forester and flew another mission with Dan Weaver before he broke his previously wounded arm throwing a football. He was sent back to the States to recover. Jerry Forester was Tom Barfoot's role model and Tom later assumed his call sign when he made aircraft commander. My role model was Chief Warrant Officer 2 (CW2) Stephen Plume. A quiet and unassuming person, I never saw him get upset at anything. Well, maybe an exception would be when he returned from R&R only to find that his hooch had burned down and his only possessions were the clothes on his back. His blood pressure probably did rise a bit that day. He was an excellent teacher and mentor. Much of what he taught me in the time I flew with him was passed on to others as I filled his role as a mentor and then later as an instructor pilot.

In Lai Khe we lived in "permanent tents" and enjoyed it. We were on our own, so to speak, and away from the headquarters at Long Binh. Maybe that's why the platoon had the nickname of "Basil's Filthy Fourth" or as the enlisted men had named it, "Basil's Bastards." The platoon had a reputation of flying hard and doing their job—albeit they tore up some equipment in the process. The leadership did not waste any time withholding morning formations, shake down inspections, etc., because there was no causal reason to do so. People were empowered to do their jobs. Peer pressure and passion ensured we met the standards. Although I never met him, the legend of "Rotor Blade" Radigan lived on in the unit after his departure. His reputation was his nickname. From what I heard, large numbers of rotor blades met their fate as he guided his machine into tight LZs to extract wounded soldiers. If the machine didn't fit, he enlarged the landing zone a bit so that he could reach the wounded. The passion and commitment continued on. Even though we had not ever heard of Stephen Covey at the time, his principles of leadership were alive and well in the fourth platoon—at all levels.

In the platoon's small operations "shack" was a posting for the Silver Star and Distinguished Flying Cross nominees. Here they tracked the names of the crew members that were nominated for these awards. I was very humbled by this listing and wondered if I would be good enough to measure up to their standards. I do not know whether any of those awards came to fruition. The awards process within the "medical command" lacked sustenance and follow through—beginning with our company commander.

Very early in my tour, I was flying with a Chief Warrant Officer (CWO) that I fully respected. We heard a mission request come over our command frequency that was directed to one of the Majors in the unit. The CWO suggested we change radio frequencies and eavesdrop on the major's radio traffic. The lesson he wanted me to learn was not to emulate this leader's methodology in working with a ground unit. The ground unit was in enemy contact, they had several wounded soldiers and you could tell by the commander's voice that things on the ground were very intense. Our "instructor for this lesson" was dictating from the regulation that governed medical evacuation of wounded soldiers. He was telling the ground commander the requirements for securing the LZ and whom he would and would not extract. In this case, he was telling the ground commander that he would not evacuate the dead soldiers along with the wounded as it wasn't our job to evacuate the dead. Our jobs were fraught with danger and we all knew it. The CWO that I was flying with didn't mince words about the conduct of this Major. "The ground commander is just trying to survive and to get his wounded and dead soldiers evacuated. You expect the LZ to be hot. What you need to know is how many wounded they have, the general direction of where the enemy is located and whether or not they are still in contact. The wounded have priority, and if there is room for the dead, take them with you. Otherwise, the units either carry the dead with them or they increase their risk by having a "Slick" come in just to extract the dead. Take the 'regulation' for what it is. It is a guide—not a document of demands to be adhered to by the ground unit. This Major gives us all a bad reputation."

In early February 1969, pilots in the 57th Med (HA) located at Long Binh and pilots from the fourth platoon were exchanged to facilitate unit relocations. Tom Barfoot and I were sent back to Long Binh ahead of the platoon to begin learning their area of operations. A couple of 57th Med (AA) pilots took our places so that they could learn their new area as well. We were there for about two weeks before the rest of the platoon joined us. I'm not sure that Tom and I did anything to benefit the platoon since we still didn't know our ass from a hole in the ground. What we did find is Long Binh was a much different environment. With the complexity of the base came the bureaucracy that is associated with large organizations. The relaxed environment of Lai Khe was replaced with rules, pressed fatigues and polished boots. REMF land!! With the platoon transitioned to Long Binh, we were learning the new area of operations and becoming integrated into the normal flow of activities. There was no Silver Star or Distinguished Flying Cross nominees posted in operations. We did have a couple of award ceremonies but the awards were for pilots in our sister detachments. The fourth platoon continued flying hard and I think led the way in the number of missions flown in comparison to the remainder of the company at Long Binh. I do not want to infringe upon the reputation of VMF 214, but the fourth platoon could have easily been designated the Black Sheep of the company. We fit, but then again, we didn't.

The leadership within the 45th Med Co (AA) during my tenure was a mixture of styles and capabilities. As a 20 year old Warrant Officer with a sum total of less than two years in the Army, I looked to senior officers to provide the vision, the passion and the modeling. Sadly, that direction was lacking during the last half of my tour—where I thought it was the most critical. Fortunately it was there during the first six months of my tour—in my formative stage. The last of the original members of the 45th Medical Company (AA) left in June 1969.[8] LTC Arlie Price and LTC John Temperelli led an excellent organization. Along with their departure went many other commissioned and warrant officers that had continued the high standards established for Dustoff units by Major Kelly. We gained a new commander for the 45th Medical Company. According to the company newsletter for that period, it appears he had just finished the undergraduate college degree program.[7] The command group had been supportive of the pilots and crew members up to this time. But this change in command caused the organizational effectiveness to quickly erode. The new commander viewed and publicly stated that Warrant Officers were scum and punks. They lacked discipline and didn't follow rules. A gross generality imposed by this commander regarding members of his command that he didn't even know. And since he didn't fly combat missions, he would have no knowledge of what was required of the crew to make instantaneous decisions in the heat of battle. Rather than listening to the needs of the crew members for their equipment needs and working to change the authorized equipment lists, he confiscated medical equipment not authorized by TO&E tables.[8] Resources remained locked in conexes, sat idle and/or were destroyed. The commander felt that the enlisted members were drug abusers and if drugs were present in the unit, he was going to find them. While the enlisted crew members were out flying, he and his leadership group would conduct unannounced inspections of the crewmembers' living area. A surprise inspection when the people are available is one thing, a surprise inspection when the people are not there is another. Such actions only erode unit morale and trust in one's leaders.

With the sudden infusion of totally new leaders for basically all positions in June 1969, leadership by example coasted to a halt. Passion for the mission didn't extend much above the level of the line pilots and crew members. The commander saw one or two parts of the operation but not how they came together through a fusion of vision and strategy. If there was a vision or strategy, what they encompassed never made it down to my level. Empowerment or the releasing of talent and energy were choked off by the grip of fear wrapped around the throats of those who possessed the talent. New pilots, especially the warrant officers, were thwarted from understanding or living up to the "expectations" of Charles Kelly. And the commander provided no modeling. Zip! Zero! Zilch! The Kelly standards were replaced with meaningless "CYA" policies.

There was discussion that our new commander actively tried to avoid being assigned to the Dustoff unit in Vietnam. Even to the point of appearing before a flight evaluation board to turn in his wings. No factual reasons were stated as to why the commander pursued such efforts in order to avoid going to Vietnam. A Freedom of Information request (FOI) revealed that he retired from active military duty in March 1971. Assuming command in June 1969 left him with twenty-one months until his retirement date. Probably too close for him personally to risk losing his ass in combat. And to a certain degree, I can't blame him with wanting to survive a complete career without having to risk losing everything right at the end. The FOI did show his decorations included one Air Medal. That's probably reflective of having flown one hundred hours or less in Vietnam. One can surely draw their own conclusions but in the interest of fairness one should assume his reasons were legitimate. For either case, having a commander who assumed leadership responsibilities under duress, so to speak, is the worse thing that can happen to an organization. Whatever passion was burning inside our commander was not aligned with the mission of our organization. In our case, empowerment, the concept of win-win, trust and modeling were all concepts taken, wrapped up in a neat wad, and given to the Vietnamese shit burner to dispose of accordingly.

Cavalrymen of time gone by knew the cardinal rule of caring for their most valuable resource—his horse. He ensured his horse was well fed, watered, curried and content. One would think that he also occasionally brought treats to recognize the horse as being special. Good cavalrymen didn't ride their horses hard and then put them to bed wet. Nor did they go to the stables the next day and kick the horse in the ass to get him going. Poor treatment of the horse generally resulted in the horse having a bad attitude. With ears laid back and with a bit in his mouth, a disrespected horse would continue with his task but his performance was often in conflict with that of the rider. We had moved from a climate of trust to one of distrust and disrespect. The horses of this organization quickly tired of being "kicked," verbally whipped and treated like common jackasses. Their ears were pinned back and they were ready to strike with a readied hoof.

It didn't take long after our commander's arrival for the "fictitious" Warrant Officer Protective Association (WOPA) to quickly become an active entity. Even though this was not a formal organization, it surely represented the bonding that occurred among the warrant officers, enlisted men and some of the junior commissioned officers. Warrant officers in my era despised stupidity and bureaucratic regulations especially if they originated from commissioned officers that didn't command our respect. The warrant officer mentality must be a genetic defect, as we all seemed to think alike in this regard. Credible lieutenants saw the reality of what was happening but at the same time had to conduct themselves as commissioned officers and implement the commander's policies as best they could. Captains and lieutenants that couldn't find their ass with both hands followed aimlessly behind their "wannabe" commander. There was an ongoing dialogue among the "members" of WOPA about the command climate, the commander having a dedicated aircraft for the purpose of hauling nurses to parties, misuse of resources, disrespecting warrant officers and enlisted men in "public," the harassment of enlisted men, as well as other issues. The more disenchanted members, after bringing these issues to light with the commander and making no headway, contacted a staff reporter from the *Overseas Weekly* newspaper in September 1969. They met together for several hours, with the reporter taking very detailed notes. A follow-up meeting was conducted between the reporter, the company commander and subsequently the brigade commander. The Brigade Commander supported his commander against all of the allegations except he didn't think it was reasonable for the commander to refer to warrant officers as scum.[9]

A few days after these meetings, the article hit the front page of the *Overseas Weekly*. Ironically, the only name mentioned in the paper was mine—and I didn't even attend the interview session with the reporter—I was out flying. But that's okay, at least the incidents were presented in a reasonably favorable light. The story was told! But there was hell to pay in the unit as the commander was on a personal hunting safari to rat out those who snitched. With my name appearing in the news article, I was considered by default to be one of the rats. Pretty much after that, I was on the mission schedule each day. Home for me became the field standbys of Tan An and Xuan Loc for the remainder of my tour. The flying was great and I was happy to be in those locations—or any place other than "REMF land" and its ambiguities. The commander's possible intent though was a real mofo. Tom Wills was a supporter of the enlisted crew members, having been an enlisted man before becoming a warrant officer. Whether he met with the reporter or not is unknown to me. However, he was sent to the 57th Medical Detachment in Lai Khe for being a possible rat. Here again, I don't think Tom cared where he was assigned. It was the reason for being reassigned that pissed him off.

Nearing the end of my tour, Captain John Mitchell, our platoon leader, DEROS'd back to the States. His tour was complete. Those of us remaining in the platoon were like trout in a pond with an eagle circling overhead. We were going to be plucked to the bone in short course. The company commander seized this opportunity to disband the infamous "filthy fourth platoon" melding its remnants into other platoons. Tom Barfoot and I were assimilated into other platoons but were the only fourth platoon aircraft commanders remaining and were allowed to continue using our current platoon call signs. When Major Kelly was killed and subsequent commanders filled his position, some chose to become conservative in how they approached flying Dustoff missions. Others chose the ways of the "wild and wooly." In the 45th Medical Company, the commander and the executive officer were vocal about their dislike for Major Kelly's style. So the "wild and wooly" mentality was replaced with a bad case of "wussatoosis." The commander would even watch how we departed the heliport. Any thing less than a "flight school" normal takeoff from a hover, we were guilty of "cowboying" the helicopter. If caught in the act, you were going to hear about it some future time—probably in a public setting. You can't be a wuss and fly Dustoff. The two are diametrically opposed.

Vietnam was a unique war. Unit leaders were rotated in and out of command position to gain "combat" experience. This was the first war since Korea and it was essential for leaders to add the combat "feather" to their resume. This attributed to commanders at many levels not being proficient in leadership and/or tactics. By the time they learned, usually after six months, they were rotated out so another officer could gain "combat command time." The average unit in Vietnam had a turnover rate of nearly 120% per year.[10] It would be reasonable to assume the 45th Medical Company was close to a 100% turnover rate per year since everyone assigned was on a twelve-month tour of duty. Progression in rank typically required one-year time in grade from second lieutenant to first lieutenant then one or more years to captain. For commissioned officers, nearly one year of that sequence was devoted to flight school and the basic officers' course. So they arrived in country as senior first lieutenants. What training prepared them adequately for their combat roles? And once they learned through trial and error, assuming they lived through their mistakes, they returned to the States with a wealth of knowledge only to be replaced by inexperienced officers who were probably going to make the same or similar mistakes in their maturation process. I know that even at my level, I didn't know squat when I arrived in country. But when I left, I did so with a great deal of experience only to be replaced by a inexperienced warrant officer who was probably going to make the same mistakes that I had already made. Hopefully, they survived as I did.

Here again from my perspective, leadership by example came from Captains like Jerry Forester, John Mitchel, and Lieutenants T.C. Greer, Dan Weaver and Tony Alvarado. They were good pilots, possessed leadership skills along with the ability to listen and learn. They flew and fought with the aircrews they scheduled on daily missions. For those officers that chose the path of least "exposure," they knew that other Commissioned Officers, Warrant Officers and enlisted crew members would pickup the slack—ensuring the mission was always accomplished.

The meeting conducted by unit members with the reporter from the *Overseas Weekly* newspaper was the epitome of disloyalty to a commander. However, the commander's disloyalty to his soldiers was a greater leadership sin. The situation had deteriorated to the point where these soldiers felt they had no other option. If the 45th Medical Company (AA) had been a naval unit at sea, the "sailors" may have mutinied and dispatched the commander from a plank into the ocean. As it was, this company commander should have been relieved of command. I have seen commanders relieved for lesser reasons. But when his subordinates challenged the commander, his superior publicly supported his actions. This clearly established the tenor for the command climate at both echelons.

And the command marched on! Naw! The command limped on!

Poof! The "AC" Orders Disappeared

Chapter 7

Being appointed as an aircraft commander was not necessarily a promotion in the sense that rank or pay increased. It was, however, a promotion in the sense that you were entrusted with the lives of four crew members and the success of any mission given to you. The only status indicators were that your name was now listed in Flight Operations under Aircraft Commander column instead of the "peter pilot" column. It also meant you had your own unique call-sign which in essence was your professional signature that ground units and others came to recognize very quickly. If you did well they remembered. If you screwed up, they remembered. In my case, I selected the call sign of Dustoff 40 that was previously held by Lieutenant Dan Weaver.

The time between arriving in-country and when a pilot was designated to fly as an aircraft commander varied by aviation unit. For some units, it was six months in-country, other units based it on having a minimum number of combat flying hours or a combination of flying hours and time in-country. Our unit guide was a minimum of 400 hours and four months. My first flight in-country was on January 15, 1969. For new pilots, it takes training time to complete day and night orientations, flights into each hospital pad, both day and night, and time to gain a general understanding of how things are done. From the time you arrive in-country until you become an aircraft commander, you are in some form of training. When you first integrate into a crew, you are more of a liability than an asset due to lack of experience. The learning curve is vertical at first and if you survive the first couple of months, you change from liability to asset. Normal scheduling for me started on January 27th. On the down days, I would sit in the cockpit and go through "blind" cockpit procedures so that I could find switches, knobs and controls without having to look at them. I would study maps to help learn the names of fire bases, villages, etc., so I didn't have to rely upon the map as much just to get from Point A to Point B. This was more for my personal development than having been directed to go through this process. I truly wanted to fly and was not happy sitting on the ground doing meaningless stuff.

January 1969 was real slow for me as I only flew 30 hours that month. Each month thereafter were ninety-hour flight months. More crew schedule time was allocated to me as I made the transition from liability to asset. By May 1969, CWO Steve Plume said I was ready to leave the nest and become an aircraft commander. The other aircraft commanders that I had flown with agreed. On May 14, 1969, I passed a four-hour check ride and was appointed as an aircraft commander. At that point, I had 325 hours of combat time logged in a little less than four active months of flying. I have never had any doubts about my skills to fly any aircraft and this was no exception. I was ready to be an aircraft commander. At age 20, I now had the responsibility to command an unarmed medical evacuation helicopter in a single ship, all weather, and all terrain mission profile. The responsibility for the lives of the other crewmen, as well as the success of the "mission," rested squarely on my shoulders. Reflecting back to this time, who in their right mind would ever think about giving a quarter-of-a-million-dollar aircraft to a bunch of unsupervised "kids" and send them out on a combat mission? I look at my own kids at that age and others who are around me today of the same age bracket. Not in this lifetime would I have ever placed these "kids" in the situation we found ourselves in during Vietnam. But there I was, age 20, designated as an aircraft commander.

From May until July 1969, I flew an average of one hundred hours per month. I felt very comfortable in how I flew and what we, as an entire crew, were able to accomplish. I took great pride in having not lost an aircraft or a crew member during six months of combat flying. In mid-July 1969, we were on standby in Tan An, south of Saigon. 1LT T.C. Greer was my co-pilot, Bill Mostek was the crewchief and Jake Bilado was our medic. While we were flying out for a non-urgent Dustoff, a call came over the Dustoff radio frequency that an ARVN soldier had been critically wounded in the neck by a booby trap explosion. By the amount of blood the soldier was losing, the American Advisor with the unit thought his jugular vein had been hit. I pulled out my map, and found the coordinates to be about a mile away out our left door. I told central dispatch that we would take the mission and be there on the ground in less than two minutes. Although this soldier had been critically wounded, this day in fact turned out to be one of the luckier ones in his life.

Once on board the helicopter, Jake quickly analyzed the soldier's condition-- he did have a serious neck injury and was losing blood. Enroute to Saigon, Jake and I conversed about the patient's status. "Fly as fast as thing will go--and maybe he will make it." I told TC to pull in as much power as we had and pull the airspeed right up to the red line. Still a few miles, we were running at about 115 knots with the red line being 120 knots. As we approached the outskirts of Saigon, we began a shallow descent heading into the 3d Field Hospital. Rather than reducing power, we just eased the nose down and brought the airspeed right up to the red line. Heat thermals rising from the buildings in Saigon produced light turbulence. As we encountered the turbulence, the airspeed indicator blipped up to 140 knots. TC made a quick power reduction and raised the nose a bit which brought the airspeed below the red line. Jake was feverishly working on the patient to keep him alive. He was urging us to 'go faster' if we wanted to save this guy. To make a long story a bit shorter, when we handed the soldier off to the docs at the 3d Field Hospital, he was still alive. We assume that with the skill those docs possessed, the soldier survived.

Did we exceed the red line of the helicopter or was it a transient indication on the airspeed indicator due to the turbulence? We didn't know for sure. When we returned to Tan An, I asked our crewchief, Bill Mostek, to locate maintenance personnel and have them inspect our aircraft for any stress or damage from exceeding 120 knots. They inspected the aircraft and didn't find any damage. They also told us they didn't have the proper equipment to fully inspect the aircraft. So, "when in doubt, write it up!" I made an entry in the aircraft logbook that we had exceeded the 120 knots indicated airspeed and the aircraft needed to be inspected accordingly. We called back to Long Binh and they brought another aircraft to us. Maintenance personnel then returned to Long Binh with our aircraft, flying it under a limited one-time flight provision.

On July 21st, having returned to Long Binh from field standby, I was sleeping "late in the morning" when a knock came on our hooch door. The maintenance officer wanted to see me. I told the runner that I had been flying most of the night and I wanted to get some sleep. I told him that I would stop by and see the maintenance officer in a couple of hours. A few minutes later the runner returned and explained to me the major meant now and to get my ass in gear. I got dressed and went to the maintenance office. There sitting behind his desk was the maintenance officer looking down at the dash-13 containing my maintenance write-up. Never taking his eyes off of the dash 13, he asked me if this was my write-up. I asked him in turn if it was my name at the end of the write up. He said it was and I in turn replied that it must be my write-up, of course trying not to be antagonistic or anything. His follow-on question was whether I knew the company commander's policy about never exceeding aircraft limitations. Now there was an oxymoron—don't exceed limitations. That was almost a daily occurrence in one way or another. We always operated on the fringe of the aircraft limitations. I said, "yes" I knew of the policy and tried to explain the circumstances around the incident. He cut me off in mid-sentence and asked me the same redundant question again. As I tired to respond, he cut me off and said that he had test flown the aircraft but could not get the aircraft to go that fast! My conclusion from this dialogue was that I was being accused of lying. This accusation caused the hair on the back of my neck to bristle.

When I first came into the maintenance office, my warrant officer attitude was already apparent. I was pissed because this non-flying toad had apparently decided he was going to make this 'write up' a major issue--no pun intended. I can only assume that he and the commander had already talked about the write-up that I made on the dash-13 and that I was guilty of 'flying like a reckless warrant officer.' I told him, still with a civil tongue, that I would be happy to take him flying and demonstrate what had occurred. Given the circumstances of that particular day, we may or may not be able to replicate what I saw on the airspeed indicator.

He finally looked up and said the commander writes these policies for a reason and they are to be obeyed. At that, I lost it and had some choice comments about the REMFs who never flew and wrote policy letters only to cover their butts. I ended my diatribe by saying that, "if the commander doesn't like the way I fly, he can take my aircraft commander's orders." After that upstanding comment, I saluted and left his office and went back to bed—knowing I had let my mouth overload my ass.

An hour or two passed and there was another knock on the door. The runner said the company commander wanted my presence in his office immediately. When I arrived, my section leader and my platoon leader were already there. It didn't take a genius to figure out that I was up to my ears in shit and in a minute or two I would be totally submerged. CWO Steve Plume was my section leader and Captain John Mitchell was the platoon leader. Both got to speak on my behalf and both had good words for my capabilities as a pilot. When it came for my turn to speak, the commander asked me if I had made the "alleged" comment to the maintenance officer. I said, "Yes sir, I did." "Are you now willing to retract your statement?" was his follow on question. "No sir," was my response. "We didn't do anything intentional and we are not even sure that we actually exceeded the Velocity Not To Exceed (VNE) airspeed limits. We wanted the helicopter inspected for reasons of safety." With that, he said he was suspending my aircraft commander's orders and I was relegated to flying as a co-pilot until further notice. My last comment to him was that by taking this type of action, other pilots, to include myself, would never be frank, open and honest with him again. At that, my newly designated "peter pilot" ass was dismissed from his presence.

When the medics and crewchiefs in the fourth platoon heard the outcome of my meeting with the commander, they were overwhelmingly disappointed. Unbeknownst to me, several of them went to the commander during his open door sessions and complained about his actions. I was surprised and very pleased at the support they provided for me. Within the next five days, I submitted two unit transfer requests to other Dustoff units and Air Cavalry units. There was no need for me to hang around this unit any longer given the command climate that was present. The company commander denied both requests. So for the next three weeks, I was assigned to fly with lesser-experienced aircraft commanders with the caveat from the company commander that if I let the aircraft commanders screw up, it was my ass that would be in trouble. Somewhat of a tenuous situation to be in. I was not in charge of the helicopter but yet I had the implied responsibility for the mission's success.

One such mission involved an "aircraft commander" who attempted to hover down through triple canopy jungle, couldn't do it and aborted the mission. I had to ask politely to see if I could try it. Maneuvering to where the wounded soldiers were located involved hovering down though an opening in the first layer of tree canopy, then moving laterally under the canopy to another open area, descending further toward the ground and then moving back toward the ground unit. The pathway was tight and it took about 15 minutes to get down into the LZ. A great deal of crew coordination was necessary to keep the main rotor and tail rotor clear of trees, overhanging branches, etc. Had we taken fire, we were dead ducks. Our only escape route out was the way we came in. Richard Dean, after reading this chapter, commented that he recalls that our gunship escort radioed to us that they were amazed that we ever got into that LZ. The accomplishment of this mission was not based on being a better pilot than the other guy. The difference was experience and self-confidence in my abilities to fly the helicopter into that LZ--and to have full confidence in my crewchief and medic who were the eyes in the back to keep the helicopter clear as we zigged and zagged our way down through the trees.

After this mission, I met informally with the commander one more time. I went over the mission that I had just flown and reiterated to him that I needed to be flying as an aircraft commander or he needed to transfer me somewhere else. He paused for a moment, and then asked me how he could be guaranteed I wouldn't screw up again? My reply to him was that I didn't think I screwed up in the first place and if I really screwed up in the future, he

54

would be the last person I would tell. The next day, which was also my twenty-first birthday and a little over three weeks after their revocation, the commander reinstated my aircraft commander orders. That night, the crewchiefs, medics and I had one hell of a party to celebrate. In the next four months, I managed to fly an additional 492 hours as an aircraft commander before returning to the US.[1]

In preparation for writing this book, I read John L. Cook's, *Rescue Under Fire!* In Chapter 6, John Cook tells the story of Captain Walter Mueller, a Dustoff pilot with the 498th

Medical Company. They had received an urgent request to extract a wounded US soldier. Once on board, Mueller asked his medic about the soldier's condition. His medic replied, "He should make it if we hurry."[2] Cook went on to say that Mueller "put the RPM gauge in the red zone"[3] and headed to Nha Trang. Cook wraps up his story by saying, "Had Sullivan [the medic] not been so quick and skilled, and had Mueller not been so willing to abuse his aircraft, the wounded man would have died somewhere on the way to Nha Trang.[4]

My only thought here is that Mueller's company commander was imbued with the spirit and commitment of Major Charles Kelly. Otherwise Mueller may have also found himself once again to be a "peter pilot."

"I have often regretted my speech, never my silence."

Xenocrates (396-314 B.C.)

"Busted"
Chapter 8

A wise mentor of mine suggested that I photocopy all of my military records before I retired. "Once you turn them in, they are gone," he said. I followed his advice and also was able to retain my original flight records as they never asked for them and I never volunteered that I had them in my possession. When it came time to prepare this chapter, each of my DA Form 759-1s chronicling my flight hours were available to me.

The *Overseas Weekly* newspaper article that lambasted the company commander was distributed in-country on October 4, 1969. Even though I was not interviewed by the news reporter, my name and the incident that I had with the commander was highlighted in the article. Shortly after the release of the news article, I found myself flying strictly first or second up at Long Binh and then being fully relegated to flying from our remote field locations. The more I flew, the happier I was. Being located at one of our remote locations meant that I was away from REMF Land, which was fine with me. The DA-Form 759-1s for October and November 1969 show that I flew combat missions for 34 consecutive days (October 21-November 23) without a scheduled day off. Over those thirty-four days, I logged 212.5 hours. Within this period, my flight crew had six days with double-digit flight hours recorded. On October 22d, my crew flew 15.5 hours, some of which was probably contiguous with the flights on the 21st. In those two days, we flew 22.8 hours, 11 hours of which were at night.[1]

By regulation, a pilot could fly a maximum of 120 hours in 30 consecutive days. With command approval and after clearance by a flight surgeon, the maximum number of hours could be bumped up to 140 hours in a 30 consecutive day period. After departing from Long Binh enroute to Xuan Loc, our platoon leader called us on the radio late in the evening of October 22d and asked how many hours we had accumulated. We knew how many hours we had remaining on the aircraft until our next scheduled maintenance check time but I had no idea of how many hours I had flown in the last month. Didn't much care, either. He said it was greater than 140 hours but they were still doing "advanced ciphering" to determine the final total. It was then that he decided that I was grounded. Halfway back to Xuan Loc and he chose that moment to ground me. "Do I continue to Xuan Loc or turn around?" was my query of him. He said he didn't have a pilot to replace me so we were to continue on to Xuan Loc but not to fly any missions. Now there was a brilliant decision. Oddly enough, I didn't see him volunteer to take my place. His decision had potentially allowed for a soldier's life to become a pawn in a process to cover someone's ass that shouldn't have needed to be covered in the first place. He instructed us that a Long Binh crew would handle any mission called in during the night.

I talked to our "Fireball" operations folks when we arrived back at Xuan Loc. On their map, I drew a circle representing the area of operations that we could respond to quicker than anybody out of Long Binh. The Operations NCO was instructed that for an urgent mission within the circled area, he was to wake our crew. No soldiers were going to be placed in harm's way during my watch if I could prevent it. The gods of good fortune smiled down upon us, as the night was quiet with no missions required in our area of operations. We were relieved the next day by a fresh replacement crew.

Once the wizards closely analyzed our DA Form 2406-12's (the aircraft log book forms we recorded our flight time on and turned into company operations) and saw how many hours I had flown, the platoon leader was really pissed. Not only had I busted the 120 hour mark, I had absolutely trashed the 140 hour mark. And nobody gave me permission to do either. Major finger pointing was occurring at this time to see where the blame would ultimately fall. Being the low man on the ranking totem pole, the fingers all pointed at me. Could this possibly be a retroactive assignment as the crew scheduling officer? I don't think so!

By the time they packed my ass off to see the flight surgeon at Bien Hoa, my 30-day consecutive total hours flown was down to 177 hours—still 43 hours over the maximum number permitted by regulation. I was interned for a couple of hours with other pilots from different units who were in a similar fix. The doc checked me out and couldn't find anything physically wrong. The only comment he made about my mental capabilities was a touch of insanity for being a Dustoff pilot. That was something he didn't have a cure for so he grounded me for three days and said to be careful. With my reprieve in hand, I returned to Long Binh assured in my own mind that after a couple of days, I would be back flying again. My naiveté led me astray again because I forgot about REMF rules. The 45th Medical Company could have been down to zero aircraft commanders and I am sure we would have played the same "games" as far as grounding was concerned. When I gave my "reprieve" from the flight surgeon to the platoon leader, he said I would remain grounded until my flight hours were under 140 hours.

Apparently it was the first time this commander had encountered a pilot exceeding flying hours limitations so he was going to follow the rules to the letter. The commander's ire had been previously focused in my direction for allegedly exceeding the aircraft's airspeed limitations. I'm sure that by my now having exceeded the maximum allowable number of flying hours, and been caught in the act, he derived some perverse gratification from having me grounded. He decided to resolve the quandary by playing what I term "REMF Roulette". A spreadsheet in the Appendix shows the "REMF Roulette" game for my flight hour scenario. For the current day of the month, flight hours for the preceding thirty-day period are summed and if the total exceeds 140 hours, I remained benched for the next day's flying activities. On day 2, or the next calendar day, flight hours were summed for the new thirty-day period. Again if the total number of hours exceeded 140 hours, I remained benched for the following day's flight activities. This process played itself out until I reached a point where I was at least under 140 hours in a thirty-day period, preferably closer to or below 120 hours. Not being a math wizard, I was still able to quickly determine that I wasn't going to be flying combat missions anytime in the near term. As you can see by the chart, it took eleven days for me to reach a point where I would become flyable at or below 120 hours. One of the commander's favorite sayings was; "Idle hands are the devil's workshop." Now he and the platoon leader were faced with having a Warrant Officer on their hands for as much as eleven days with nothing for his idle hands to do. Suddenly, as if by magic, an interim cure appeared to convert idle hands to busy hands. I had become the company's assistant fire marshal. Now what do you imagine the role of an assistant fire marshal would be in an area consisting of plywood shacks that we referred to as home? Possibly empty the water-filled, manually pumped fire extinguishers that were located throughout our area ensuring they were all operationally ready? Absolutely! A noble job indeed as it was time to remove the build up of crud that had accumulated in the bottoms of the extinguishers and see if the damn things really worked or not.

Civilian labor in Vietnam came very cheap. There was no reason for the fire extinguishers to have been neglected for as long as they were. For a few extra piasters, they may have been able to convince the shit burner to work on the extinguishers. A much cleaner task than his primary duty!

I set about my task with eager anticipation. Within two days, all of the fire extinguishers were repaired, refilled and functionally checked for operation. I reported a green status to our platoon leader and looked forward to my next assignment—since I still had a few days left in my grounding status. Oh, the games people can play when they screw up and you are the culprit of their angst.

Now that the fire extinguishers were operational, my next task was to ensure they had fresh water—on a daily basis. You would have thought we were growing a garden or something. Fresh water on a daily basis for the fire extinguishers? You gotta be shitting me! We didn't have fresh water in our showers. Vietnamese were cooking with worse water than what we had in our fire extinguishers. It must have been the "idle hands" syndrome that drove them to decide to have me replace the water on a daily basis. After eleven months of combat flying, I didn't need to participate in petty harassment programs to occupy my idle time.

During my tour to this point, I had not taken either an in-country or out of

The "Officer's Ghetto Burns." Would operable fire extinguishers have prevented this?" 1969

country **R&R.** So I requested and received an unscheduled **R&R** trip to Australia. Tom Barfoot and I sat on the beach, drank plenty of Aussie beer and checked out the round-eyed women at Surfer's Paradise. Nothing like wrapping idle hands around a cold brewskie. Beat the hell out of refilling fire extinguishers.

Photo taken at Surfer's Paradise Austrailia-- 1969. "I wonder if she looks this good now?"

"Fill what's empty, empty what's full and scratch where it itches."

Duchess of Windsor

Awards the Commander had the
Authority to Pursue on
Behalf of his
Soldiers

"No Stinkin' Badges"

Chapter 9

If you have never been exposed to the teachings of Dr. Stephen Covey, the *Seven Habits of Highly Effective People* may seem a strange lead in to a chapter titled "no stinkin' badges." The basic tenants of the Seven Habits are Principles and Values. *Principles* are the natural laws or fundamental truths that are universal and timeless tending to produce predictable outcomes.[1] *Values* are the worth or priority we place on people, things, ideas or principles.[2] Stephen Covey says, "Our paradigms or perceptions of people influence the way we treat them." He goes on further to say that the most important resource available to any organization is the relationship among its people.[3]

The chapter entitled "Where are the Leaders?" outlines my perspective and that of others in the unit regarding the leadership climate during our time within the 45th Medical Company (AA). The commander created an environment where he openly referred to his people as "scum" and "punks." His pervasive perception served to influence the way the command treated its most valuable resource—the pilots and enlisted crew members that maintained and flew unarmed helicopters into harm's way to rescue others. Punishment and harassment came often. Rewards came infrequently. His unwritten rule stated that if a member of the command extended their tour by six months (for a total tour length of 18 months), they might receive an Army Commendation Medal (ARCOM). I am not sure what his requirements were to receive a Bronze Star (BSM) for meritorious achievement—I never witnessed one being given. Tactical units in Vietnam typically awarded their soldiers an ARCOM for their first six months and a BSM for the entire tour. The award of both medals for a tour was not always the case----but at least one of the awards would be given during the tour. The Army Commendation Medal can be awarded for acts of valor performed under circumstances which are of a lesser degree than required for the award of the Bronze Star. The ARCOM may also be awarded to soldiers who distinguish themselves through extraordinary achievement or meritorious achievement.[4] Doesn't it seem odd, if not pathetic, that a commander could not find anyone in a combat medical evacuation company that he could cite for extraordinary achievement or for meritorious service? By not recognizing his soldiers with these awards, when their service warranted it, conveyed the message to all that either their service was not meritorious or their service was not valued.

Highly effective organizations in today's business world continuously strive to improve the environment for their most valuable resource—their people. They value the differences their staff members provide to the organization. They seek ways to create synergy and operate with an abundance mentality—there is plenty of everything to go around. Southwest Airlines touts their employees as being first priority, with their customers following in a close second place.[5] Their premise is, if they have a satisfied work force, their employees will ensure the customers are satisfied. Les Schwab takes a similar approach but places their customers first and their employees second. The Les Schwab Company is an excellent organization. The difference between them and Southwest Airlines may only be in how the products and services are marketed rather than who is designated as the organization's first priority.

Yeah, but this is the Army, not Southwest Airlines. How can I compare apples and oranges? Warriors like Tom Tait, JE Hamby and Beau Bergeron never failed to recognize a soldier for an accomplishment whether by a one-on-one type pat on the back, through a personal note saying thanks, or by personally presenting a certificate or a medal. Unlike a civilian organization, the military constantly functions at high operational tempos. Commanders continually "ask" their soldiers to step it up another notch. It is much like going to a pail of water and repeatedly dipping out a cup or two. Soon the bucket will be empty

unless there is some means to replenish the resource. For these three leaders, their soldiers would go to the well time and time again, never depleting their willingness to go further. These leaders were not able to offer monetary performance bonuses, stock options, free trips or other tangible rewards. Why could they do this? What causes the well to be replenished?

The answer is simple yet very complex. Tait, Hamby and Bergeron learned to care for soldiers. They generated trust and respect with their soldiers. They understood leadership! The cavalryman knew that his most valuable resource was his horse. No horse, no mission capability! Good cavalrymen never rode their horses hard without caring for it properly at day's end. If they did, the mission capability of their horses would have been degraded on the short term and would have been unavailable for the long term.

Why couldn't the leadership of the 45th Medical Company (AA) get it right?

With the exception of the 1st Air Cavalry Division, which had its own organic medical evacuation company, Dustoff units were predominately assigned in a general support, rather than a direct support role. Dustoff units were organic to the medical system and its infrastructure. A unit recommending a Dustoff crew for an award would submit their recommendation through their reporting chain of command (company, battalion, brigade, and division). Once approved by the tactical unit chain of command, the recommendation would be forwarded to the responsible medical headquarters then work its way to the flight crew's respective organization. A commander at any point in the chain of command could recommend disapproval or downgrade of the award recommendation. How many in-boxes, routing slips and "give a shit-less attitudes" do you imagine an award recommendation encountered before it could be presented to the flight crew in our unit? The old adage of, "it got lost in the shuffle" is not a military axiom because paper flows efficiently. Being so far removed from the originating unit created an opportunity for paper work to be lost in the shuffle. How many other awards destined for pilots and crews in the 45th Medical Company (AA) were downgraded by the commander or tossed aside out of contempt?

The medical community did nothing to garner support for the Dustoff medics to be awarded the Combat Medics Badge (CMB). The CMB was conceived primarily for medics assigned to an infantry unit as a parallel award for the Combat Infantryman's Badge. The CMB served as recognition for medical aid men who shared the same hazards and hardships of ground combat on a daily basis with the infantry soldier. To be awarded the CMB, the infantry unit to which the medical personnel were assigned or attached must have engaged the enemy in active ground combat. Medical personnel must have been personally present and under fire to be eligible for the CMB.[6] The criterion was changed in Desert Storm to allow medics in armor and cavalry units to qualify for the award of the CMB. Ironically, a medic in Desert Storm may have never had to treat friendly casualties but yet still have qualified for the award. The medics in our unit were not eligible for the award because they were not assigned to an infantry unit. Medics in Dustoff units, actively flying combat missions, probably saw more hostile fire than their counterparts in the infantry units.

Webster's dictionary defines a hero as, "an illustrious warrior or one that shows great courage." Borrowing from Webster's one more time and looking at heroism, we find the definition to be, "heroic conduct as exhibited in fulfilling a high purpose or attaining a noble end." I'll let you be the judge but if I were to choose a percentile to represent the number of Dustoff crews who laid their asses on the line or gave their lives in an attempt to save another person, the percentage would be above 98%—and that is probably conservative. Within our unit, I could easily name those that preferred not to lay their asses on the line. The others laid it on the line every time they flew and asked for nothing in return.

While the aircrews in other aviation units were recognized for achievements that would pale in comparison to the missions accomplished by Dustoff crews, our crews were seldom recognized. Pilots like Steve Plume (who I fully believe was recommended for a Distinguished Service Cross for his participation in extracting the wounded when fire support base Oran was under siege), returned to the United States receiving little or no recognition.

Even though this chapter is short, it contains what I feel are very powerful learning points. The first point is an affirmation to any Dustoff crew member reading this book that their service in Vietnam truly fulfilled Webster's definition of a hero. Those who flew Dustoff missions, and the soldiers that were rescued, inherently know that we served a higher purpose.

The second point is that, whether we are leaders, managers or parents, the creed of the cavalrymen should be understood and practiced. The most valuable resource anyone will ever have, regardless of the situation, is people. Understand who your horses are and care for them properly.

And the third point is that a person's character is more important than any badge, ribbon or title that has been awarded. In the case of most former Dustoff crew members, when someone asks us about "Badges," the best reply is, "We have character, we don't need no stinkin' badges."

> "It is better to deserve honors and not have them, than to have them and not deserve them."
>
> Mark Twain

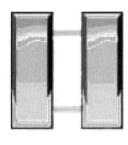

SECTION

War Stories

FSB Oran

Chapter 10

January 1969, was my first month in country. In processing, local area orientation rides and just stuff in general caused the month to be slow for really getting my feet wet in combat. Toward the end of the month, I became integrated into the normal mission schedule and the pace of flying increased significantly.

On February 1st, I was flying standby out of Dau Tieng with Steve Plume. Shortly after midnight, a mission came in for extraction of US soldiers from Fire Support Base Oran which was located approximately sixteen kilometers to the east-northeast of Dau Tieng. For the most part, this standby was my first introduction to night combat missions. Up until that time, I had a total of ten hours of night flying in Vietnam—hardly enough to even be marginally mission capable. My night time "training wheels" were steadfastly affixed to my "chariot."

FSB Oran was occupied by the 1st Battalion, 28th Infantry (Black Lions) along with other units from the 3d Brigade, 1st Infantry Division. The fire support base was a short distance away from Dau Tieng and was easy to find—the sky was illuminated by several parachute flares slowly descending over the ensuing battle. In just a few minutes, we were over the battle area. I was flying and Steve was talking on the radios. He pointed in a direction and that's where I flew the aircraft—kind of a point and drive method. The FSB was under siege from a northerly direction by the 101st NVA Regiment.[1] The ground unit was still in heavy contact and was not yet ready for us to come in for the extraction. Steve had me setup an orbit well to the east to remain clear of artillery gun target lines and to remain well outside the area of "confusion" that occurs in the airspace above an ongoing battle. Watching what was going on was enough to pucker the cheeks of my ass.

Aerial View of FSB Oran--January 1969

To the west, an NVA 51 caliber anti-aircraft gun had shot down a gunship belonging to the 11th Aviation Battalion and was engaged in a gun battle with another AH-1G crew. Both the crew members of the AH-1 and the NVA soldiers operating the anti-aircraft gun had huge pairs of balls. A fiery red stream of mini-gun 7.62 mm tracers formed a continuous link from the helicopter to the ground. Coming up from the ground and through the red tracers were the green tracers of the enemy 51 caliber anti-aircraft gun. These guys waged one hell of a duel. Both fell silent as the AH-1 put that enemy anti-aircraft position out of business and in turn the AH-1 had to limp home to patch his wounds.

The Recon element was the first unit to have contact with the enemy force moving about 2000 meters south-southwest of the FSB. They were moving back toward ORAN using fire and maneuver since they were still in contact with the enemy. Recon called for the medical evacuation at six minutes after midnight as their initial contact with the enemy resulted in two of Recon's soldiers being wounded. This evacuation was going to be doubly difficult. For the unit that was still moving and attempting to break contact with the enemy, having a helicopter land in their position was going to place them back in harm's way almost immediately. For our crew, locating the Recon element at night and then squeezing into a hot landing zone would increase our vulnerability by two fold. Leaving our initial orbit pattern, we made contact with the Recon element and safely extracted their two wounded without taking any hits from enemy automatic weapons fire that was being directed at us. After we departed, Recon continued to move toward the 'security' of FSB Oran.

We made a quick patient drop off at the 2nd Surgical Hospital across from our heliport at Lai Khe and then headed back to Oran. The FSB had come under ground attack and more soldiers had been wounded in the ongoing battle. Rebel 61 along with his light fire team were on station attempting to fend off the NVA's efforts to overrun Oran. While the air to ground battle ensued, the ground unit radioed they were ready for us to make our first evacuation effort. They were still in heavy contact but they had wounded they needed to have evacuated. They were going to mark the landing spot inside the fire support base with a strobe light. Turning our attention to the fire support base, we tried to visually locate a strobe light. The area was well illuminated by the many mortar and artillery flares suspended in the night sky by small parachutes. There were explosions inside the fire support base from incoming mortar or other types of enemy high explosive rounds. Friendly and enemy automatic weapons fire crisscrossed the landscape with every third round fired marked by a tracer round. Flashes illuminated the ground both inside and outside the perimeter of the base. In the melee of combat we didn't have the strobe light in sight when Steve started the approach. He figured that the fire support base was not that big--we should be able to find it as we got closer. Our intended point of landing was on the east side of the base.

Even though we turned our aircraft navigation lights off as we approached, there was so much illumination created by the artillery and mortar flares, there was no place to "hide" when we flew under the umbrella of descending flares. This caused the enemy to focus part of their attention on us. We also found a new anti-aircraft battery as they selected our helicopter for their first target of the night. Steve asked me if I had the strobe light on the ground. I said, "It looks like there is one on the east side of the fire base, but there are all kinds of flashes on the ground that make it difficult to keep it in sight." Steve pressed on with his approach still looking for the elusive strobe light. If we can't find the strobe light, we always had the option of aborting the approach and going around for a second attempt.

On short final, Steve felt confident he had the strobe light in sight. I was looking, but with the confusion on the battlefield, the strobe light wasn't jumping out at me. Crossing the outer wire perimeter at approximately forty feet above the ground, dead and wounded enemy soldiers could be seen entangled in the strands of concertina wire and other obstacles, which surrounded the fire support base. The wounded enemy soldiers who were possibly in the light grasp of the grim reaper found enough fortitude to send some automatic weapons fire in our direction—albeit not that accurately. They made a gallant effort to shoot us down. You could see other enemy soldiers within the 'wire' defenses lobbing hand grenades into the fire support base.

Steve had a good fix on the strobe light and brought the helicopter in for the landing. The other flashes that we were seeing were actually incoming mortar rounds. Shit! If they have a target fix that close to the strobe light location, we were prime beef waiting for the slaughter. Right at touch down, the medic and crewchief jumped outside the aircraft ready to load the wounded soldiers on board. The ground troops were not anxious to come out from behind their protective cover to assist—and I sure the hell couldn't blame them. Their asses had taken a pretty good "whupping" at the same time putting up one hell of a fight. Our medic and crewchief gathered some of the wounded along with the ground troops who over came their initial hesitancy and carried the rest of the wounded to the helicopter. In what seemed like an eternity, the six litter patients were loaded and we were again airborne. Our helicopter was not configured for that many litter patients so the three most critical remained on litters and the other three had to tough it out by laying or sitting wherever we could find room for them.

Clear of the fire support base, Steve turned the controls over to me and we headed towards Lai Khe Obviously we had the most critically wounded soldiers on board so we headed to the 2d Surgical Hospital (MASH) at Lai

Khe. They could be stabilized there and if necessary we, or another crew, would transfer them to Long Binh. The close proximity of the 2d Surgical Hospital allowed a quick turn around for us.

The 2nd Surgical Hospital at Lai Khe, which was located just across the helipad from where the 4th Platoon was located. Picture taken January 1969

Shortly after our departure, Bulldog 234, a UH-1 'slick' came in for a resupply drop of small arms ammunition and left ORAN with two more litter patients and one ambulatory patient. Rebel 61 was nearing his maximum time on station and was awaiting the arrival of Rebel 51. The preponderance of mortar fire coming into Oran was coming from the south and the southwest. The NVA had ringed the north to south quadrants with caliber 51 gun emplacements that served as their anti-aircraft defenses. The NVA were successful in bringing down one of our gunships. There was a mad frenzy by all aircraft in the area to get an exact location on the downed gunship and to provide security for the crew.

With the pressure being applied by the enemy through ground assaults, mortars, rockets and rocket propelled grenades, the military's ultimate weapon, of that era, was summoned to provide assistance. Spooky 71 reported on station at 0230 hours in the morning. The NVA were in for a major pummeling from the massive fire power that this AC-47 could impart. In between our extractions, resupply helicopters were able to get into the FSB, drop off small arms ammunition and at the same time extract wounded soldiers. After Spooky worked over the area, the assault on the fire support base was halted.

CH-47s then began resupplying Oran with badly needed artillery and mortar rounds. They were able to get five resupply lifts in during the nearly one hour lull in the battle. Dustoff 48, CW2 John Murray, was alerted at Lai Khe and he joined us to airlift more wounded soldiers out of the fire support base.

Throughout the night and early morning, we made five trips into the fire support base. Our total mission time devoted to FSB Oran was 7.5 hours.[2] We hot refueled every two hours or as the sequence of extracting the wounded allowed us. Just before sunrise, the enemy had broken contact and withdrew into the surrounding jungle trying to become invisible. Hunter-killer teams were hovering around trying to pick up blood trails or other signs of the fleeing enemy. With just a hint of cynicism, I might add that if the NVA regiment was augmented with any local Viet Cong forces, they probably broke contact so they could still make it to their day jobs and not be "docked" any time for being late to work. Our last flight into the fire support base was just after sunrise to pickup the last of the of the seriously wounded soldiers. While we were making our last flight into the FSB, a CH-47 Chinook was on short final to the west side of the fire support base to pick up the walking wounded and the soldiers that were killed in action. The American forces suffered two killed in action and thirty-three wounded.[3] We made two trips from Lai Khe to Long Binh for patient transfers of the wounded that we

Troops boarding a CH-47

had flown in there early that morning. Steve Plume, the crewchief, and medic did a superb job that night. I was along for the ride, still too little time in the saddle to really be fully effective in my role. Liaison officers from the 1st Infantry Division called back to our operations staff and obtained our names and service numbers to submit us for an award. When we returned to Lai

Khe, our names were posted in the Flight Operations Room as "Silver Star" nominees. A month or so later, we heard that the CH-47 crew received Silver Stars for their trips in to drop off their sling loads of ammunition during the lulls in the battle. We heard that our awards were upgraded to Distinguished Service Crosses. No paper work ever filtered down to our level and what started out to apparently be awards for valor never materialized. Whether the rumors of DSCs were in fact valid, we will never know. When we checked through the system, we found nothing but a cold trail. When Steve was back in the states, he ran across one of the Chinook pilots who confirmed their awards. This was not a unique occurrence for Dustoff crews as we typically had no champion for us that could follow such an award through multiple systems. I feel shortchanged not for myself, but for Steve and the two enlisted crew members. Everybody laid their ass on the line during the mission, but Steve Plume really made it happen. As the aircraft commander, he flew that helicopter into the fire support base numerous times while the battle raged on. The crew members directly exposed themselves to enemy fire in order to get the wounded into the helicopter. But then again, our job was to rescue the wounded and that was accomplished. We were very fortunate that night. Even with the tracers coming at us from all directions and with the incoming mortar explosions landing nearby while we were on the ground, we only received two hits from 51 caliber anti-aircraft fire.

FSB Oran was built on January 24, 1969. In the days following the attack of February 1st, elements of the 1st Battalion 28th Infantry came across a NVA base camp within two thousand meters of the FSB. Within the captured documents was a hand drawn map with a route from the Michelin Plantation into FSB Oran. The 'map' also contained a diagram of the layout for the FSB. Given the size of the enemy force that attack this FSB, it is a miracle more lives were not lost.[4] God was surely watching over everyone that night.

"Glory is fleeting, but obscurity is forever."

Napoleon Bonaparte

The aftereffects of NVA attack on FSB Oran The close-in-damage resulted from mortar rounds landing in the soldier's living "quarters" commonly referred to as tentage.

Outgoing artillery from FSB Oran after NVA were spotted earlier in the day.

Mission Area of Operations
For FSB Oran

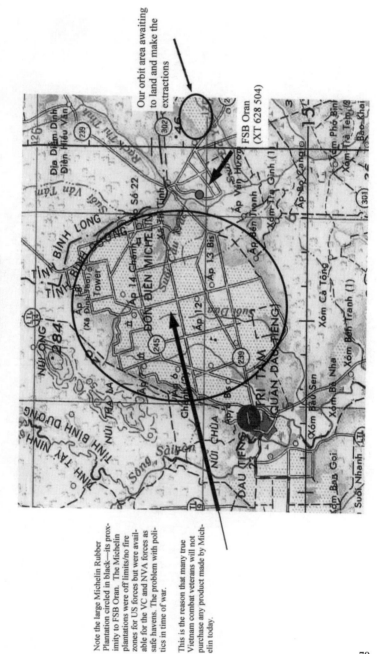

Our orbit area awaiting to land and make the extractions

FSB Oran (XT 628 504)

Note the large Michelin Rubber Plantation circled in black—its proximity to FSB Oran. The Michelin plantations were off limits/no fire zones for US forces but were available for the VC and NVA forces as safe havens. The problem with politics in time of war.

This is the reason that many true Vietnam combat veterans will not purchase any product made by Michelin today.

"Beware of the Boogyman"

Chapter 11

When our children were very young, they had this innate fear that the boogyman came out at night. Even though we could never find him, they were convinced that he lived underneath their bed at night. The inevitable question would always arise, "Dad is there really a boogyman?" Even though I knew the real answer to be true, I always told them he didn't really exist. The boogyman really lived in Vietnam. Where he slept was a moot point but I do know that he was around during our night missions. He would seemingly hang around waiting for the opportunity to present us with a challenge. Or better said, he threw challenges at us to see how messed-up we could get and still survive.

In flight school, my flight log shows a total of 19.1 hours of night flying.[1] Most of that time was dual with an instructor, in and around a stage field (student training heliport), cross-country or two hours of night hooded flight. Hooded flight is where the pilot undergoing training wears a small hood affixed to his flight helmet thereby removing any visual reference outside of the cockpit. Reliance upon his flight instruments then are his only means of flying and navigating. For the second phase of flight training at Hunter Army Airfield, Georgia, we flew UH-1's for the contact portion as well as what was termed tactical training. In the contact phase, night flight time was confined to the stage field and involved landing approaches to a lighted helipad and "emergency procedures" to a short lighted runway. For the tactical training segment, we made a very limited number of night landing approaches using a tactical VASI and beanbag lights arranged in an inverted "Y". We would overhear our instructors telling "war stories" to one another about making approaches in Vietnam without landing lights to non-lighted LZs except for a flashlight or cigarette lighter. Just war stories, we thought!

So what was flying at night like in Vietnam? When I am asked that question in mixed company, I gather them together in one of our kid's bedroom. We close the window shades, and turn out all of the lights. After a few seconds, the first comment heard is "Wow, this is really dark." "But what about the stars and the moon," they would ask? On top of the dresser, our son had a collection of small glow-in-the-dark toys that could be affixed to the ceiling or walls of a room. I put these up on the ceiling to represent the stars. "Wow, its still dark, but at least you know up from down," would be one of the comments. "And with the moon," some smart-ass would ask? Bed sheet in hand, I made one wrap around the over head light fixture for a full moon effect and turned the light on. "Flying at night, with the stars and a full moon out." "Not too bad, eh?" Some ho-hums would come from the group in response to my question but nobody seemed eager to try their hand at this type of flying. In non-mixed company, especially in a group of aviators, I would simply respond to the question of what it was like flying at night in Vietnam with, "It's like flying up a well digger's ass while he is digging at the bottom of the well." Smiles and nods come forth from the group, as they are able to visualize the experience.

About thirty percent of my flight time as an aircraft commander in Vietnam was at night. I never saw a VASI approach indicator system or bean-bag lights arranged in an inverted "T" during any night mission that I flew in Vietnam. The LZ marking methods that I encountered and the frequency of their use during my missions were: strobe light, flashlight, cigarette lighter, ground flare, jeep lights and nothing. Hospital heliports, hospital ships and other airports all had some form of standard lighting patterns. The biggest detractor to flying at night was the lack of a visible horizon.

We had the appropriate aircraft instrumentation to handle these conditions but the boogyman had the potential to induce vertigo when we were least expecting it. None of the LZ marking tools (strobe light, etc) provided any depth perception during a landing approach so that we could judge rate of closure or our height above the ground. The use of the landing light provided depth perception as well as rate of closure cues, but it also visually exposed the ground personnel to the enemy lurking in the area. Another reason for not using the landing light during night approaches in the Delta was to reduce the effects of "whiteout." In the dry season, dirt, dust and debris in the fields was picked up and swirled through the rotor blades during landing. The landing light refracting off the debris magnifies the intensity of the whiteout conditions. Even in the rainy season, the water in the rice paddies would be drawn up into the rotor blades and appear as a swirling watery mist in the rotorwash. The landing light then would reflect off the water particles creating potential whiteout conditions.

Flying at night did have its benefits. Darkness was also concealment for us as well as the enemy. No one had night vision devices at that time so everyone was on a similar footing. If we stayed blacked out (no lights at all visible on the aircraft), we could often sneak in and out of an LZ without being directly pinpointed. The noise from our turbine engine and the rotor blades signified our presence in the area but all they could do was shoot at the sound. Depending on your personal perspective, during the daytime it was more difficult to see the enemy firing at your helicopter. At night, you could see all of the tracer fire. Ground fire aimed at the helicopter was much easier to detect at night but it increased your fear factor knowing someone really had a target fix on you. But it also gave you an opportunity to evade it.

Flying at night was also lonely. With the exception of gunships flying in support of a unit in contact, the Dustoff crews were generally by themselves, especially as the night grew longer. And if the weather was bad, you might have been the only helicopter operating in the sector. It was not uncommon for us to be already on site to complete an extraction only to hear that our gunship escort cancelled their mission due to weather. In the southern portions of the Delta, the US Air Force's area radar control known as Paddy Control provided radar vectoring for aircrews. I used their services several times when we were flying near the Cambodian border. In the Saigon area, there was Paris Approach Control but they were geared more for the Air Force than they were for us Army guys. The radar transponders on our helicopters were seldom operational. Also, our helicopters were not, for the most part, equipped with VOR navigation radios. The first time that I tried to work with Paris Approach Control, we came up on their UHF frequency with the contact going something like this.

"Paris Approach Control, Dustoff 40, over."

Dustoff 40, Paris, go ahead."

"Roger Paris, Dustoff 40 is a UH-1 about 65 nautical miles northeast of Saigon, at 3000 feet, inadvertent IMC in a thunderstorm requesting vectors to Bien Hoa, over."

"Roger Dustoff 40, squawk 1200 on your Parrot and give us your DME fix off the Saigon TACAN, over."

Here we are, up to our asses in alligators and this air force guy is talking about parrots and TACANs. Neither my co-pilot nor I had a clue as to what he was talking about. And we sure weren't going to ask him what he meant.

My response was: "Paris Approach, Dustoff 40—that equipment is not operational, over."

"Roger, Dustoff, we are not going to be able to provide assistance, radar service terminated, over."

We worked our way out of the weather but through no assistance from the radar approach controller. Later, I found out that a parrot was Air Force terminology for an aircraft's transponder. Even in my ignorance, my reply to the controller was correct, the equipment was not operational primarily because it wasn't even installed in the helicopter.

Bearcat Army Heliport located seven miles, south-southeast from Long Binh provided excellent radar service for me during the monsoon season. If we were working in and around the Xuan Loc area and ran into bad weather, they were able to bail my butt out of trouble. I worked with them several times for an Area Surveillance Radar approach to our heliport in Long Binh. They could get us lined up with our very short and narrow runway, put us on a quarter mile final approach, and still be within their comfort zone for safety. They couldn't provide glide slope information but they gave us safe vectoring altitudes to avoid the known obstacles in the area. It was an excellent "out" if we were in trouble. We always had the option of taking a full GCA into Bearcat if the weather really got below safe minimums.

Early in my tour, I was flying with CWO Jones on the Saigon field standby rotation. Of the "field standby" locations, this was the most relaxed and comfortable. We didn't receive many missions, had hot showers, decent beds to sleep on, good chow and plenty of round-eyed nurses to visually overdose on. One of the missions we were given was a night mission for a US force that was hit hard. Their location was about 11 miles Southeast of Saigon on what was termed Tomahawk Island. The "island" bordered the canal and marsh area that fed into the South China Sea. Ground surface consisted of bamboo and nippa palm trees along with other marsh type grasses. Once in the area, we learned the unit was a Long Range Reconnaissance Patrol (LRRP) that had been ambushed. The soldier on the radio reported everyone had some form of injury or had been killed. They were not sure whether the enemy ambush force was still in the area. There was no LZ but he thought we could get a helicopter in to get them out. I was the co-pilot and talking with the ground unit. Jones was flying the helicopter. Our helicopter was named Flower Power with Mike Casper and Rick Blackwell flying as crewchief and medic respectively. I asked the unit to mark their area and the response was they had no lights other than a cigarette lighter. Here's a new challenge—find a LZ marked by a Zippo lighter. We had our navigation lights and rotating beacon on. Once we got close to his position, the soldier we were talking to on the ground was able to see us and give us general heading changes until we were able to detect his cigarette lighter. Not much illumination from a cigarette lighter. CWO Jones made the approach and on short final we turned the landing light on. There was no LZ. The soldiers we could see were hunkered down in an area containing nippa palm plants. CWO Jones decided that he was going to improvise a bit on the no landing zone option. I radioed the ground unit, told them to keep their heads down and we were going to make a LZ. CWO Jones repositioned the helicopter over a small canal and then smoothly eased the helicopter forward using the rotor blades to cut a "pathway" into the nippa palm plants far enough to where we could place the skids on the ground. When the rotor blades made contact with the soft nippa palm trees, shredded green fibrous plant was flying every which direction. In a quick few seconds, we were on the ground. Mike and Rick unplugged from their radio/intercom cords and went out to gather the dead and wounded LRRPs. We extracted everyone we could find on that first lift and then headed back to Saigon.

Between the time we returned to Saigon and refueled, the sun was beginning to rise. We decided to make another trip out to the extraction site just to ensure nobody was left behind in the landing zone. Coming to a high hover over the area, we used the down wash of air from the helicopter's rotor blades to part the grass so we could see anyone lying on the ground. We hovered around for five minutes or so and couldn't find any one else. Time to head home and get out of harm's way. While exiting the LRRP landing zone for the last time, Mike and Rick laid down suppressive fire with their M-16 and a M-79 grenade launcher—more for the John Wayne effect than out of a need to counteract enemy fire.

Staying at the 3d Field Hospital, as I said, was pretty nice. Along with the military policemen assigned to the hospital as a security force, the Dustoff crews were the only ones allowed to carry weapons in the hospital compound. After a brief time back on the ground, we received another mission. Heading out of our building and in the open compound area, Rick said he forgot something, tossed his M-79 to Mike and then hustled back to the room to retrieve the forgotten item. While we anxiously awaited Rick's return, Mike was fidgeting with the trigger on his M-79 when it suddenly discharged sending a 40mm grenade for an unintended flight in the hospital compound. Fortunately for everyone in the hospital area, the barrel was pointed towards the ground. The round hit the ground with a trajectory somewhere between a 45 and 60 degree angle, was then deflected upwards, striking my shoulder with a glancing blow and continuing vertically upwards in the air. As if caught in some kind of time warp, we watched as the grenade flew up, lost momentum, stalled and came back down towards us. The three of us were like deer frozen in the headlights of an oncoming car. Thump! The grenade hit the ground and we all flinched expecting to be riddled by flying shrapnel. Nothing happened! No explosion! The arming distance for a 40mm grenade is about 40 meters (it is spin armed). Why it didn't detonate, I have no idea. I can only assume that its impact with the ground caused the warhead to be damaged. The grenade rolled to a stop just for a quick moment. Mike had thought about catching the grenade as it came back down and then decided against self-annihilation. Quickly to the rescue, an apparent Medal of Honor wannabe dressed in green surgical scrubs appeared out of nowhere and kicked the grenade sending it tumbling across the asphalt courtyard. "Shit, we are all dead now!" Still nothing happened. No explosion! I walked over to it and stayed there until an MP arrived to secure the area. We had a mission to fly and left the MP in charge of our errant M-79 round.

The sandbags can be seen about midway in the compound that the EOD folks used to cover the grenade.

The bomb disposal unit was summonsed to come and blow the grenade in place. By the time we returned from the mission, EOD had just finished sandbagging and placing C-4 on the round. We had the opportunity to see them detonate it with an electrical timing device. The next explosion we heard came from the hospital commander's office. CWO Jones and I were called down to the commander's office to explain what had happened. There wasn't much that could be offered in our defense. The crew didn't clear their

The aftereffects of the C-4 and the M-79 grenade being detonated. One can only imagine what would have happened to the four of us had the grenade gone off when it hit the ground the first or second time.

weapons, and the M-79 grenade launcher was accidentally discharged. After a brief exchange of salutations, the commander proceeded to discharge on CWO Jones. That was one time when I was glad I was not an aircraft commander. I felt the impact of the explosion and I wasn't even the target.

The first part of May 1969, I was recommended for advancement to aircraft commander (AC). I had one more field assignment flying with an aircraft commander from the third platoon. We were flying the field standby out of Tan An and had been there for a few days. The aircraft commander was Lt. Tom Camp. I had not previously flown with him so it would be a learning experience for both of us. Before this particular night mission to extract wounded soldiers west of Tan An, the field standby did allow us to fly several missions together thereby becoming more familiar with how each of us flew. The aircraft assigned to this mission was once again, "Flower Power" (66-16429) crewed by Mike Casper along with his medic, Rick Blackwell.

Since I was about ready to take my AC check ride, Tom said this mission was mine to fly. We headed west out of Tan An and climbed into the darkness of the night. Tom made radio contact with the ground unit. They had three soldiers with serious gunshot wounds. The unit had just broken contact so the enemy was still in the area. They were going to mark the LZ with a strobe light and recommended an east to west approach direction with a departure to the east. The unit was located in an area of dry rice paddies. As we approached the area, the ground unit called and said they had the lights of a helicopter off to their southeast. We asked them to turn their strobe light on. The pulsing white flashes of the strobe against a pitch-black background made it easy for us to locate their position. With the exception of the two to three foot berms around the rice paddies, the area was reported to be clear of any obstacles. This is about the point where the boogyman decided to help us out a bit—give a challenge or two for the mission. We agreed that because it was so dark, we would use the landing light on short final approach to get a quick look at the LZ and then turn it off before we landed. On short final, I called out that the landing light was coming on. No sooner had I turned the light on than the sky lit up with tracer rounds flying towards our helicopter. I quickly turned the light back off but the tracers continued so I aborted the approach less than 50 feet off the ground and started a go-around for another approach attempt. Lt. Camp said, "I have the controls" which means we switched duties. He finished the go around while chewing my ass for not continuing the approach. Camp brought the helicopter around and set up for another approach. I called out his airspeed and altitude so he would be able to judge his position in relation to the ground. On final approach, his approach angle was too shallow and placed us very low over the ground. His airspeed was also too high. Tom said he didn't want the landing light turned on—he intended to make a blacked out approach. Probably the wisest decision given the tactical situation. Here again, the strobe light makes depth perception and rate of closure difficult to determine during a night approach. We began to receive fire from our three o'clock position as called out by Mike over the intercom. About the time I yelled at him to "go around" we impacted the rice paddy dike. Wham! We hit the dike with about 40 knots of forward airspeed. This bounced us into the air and we continued flying forward. The force of the impact when we hit the paddy dike locked our shoulder harnesses so we were ready for the subsequent touchdown. It seemed like an eternity before we came back down to earth. Mike thought we had crashed and was grabbing for his M-16 and bag of ammo to exit the helicopter. Remember it is pitch ass black so in the few seconds from the time we hit the paddy dike until we came back down, we had no visual cue to detect motion or the aircraft's flight attitude. Dust and shit were flying through the open windows and cargo doors. Fortunately for the soldier holding the strobe light, he caught a glimpse of our helicopter and realized he was about to become a hood ornament. He was able to jump out of the way at the last second. I caught flashes of human silhouettes scattering out of our path as we impacted earth for a second time. We slid a short distance across the rice paddy coming to a full stop a little ways from our intended point of landing.

Literally after the dust and shit settled, Mike and Rick loaded the wounded soldiers on board and we headed off to Tan An for our patient drop off at the aide station. The helicopter required a little more left pedal to fly after we had hit the ground. Also our FM radio transmissions were weak and scratchy sounding. Landing on the medical pad at Tan An, the helicopter was sitting abnormally tail low. After off loading our patients, we repositioned the helicopter to our normal parking area, shut it down and did a walk around

Tom Camp (L) and David Jones (R) standing in front of
Flower Power

inspection to check for damage. The top of the vertical stabilizer is about 10 feet above the ground. When I walked to the end of the tail boom, the tail rotor that sets atop the vertical stabilizer was at eye level. We hit the ground with such impact that the rear skid crossover tube underneath the helicopter was spread nearly flat. The cross tube normally has a fairly smooth arc to it. The FM radio antenna, located on top of the vertical stabilizer (tail) had flexed laterally to the left and made contact with the tail rotor blades. This contact severed the FM radio antenna leaving us with about half a length of antenna with strands of broken fiberglass threads as the only remnants of the missing part. Now the mystery was resolved as to why our radio communications were garbled after our controlled crash in the LZ. The tail boom appeared to have flexed and bent which may have contributed to our tail rotor control input difficulties. LT Camp called back to Long Binh and reported the aircraft damage. In the daylight hours of early morning, we looked at the aircraft for a second time. We were amazed at the amount of damage done during this landing. The boogyman really worked his magic on us this round.

Another helicopter was flown down to us the next morning. The maintenance crew determined the helicopter was not flyable and coordinated for it to be airlifted by CH-47 back to Bien Hoa. I cannot fault Tom Camp's skills as a pilot in this incident. Combat flying places the crew on the operational edge between success and failure. It is a very fine line with circumstances often beyond the crews' control. We obviously damaged the aircraft. But we successfully completed the mission while receiving enemy ground fire throughout the process. This mission was no walk in the park exercise. It tested our personal limitations in many different respects.

Flower Power was airlifted from Tan An to the maintenance facility at Bien Hoa. The helicopter never returned to flying service with our unit. We received a new helicopter in return. Mike Casper's pride and joy had been mortally wounded. The soldiers we successfully evacuated recovered from their wounds including our feeble attempt to land on them in the rice paddy. And just as important, the four helicopter crew members were able to walk away from this incident. On a comparative basis, the mission sounds like success to me. What do you think?

Mike Casper standing in front of Flower Power

"Black holes are where God divided by zero."

Steven Wright

Hoist Bird—2d Up in Long Binh
Post January 1970

256 feet of cable of which 200 is a safe guide for fully useable cable length.

Jungle Penetrator with the paddle seats that fold down

Hoist is powered via the helicopter's electrical system.

Hell-Hole where soldiers who are not seriously wounded are placed.

Note that the cargo doors are removed. Why I cannot say—it eliminates the red cross markings on each side plus "allows" for a soldier to fall out of the helicopter.

"Beam Me Up, Bubba!"
—The Hoist Mission—

Chapter 12

"Hovering is for pilots who love to fly but have no place to go."

The terrain that I operated in during my tour was divided between the rice paddies of the delta and the thick canopy jungle in the transition zone between the delta and the mountains. In the delta, the terrain in my area of operations was flat and consisted of rice paddies, canals, rivers with the land being crisscrossed with a rudimentary road network. During the monsoon season, the whole area seemed like one vast rice paddy interspersed with small hamlets or villages. While I flew in the delta, we never carried an internal hoist in the aircraft nor did we really have a need for a hoist. The one or two times a hoist would have been nice to have, we were able to "use" the helicopter as an oversized weedeater to make our own LZ.

Triple canopy jungle interspersed with mountains in the eastern and northern areas of operations provided extraction challenges for the flight crews. Natural landing zones were generally not available. Damage from B-52 air strikes created ready made LZs. Ground units could create a LZ by detonating explosives to clear an area. But in many cases, time, as well as the tactical situation, did not allow for engineering operations of this magnitude. The hoist quickly became the most valuable piece of equipment available to the Dustoff crews. Our unit was equipped with the electrically powered Breeze hoist. The hoist contained a maximum of 250 feet of *twisted* cable, which allowed us to reach all of the soldiers that I personally extracted. The hoist was capable of lifting 600 pounds. The amount of weight we could hoist during one lift sequence was limited more by the helicopter's lateral center of gravity than by the capability of the hoist. We installed the hoist behind the co-pilot's seat, which was located forward of the helicopter's longitudinal center of gravity. From a flight control perspective, there was a danger of having insufficient lateral and longitudinal control for maintaining a stable hover position.

Jake Bailado and "Hover Lover" in 1969

Although the Breeze hoist had its problems, it was, for the most part, a valuable piece of equipment. Its weak link was the twisted cable. When the jungle penetrator was being reeled in with patients on it, there was a tendency for the penetrator to rotate on its horizontal plane. This combined with general wear and tear on the cable, the strands of twisted cable would tend to separate at the most inopportune time—while hoisting a wounded soldier from the jungle. The separated cable strands would bind up in the control arm not allowing the cable to be extended or retracted. The crew was then faced with having a wounded soldier suspended beneath the aircraft and unable to extend or retract the hoist cable. The choices available to the aircraft commander were to electrically cut the cable, separating the soldier from the aircraft, or to fly the wounded soldier, while dangling below the helicopter, out of the hoist site to an open location. My unspoken guarantee to the soldier on the jungle penetrator was that we would never cut the cable on him once he left the ground.

Flying unarmed medical evacuation helicopters was a highly dangerous job to begin with. The hoist mission doubled the risk factor. Add darkness along with poor weather conditions, the mission approached the fringes of being suicidal. During my tour, I flew 26 hoist missions. Each hoist mission was an "E-ticket ride." Some went smoothly and some turned to absolute shit in a heartbeat. Weather in the form of high-density altitude, cross winds, and low clouds with rain or fog provided a complicating set of challenges. The experience levels of the crew and their ability to perform as an effective team were other factors determining whether the hoist mission was a success or failure. And finally, let us not forget our worthwhile enemy who found the helicopter to be very vulnerable during a hoist mission. The Dustoff helicopter was the enemy's prized target for destruction.

Flying with Captain Jerry Forester on my second mission in Vietnam, we hoisted two wounded soldiers from a First Infantry Division armored unit. With a total of about two hours of combat flying experience under my belt at the time, I was pretty much an observer to the process. Captain Forester did the flying while handling the internal communications within the crew. I handled the external communications with the ground unit. I was on the controls lightly following him through the motions to sense control inputs as well as to provide a backup in case he was incapacitated. Though there was incoming ground fire, we made the extraction without being hit. Even in the supporting role that I played in this first hoist mission, the adrenaline rush was intense. After 30 minutes or so of being back on the ground, there was a sense of being more fatigued than normal.

My next involvement in a hoist mission came when flying on February 4, 1969. I was part of the fourth platoon contingent at Long Binh learning the area of operations. I was flying with Captain Langhorn from the 57th Medical Company that was assigned to Long Binh and was projected to replace our fourth platoon at Lai Khe. At the noon hour break, we ate lunch with the crew who was flying second up—the hoist ship. The co-pilot, WO William Hix and I

RPG 7

had gone to flight school together. Captain Otha Poole was a good friend of Captain Langhorn. Within the hour, Captain Poole, WO Hix, Specialist 4 James McNish and Specialist 4 Gary Johnson were performing a hoist mission northwest of Xuan Loc. The helicopter was at a stationary hover, with the jungle penetrator near the ground when the VC fired the rocket propelled grenade hitting the helicopter in the primary fuel cell. The resulting explosion totally obliterated the aircraft. We were airborne at the time and flew to the scene to see if there was anything we could do. There were no survivors. Another aircraft was dispatched at a later time to hoist the wounded soldiers from the LZ. This experience burned in my mind, the vision of the crew's added vulnerability when performing a hoist mission. I do not believe it ever caused me to fear a hoist mission. It did, however, build a very healthy respect for this type of mission. No aspects of the tactical situation could be taken lightly as the crews were literally hovering at death's doorstep.

Prior to arriving in the area of the hoist mission, we would contact the ground unit for a tactical situation update and to confirm the number and status of their wounded. If gunships were on station, we would exchange information with them to ensure we were all on the same sheet of music. Once we understood the tactical situation, we briefed the gunships on our mission plan. I preferred not to orbit over the intended hoist site. Staying in a loiter area a couple of miles away kept us away from artillery gun target lines, command and control helicopters and whatever else was ongoing in support of the operations. When the unit was ready for us, we asked them to "pop smoke." Leaving our loiter area when we called for smoke, we were able to easily locate the site, make an orbit or two for a visual check of the area, determine wind direction, and then move away to begin our low level approach. My desired approach profile was to quickly descend from our orbit altitude approximately one-half mile from the landing zone in the opposite direction of the enemy contact, make a steep tight turn and head back towards the landing zone for our brief final approach. In our descent, we would ask the ground unit for another smoke of the same color. The additional smoke was to ensure we didn't lose site of the landing zone during the approach. When we reached a "tree top" altitude, we began a gradual deceleration from a 100-knot airspeed until arriving at a hover over the smoke. On very short final, the pilot flying the helicopter, the medic, and crewchief would come up on "hot mike"—open intercom—so we could all talk and listen without having to use a "transmit switch". The non-flying pilot was not on hot mike and was in charge of the UHF and FM radio communications.

Hovering over the pick-up site, the crewchief who was the hoist operator directed the aircraft into its final position. Both the crewchief and medic cleared the main rotor blades and the tail rotor from making contact with the trees. The downwash of air from the rotor blades caused the trees to sway about thereby making it difficult to establish a steady hover reference point. I really liked to hover below the surrounding treetops so that I was in and among the trees for better concealment. Yes, the enemy could hear us hovering in the area, but I hoped that by being down in the trees, we would be more difficult to find. Plus the lower we were, the less time it took to hoist the wounded out of the LZ. When hovering in the trees, I preferred to find a tree that I could set the nose of the helicopter against—aircraft skin to tree leaf contact. This tree then became our constant hover reference point making it easier for us to stay directly over the site.

Once we had a stable hover over the site, the crewchief would report "penetrator going down" and "penetrator on the ground." Getting the jungle penetrator on the ground was fairly easy. The hard part was bringing the wounded back up to the helicopter. We could hoist two soldiers at a time depending on their size. Small and large often had different meanings to people. While the ground unit was securing their wounded soldiers to the penetrator, the crewchief would be talking to the pilot about the helicopter's positioning over the site, how many wounded were coming up and obstacle clearance. When the crewchief was ready to "break ground" with the penetrator, he would announce "coming light"—pause—followed by "breaking ground." When the crewchief would announce coming light, the pilot who was on the controls would begin applying opposite cyclic control input—in this case to the left. When the crewchief broke ground, the lateral center of gravity moved to the right necessitating the left cyclic control input to remain stationary over the hover point. The crewchief paused just after breaking ground to ensure there was enough cyclic control remaining for the pilot to stabilize the helicopter. If there weren't, the helicopter would begin to drift to the right requiring the patient to be lowered quickly the foot or two back to the ground. If we didn't follow this procedure, we risked crashing into the trees or dragging the wounded soldier(s) through the trees as we attempted to fly the helicopter. After breaking ground and with the helicopter's hover stabilized, the crewchief would begin raising the penetrator with its valuable cargo up toward the helicopter. Frequently, the wounded would get hung-up in the trees, so close coordination was required by all crew members to maneuver them away from the obstacle. Keep in mind, the pilot cannot see the patient or the ground--he is relying totally on verbal directions from the medic and crewchief. When the wounded were on board, the medic took over the responsibility for the patient(s). The medic and crewchief would situate the "patient" in the helicopter so the medic could administer first to him and at the same time keep the helicopter within

the center of gravity. Flying the hoist "sequence" demanded a great deal of emotional and physical energy. After the first "lift" of the wounded, I generally switched controls to the non-flying pilot for a break from the tension. When flying with an inexperienced co-pilot, I always monitored the ground communications on the FM radio whether I was flying or whether I was the back-up pilot. With an experienced pilot, I evenly divided the radios and flying duties as the trust factor had already been established with him. The experience level of the crewchief and the medic also dictated how tight I set the helicopter into the trees. The break in duties was always welcomed especially if you had been flying for ten hours or so. Fatigue and the stress of flying the hoist mission could jump up and bite you in the ass when you were least expecting it.

If you were afraid of the "boogeyman" when you were a kid, you would not have enjoyed the night hoist missions. With the night version of the hoist mission came additional gremlins wanting to help you to make a mistake. Darkness obscured cells of bad weather, low clouds, fog and terrain creating problems in even reaching the LZ. A strobe light was used to mark the LZ and could only be seen from overhead in the jungle terrain.

Gunship escorts at night would often have a UH-1 with a high intensity Xeon searchlight mounted in the cargo compartment. The searchlight when properly employed made it seem like it was daylight in the LZ. When improperly employed, it was a liability. The chances of having a gunship escort at night was a 50-50 probability. Without the gunships, the Dustoff helicopter was an extremely vulnerable target. On approach to the hoist location, I turned off the navigation lights and the rotating beacon. On very short final, we turned the landing and searchlights on. Even though we had the landing

UH-1 with a door mounted Xeon Searchlight
and a 7.62 mm mini-gun.

lights on, by turning the red, green and white navigation marker lights off, I felt that we were less of a pinpoint target for snipers or other enemy ground fire. At night, the helicopter's landing light and searchlight were used for LZ illumination. The landing light was pointed directly beneath the helicopter so the crewchief could see the ground

and the jungle penetrator. The searchlight was pointed at a 45 degree angle in front of the helicopter so the pilots could find something to use as a hover reference point. The airflow from the rotor's downwash caused the trees to sway and appeared to dance in the lights. For the crewchief and medic, the reflection from the landing lights illuminated the tip path plane of the main rotor and tail rotor, making it easier for them to judge distance from the turning rotors to the obstacles. A moment's lapse in concentration can result in the pilot being overcome by vertigo. Here again, if I could find a tree to stick the nose on, I did it. The tree and the helicopter became one, making it easier to remain over the hover point.

Of the 26 hoist missions I flew, the following short stories represent the most rewarding and the worst of the worst. These two missions provided gratification in one instance and deep regret in the other. The early 1990's were famous for the saying, "When Shit Happens" or "Shit Happens." There is a substantial difference between having the decal on the back of your VW Micro Bus and not being involved in life versus being in the driver's seat of life when things really turn to shit. People die and you have no control over the events other than it continues to pile up. After digging yourself from beneath the "pile," you still have to find some salvation for the situation.

> "Anyone can do the job when things are going right.
> In this business, we play for keeps."
>
> Ernest K. Gann

Soldier being hoisted using a rigid litter. The rigid litter was used for severe neck or back injuries where the wounded needed to remain immobile.

"A brave soul riding the hoist up during a demonstration for the
101st Airborne Division"

"Doing What's Right."

The documentation for this segment is derived from a personal letter to me from the Commander, 4th Battalion, 12th Infantry, 199th Light Infantry Brigade (Sep)(Lt), dated December 31, 1969. Our crew received no other recognition for this mission. The action occurred on December 28, 1969 about nine days before I was scheduled to return to the states. To be able to tell the story, I have had to ad-lib with the call signs in order to add interest for you, the reader. The sequences of events are accurate.

We were flying out of Xuan Loc when we received an urgent hoist mission request in support of Company A, 4th Battalion, 12th Infantry, 199th Light Infantry Brigade located northeast of Dinh Quan. The hoist mission came in around 1:00 PM. Flight time was estimated to be about 15 minutes to reach the extraction site. Enroute, we made contact with the ground unit and received a situational briefing. The unit had encountered enemy contact resulting in one US soldier with critical injuries requiring extraction using a hoist. Gunships had been requested but were not yet on station. The platoon with the injured soldier was moving to the company's location for better security during the extraction.

Arriving on station, we found two other aircraft in orbit over the unit, an OH-58 with the unit's battalion commander, LTC Robert Clark, on board as well as an OV-10 Bronco. The gunships were supposed to be enroute but there was no ETA for them. Discussing the tactical situation with the battalion commander, I told him we were comfortable with the OV-10 providing air to ground target suppression if we were engaged by the enemy. Although a single OV-10 is not necessarily a daunting force, the pilot would be able to place enough suppressive fire on the location to enable us to egress from the site. If nothing else, the sight of a multi-engine aircraft diving on the enemy's location at 300 mph would be enough of an imposing threat to cause them to redirect their fire towards him or just quit firing altogether and hide until the aircraft passed their location.

We radioed the ground unit saying we were ready anytime they were. Following on the heels of that radio transmission was the battalion commander coming up on the radio telling us the wounded soldier had died. Well, that was a real downer for us and I can expect the same for the ground unit. The unit didn't have any other wounded soldiers that needed our assistance so I radioed back to them that we were going to break station and return to Long Binh. Before I could say anything else, the battalion commander was back on the radio to ask me if I would be willing to hoist the dead soldier. Carrying a dead comrade for the remainder of the day until they could get a resupply helicopter into their location would be demoralizing to the other soldiers and a physical burden for the unit until a resupply helicopter could reach them.

The commander knew the rules that prevented us from placing the crew and the helicopter in harm's way to hoist a soldier that we couldn't help. We had a real ethical question on our hands! Not only did I have just nine days left until my Vietnam tour was complete, I also had the responsibility for safeguarding my crew members from unnecessarily risking their lives. It's now "Monday morning" and you are the "quarterback." What are you going to do? Hoist him or leave him? Keep in mind the motto of: "No Compromise! No Rationalization! No Hesitation! Fly the Mission!"

For our crew, it was a three second internal survey over the intercom— "let's hoist him," came the joint statement of agreement from the crew. I radioed the battalion commander and said, "How about checking the soldier again just to see if there might be some sign of life in him."

"Roger, standby!" After a short pause, the battalion commander came back on the radio. "Dustoff 40, our medic has detected a sign of life in him and they are requesting an immediate extraction."

"Roger 6, have the unit pop smoke and identify for us."

"Roger Dustoff, yellow smoke is out."

"We have the yellow smoke and we'll be over their heads in 30 seconds."

Approaching southeast to northwest, we arrived over the area, came to a hover and the crewchief started the jungle penetrator down through the canopy. After a few seconds, the dreaded words were heard over our hot mike intercom.

"Hoist cable is not going down. It's stuck!" said the crewchief.

"Try bringing it back a bit and then lowering it again," I told the crewchief.

"Sir, it ain't fucking moving either direction and its seventy-five feet below us."

"Okay, we'll fly the penetrator out."

"D-22, Dustoff 40—the hoist cable jammed about halfway out. We're going to lift out vertically to clear the penetrator from the trees and if we can find a LZ close by, we'll land and try to fix the damn hoist."

"Roger, four-zero, we'll standby."

Decision time once again for you Monday morning quarterbacks. Do you leave and head back to Long Binh or do you finish the mission?

The OV-10 was quick to react and found a suitable LZ within 500 meters of the hoist site. He made a couple of low passes to see if he could draw any enemy fire, but he came away clean. We flew at less than 60 knots, with the jungle penetrator dangling seventy-five feet below us. Coming to a high hover over the open area, we set the penetrator on the ground and then quickly landed next to it. "Can you pull more cable out of the hoist?" I asked the crewchief.

"We'll try," came his response. He and the medic were successful in pulling more cable out so we had about 150 feet of cable extended. The crewchief and medic each grabbed an arm full of hoist cable along with the jungle penetrator and laid it all on the cargo floor. With them climbing hastily back on board the helicopter, we were ready to give it another try.

"Ready on the right! Ready on the left," came the crews response. They were set to head back to the LZ.

"D-22, Dustoff 40. We are inbound to your location. We have enough cable reeled out to get the penetrator to the ground. We'll see if this will work so that we can lift the soldier out of the LZ."

"Roger 40, smoke is out."

Arriving directly overhead of where the smoke was rising through the treetops, the crewchief guided us back into position, and once at a hover, the crewchief and medic hand fed the penetrator and cable from the cargo compartment down towards the ground.

When we initially departed Xuan Loc area, we estimated that we had one hour of fuel to accomplish the mission and still get back to Long Binh. As we eased into a hover over the site for our second attempt, we had been on station for about 50 minutes. Our fuel on board at this point was now reaching the critical point and there would be doubt as to whether we could make it back to Long Binh. We were watching the fuel gauge and 20 minute fuel warning light which we expected to be illuminated very soon. Every minute we remained on station, our risk factor increased. Each crew member's adrenaline level was on the rise. "Sir, the soldier is on the penetrator, anytime you are ready," announced the crewchief.

The task now facing us was to vertically climb 200 feet while remaining stationary at a hover while raising the soldier out of the jungle. As the pilots, we are flying "blind" and had total reliance upon the directions and guidance of the crewchief as we eased the soldier up through the trees. Even though we knew the soldier was already dead, there was no reason to treat him in a disrespectful manner by dragging the body through the trees. Once clear of the trees, we flew at 60 knots to the same LZ we left just minutes before. The OV-10 was overhead; performing simulated strafing runs in an attempt to draw any enemy fire that may be intended for us. Once we had the soldier on the ground, we quickly descended and landed next to him. The cable, penetrator and the dead soldier were quickly loaded on the aircraft and we were on our way—five minutes beyond our allocated on-station time fuel limit.

"D-22, Dustoff 40. Off your location heading back to Long Binh. We will be taking your soldier into the 93d Evac."

"Thanks for everything, Dustoff."

"Our privilege, Sir! We are QSY to the Arty boys at this time."

Heading back to Long Binh, we adjusted our airspeed and power settings trying to maximize our fuel economy. The medic worked on the soldier and confirmed he was a KIA. We called Wide Minnow and were advised to take the soldier into the 93^d Evac in Long Binh. We radioed back to our base operations and told them to have either an aircraft or a vehicle available to bring 20 gallons of fuel to us somewhere in the proximity of the Long Binh perimeter—the exact location was yet to be determined. We requested them to have either the first or third up crew rendezvous with us for a possible patient hand-off. The fuel gauge was painting the picture that we were not going to make it to the 93d Evac. And there sure wasn't any AM/PM Mini Mart nearby to stop at and refuel.

My visual focus alternated between Long Binh in the near distance and the fuel gauge--as well as the 20 minutes of fuel remaining caution light that was now illuminated. Arriving at the outer perimeter of Long Binh, we were about 21 minutes into our 20-minute fuel reserve. We had already made radio contact with the first up crew out of Long Binh and now confirmed the coordinates of where we intended to land our aircraft. We elected not to risk hitting fuel exhaustion and having to autorotate into "down town" Long Binh. I'm sure the way our day had gone, if we would have had an engine failure due to fuel starvation and had come crashing down through some REMF's building, there would have been hell to pay. And I'm not sure I had enough 'money' to pay for hell.

Thirty minutes after we shut the helicopter down and made the "patient transfer," a maintenance helicopter showed up with 25 gallons of JP-4 loaded in five-gallon 'jerry cans.' The "insulting" task of having to refuel our helicopter, five gallons at a time, lasted about 30 minutes. We loaded enough fuel on board to ensure we had the capability of making the five-minute flight to our heliport where we could take on a full load of fuel. After we refueled, we headed back to Xuan Loc to finish out our holiday season field standby.

And now you are asking, "Where is the positive outcome? Looks like a screwed up mission to me that didn't get any better." The soldiers on the ground were the benefactors of the positive outcome. They didn't have the burden of carrying their fallen comrade for the rest of the day and having him as a constant visual reminder of how dangerous their job was. For the crew, our satisfaction came from completing the mission and helping the ground unit in the only way that we could. Once again, we operated on the fringes of disaster, but that was a daily occurrence for us. For those Monday morning quarterbacks who made decisions to turn back and not complete the mission, I hearken back to Major Kelly's credo of "No Compromise!" "No Rationalization!" "No Hesitation!" "Fly the Mission!" Given the same circumstances today, I would *still* fly this mission.

"Do or not do. There is no try."

Yoda

"Max Velocity, Zero Direction"

This title comes from a saying that I assimilated in my military career which in essence implies you are going around in circles as fast as you can thereby getting nowhere while doing it. As I reflect on the mission where everything turned to shit, (nobody gave a damn about the situation we were in and couldn't get off their collective asses to help solve the problem), the old saying seemed to fit the situation.

This mission again occurred while I was on field standby in December 1969 with approximately 15 days remaining in my combat tour. Our problem arose in part from the lack of crew training and crew coordination. The company commander opted to disband the integrated crews and mix and match "players" hoping they could function as a cohesive team. The crewchief and the medic assigned to our standby mission had never worked together, nor had I worked with the crewchief. The crewchief was very inexperienced and had never flown a hoist mission.

Because I had experienced several incidents of the twisted hoist cable coming apart causing the cable lockup inside the hoist's control arm, I made a point to do a "dry hoist" after installing the hoist in the helicopter. This gave the crewchief an opportunity to check the cable for any frays and signs of damage. This dry hoist exercise also served as a training session for our new crewchief.

Even though the Xuan Loc field standby routinely performed the greatest number of hoist missions, the command group refused to place a second backup hoist on site in case the primary hoist failed. By locating a backup hoist at Xuan Loc, the amount of turn around time saved would be substantial in the event a problem was encountered. Command mentality preferred to keep the spare hoist at Long Binh for their second up mission crew.

Our mission came in around 10:00 PM. An infantry battalion had engaged a larger sized enemy force and had incurred four casualties with gunshot wounds. One soldier was in critical condition. As we headed to the aircraft, we could see the illumination flares well east of Xuan Loc, so we knew right where we were going. Once airborne, we made contact with the ground unit, confirmed their location, number of wounded and status of the LZ. Indeed, the ground unit was located where we could see the flares in the distance. They had four wounded that would require a hoist extraction and the LZ was currently "hot." Gunships were on station flying in support of the ground unit. They were using their "firefly" to illuminate suspected enemy targets with the gunships then applying the ordnance on designated target areas. I advised the ground unit we would loiter just west of their position until they were ready for us. Most importantly, I told them I wanted their most seriously wounded soldiers to come up first in case we had to abort the mission for some reason. While we loitered in the area, I briefed the crew that we would use a high overhead approach so we could keep the strobe light in sight. Our final approach would be from west to east. The crewchief and medic would then guide us to the exact location for the hoist extraction. The "gun drivers" had a third helicopter with them, a UH-1 equipped with a high intensity Xeon searchlight mounted in the cargo compartment. For our purposes, the light bird would be used to illuminate our area so we would have plenty of light to see what we were doing.

The ground unit radioed they were ready for us and we left our loiter point with a two minute ETA. A quick call to the guns let them know that we were going to slip through their orbit pattern and approach the LZ from west to east. We had the LZ pinpointed and arrived over the site, making adjustments in aircraft positioning to get directly above the strobe light.

"We're taking fire," yelled the crewchief.

"Chief, we are not taking direct fire. The ground unit is shooting and they are still in contact. Get the penetrator on the ground so we can get the wounded hoisted out." You could hear the fear in his voice and his uncertainty of being there. We are nestled in the trees trying to maintain a steady hover. The crewchief's strict focus was on trying to operate the hoist. Due to his inexperience, he was task-saturated at this point.

"Tango one six alpha, reminder that we want your most serious on the penetrator first, over."

"Roger, Dustoff 40."

"Penetrator on the ground. Sir, I don't think I can do this."

"Chief, you did fine with your dry hoist today. This is a piece of cake. Everybody's ass is hanging out here and we are depending on you. You can do this hoist. Remember to tell us before you break ground, then ease him up, stop so we can stabilize the helicopter, and then continue on up. Just like we did today," I said.

"Sir, they are still shooting. Okay, the ground guys are ready, coming up."

"Easy, Chief. Stop! Okay we are stable, bring him up," I said.

"He's spinning in circles," said the crewchief.

"Stop bringing him up. Wait until he quits spinning. Chief, what's going on back there---talk to me."

"Sir the hoist won't come up, what do I do?" cried the crewchief.

"Doc, slide over and see if we have his penetrator stuck in the trees," I directed.

"Penetrator's clear! Control switch won't raise the penetrator," Doc replied.

"Check the circuit breaker," I told Doc.

"Circuit breaker is in and set," Doc said.

"Tango 16 Alpha, Dustoff 40. Our hoist is tits-up. We're gonna fly your guy out of here the way we have him now."

"Roger, Dustoff, we still have the most serious guys here with us."

Now we're fucked. The penetrator is half between us and the ground and we don't have their critical guy with us.

A quick call to the gunships to tell them our hoist is tits-up. They will need to find a place for us to fly this guy so we can set him down safely and land next to him. Once we are on the ground, we can load the soldier on board and determine if we can do anything with the hoist to make it operational.

The gunship escort along with their light ship departed the LZ before we did in order to locate a suitable landing zone to the west of our location. West was towards Long Binh thereby reducing our enroute time to the hospital.

"Okay, let's get this guy up and outta here. Chief, you and Doc keep talking to us so we don't drag this guy through the fucking trees. And you keep your hands off the cut switch," I said.

"Ease it up. He is hitting tree limbs but he's free. Okay! Come on up."

Okay, he's clear of the trees," the crew said as we were climbing vertically at a hover.

Once clear of the trees, we picked up the lights of the gunships to our west and headed towards where they were illuminating an area and laying down suppressive fire.

"Okay guys, the gunnies are heading to the west, they will find an area for us to land in and recover our wounded soldier. We're gonna come to a hover, set this guy on the ground and then land next to him. Doc, you get him in the chopper; Chief, you pull the cable all the way out to the red line. Understand?"

"Roger, sir," came the reply from the back.

"Long Binh Dustoff, Dustoff 40."

"Four-zero, Long Binh, go ahead."

112

"We are off site now, the hoist is tits-up. I need for you to dispatch one of the Long Binh aircraft to Xuan Loc with a spare hoist for us. At Xuan Loc, I'll transfer my patient to him, put the new hoist in our aircraft and go back out. They still have wounded that need to be hoisted."

"Roger, four zero."

The guns were working over the LZ; firefly had the LZ illuminated for us. With all of the lights and "fireworks" going off, it looked like a grand opening for a Cal Worthington car dealership in Southern California. We came to a high hover over the LZ and eased the wounded soldier down to the ground. After he reached terra firma, we quickly landed close by. Doc went over to the soldier, who was somewhat ambulatory. Chief was working mightily trying to pull more cable out. The hoist wouldn't electrically feed the cable in either direction and Chief couldn't pull it out. Whatever happened inside the hoist, it was frozen in place. So any effort to lower the penetrator and use the hoist like a Macquire rig, to essentially repeat the process we just completed, was no longer an option for us. With the cable, penetrator and the wounded soldier on board, we headed to Xuan Loc to link up with the inbound crew. Nearing Xuan Loc, the first up crew contacted us and we exchanged ETA's. When I asked him if he had the spare hoist with him, he said that he didn't. They couldn't find the guy with the keys to the connex where they stored the spare hoist. From this point on, my normally cool and unassuming demeanor went to hell in a hand basket. If there was a rule or policy within 40 miles of me, it was probably going to be violated within the next two hours. "Couldn't find the guy with the connex keys. Give me a fucking break!" I told the first up crew they were on their own and they might as well turn around. They were as useless as tits on a boar hog for this situation.

"Long Binh Dustoff, Dustoff 40."

"Dustoff 40, Long Binh, go ahead."

"Okay ladies, you guys fucked this up. Now listen carefully. We are about 20 minutes out of Long Binh. I'm going to patient drop at the 93d, and then I am going reposition to the engine run-up pad. I want a hoist sitting on that pad, waiting for me. Is that clear?"

"Roger, Dustoff 40."

Doc was working on the patient who was going to survive. Doc said the guy's eyes were as big as saucer plates when we picked him up off the ground. That didn't surprise me. Here we lifted him out of a LZ, dangling seventy-
five feet below the helicopter, in the pitch ass dark and flew him into a LZ that was being prepped by gunships. If I had been in his shoes, my eyes would be as huge as saucer plates in addition to having a brown load in my shorts.

"Long Binh Dustoff, Dustoff 40. One mile final landing Long Binh, patient drop-off at the 93d. You guys got my hoist ready?"

"Dustoff 40, Long Binh; cleared to land, winds calm, hover direct to the 93d. Uh, we haven't found the guy with the keys to the connex yet, over."

Keying the mike switch, I asked, "Everyone at the O'Club?"

"Yes, Sir!"

"Okay, Long Binh, this is four-zero, I'll take care of it. After the patient drop off we will be repositioning to the run-up pad."

"Roger, four-zero!"

With the patient now in the hands of the medics at the 93d Evac, we hovered over to the engine run-up pad which was right next to the connex containing the backup hoist. The connex was near the front of the officer's club Quonset hut. I told the medic to go and check to see if there was a lock on the connex. I also told him to take his weapon and if the connex was locked, I wanted him to shoot the lock off. With the helicopter running that close to the officer's club, the noise and vibration we generated disrupted whatever was going on inside and several of the officers came outside to see what was going on. When the medic shot the lock off the connex, the officers standing outside scattered like spooked quail. The medic and crewchief quickly had a new hoist for us and the exchange went quickly. We did a quick electrical check to make sure everything worked. It checked out fine. Lord only knows what kind of condition the cable was in, but we would be finding out very soon. Before heading back to the extraction site, we needed to hot refuel. In lieu of hovering back out to our short runway and then hovering west to the hot refuel point, I just snatched the helicopter up from the pad to a one-hundred foot hover. From there I proceeded on a straight-line course to the hot refuel point passing directly above the parked helicopters that were below us.

I am not sure whether shooting the lock off the connex or the high hovering over the parked helicopters was the precursor for the radio to crackle back to life, but it did and there was an angry major on the other end. I just ignored his radio chatter. I think that really pissed him off more. When we finished refueling, I called Operations for takeoff which only provided an "advisory service" after our small control tower closed. Instead of hovering out to our small runway, I just did a vertical takeoff from the pad, cleared the surrounding wires, and nosed it over. We were on our way back to the hoist extraction site. I was extremely pissed at the command group and I wanted them to know it not only by my physical actions but through my comments directed back to the major in the operations building. The summation of my comments over the radio politely boiled down to reminding the major that if anyone had any brains around there, they would have placed the second hoist at Xuan Loc and we wouldn't be having our current word exchange over the radio.

We got back to the hoist site, the guns had departed station to rearm and refuel and the critically wounded soldier had died. We went in, hoisted the two wounded and the one dead soldier in turn flying them to the 93d Evacuation Hospital. Back in Long Binh, radio communications were simple and concise avoiding any mention of the circumstances surrounding this mission. We refueled and headed back to Xuan Loc.

I was down to about fifteen days remaining in-country. On the quiet flight back to Xuan Loc my mind was spinning around trying to determine if I did the right thing and whether the "right thing" was going to get me court martialed. Oh, well! What's done was done. The worse they could do is keep me in Vietnam. I said a silent prayer that it wasn't going to be in the infamous Long Binh Jail.

After doing a post-flight inspection on the helicopter we headed back to our operations building to await another mission. The crew chief said he would follow along shortly after he did some work on the helicopter. You're thinking the conclusion of this story has arrived. Not so! There was still plenty of room to throw another shovel of shit onto the pile just to make the day "pleasurable."

While lying on our bunks, winding down from the last mission, the telephone rang in our operations room. The RTO answered and shouted out that we have an evacuation request from the aid station right there at Xuan Loc. One US soldier with a self-inflicted gunshot wound to the foot. The aid station will meet us at our helicopter for a patient transfer. We hurriedly gathered our stuff and beat feet for the helicopter. The crewchief wasn't at the helicopter when we arrived. The medic untied the rotor blades and we cranked up the Huey. Even if the crewchief didn't show up, we could handle the flight to Long Binh without any difficulty. The medical aid vehicle arrived moments after we had the helicopter ready for departure. The medics swung open the back doors of the ambulance and guess who was lying on the stretcher? Yep, our crewchief! Seems he was "clearing his weapon" with the barrel muzzle resting on the toe of his boot, when the M-16 suddenly discharged.

Obviously the crewchief was not going to fly anymore for awhile so after dropping him off at the hospital, we picked up a new crewchief and headed back to Xuan Loc for the remainder of our field standby.

"I do not feel obligated to believe some God, who had endowed us with sense, reason, and intellect, has intended us to forego their use."

Galileo Galilei

"No Gunship Cover"
Non-Secure Night Hoist Mission
Chapter 13

In reviewing the stories in previous chapters and those following this one, you as the reader may have drawn the conclusion that I was some kind of recalcitrant Warrant Officer. Obstinately defiant of authority or generally disobedient in my disrespect for written policy letters and/or regulations that impeded our mission capability. Mentors told me about the policies and regulations; that they were guides, not etched in stone. The situation always dictated how the mission would be accomplished with no two missions being identical. The Army, in its infinite wisdom, selected high quality people to train as Warrant Officer pilots. We were taught to think and to fly helicopters into situations where others couldn't or wouldn't go. Otherwise, they would have strapped chimpanzees into the cockpit, much as NASA did with their early "astronaut" program. Our company commander, I believe, would have preferred the Army train chimpanzees in lieu of sending him Warrant Officers. But life is a bitch in the fast lane.

This story fits a similar theme of disregarding the "gospel," as set forth by the commander of the 45th Medical Company (AA), which dictated that a pilot would not perform a hoist mission without having gunship coverage for security. This wasn't the first time that I violated this policy nor was it the last, albeit my tour was coming to an end. The chances of having gunship cover at night were a 50-50 proposition. If the gunships were already on station or we were talking with them while they were enroute, one part of the "50%" was assured. If they were not on station and/or we weren't talking to them, we were guaranteed the other "50%" would be in effect. Without the prospects of gunship support, we had to make a decision on the significance of the tactical situation, in comparison to how urgent the soldier's condition was. The aircraft commander basically had the decision of life and death for the soldiers on the ground and for his crew. At age 21, with eleven months of combat flying under my belt, policies written by REMFs

Rob Spitzer and myself on field standby. You can see the hoist over Rob's left shoulder. Photograph was taken in late 1969 with the helicopter parked on the number 2 hotspot at Long Binh.

who didn't fly combat missions were meaningless. The decision had to be made on site—not in the O'Club.

On the night of December 19, 1969 while flying standby out of Xuan Loc, we were alerted by Fireball Operations that we had an urgent hoist mission 15 kilometers southeast of Xuan Loc to extract four US soldiers wounded by enemy contact. We launched out of Xuan Loc, quickly covered the fifteen kilometers and picked up an orbit west of the coordinates of YS 559 999. Our mission sheet gave us a frequency of FM 45.60 and ground unit call sign of "B-50." We spent seven minutes on this frequency attempting to contact B-50 or any other unit within that organization to no avail. Switching back to the Fireball Operations frequency, we asked them to check with the tactical operations center to see if they had a different frequency we could try. They came back with a new frequency of FM 44.45. Initial contact was made with B-50 X-Ray eight minutes after we departed Xuan Loc. They informed us the ground unit in contact was call sign B-100 and they could give us a run-down on the tactical situation. Also, the ETA for the "Sidewinder" gunships was ten minutes. Eleven minutes into this mission, B-100 said he had four wounded soldiers, two critical. They were not sure what hit them. It could have been an RPG or a reversed claymore mine. In either case, someone fired the RPG or there was something on the ground that caused the claymore mine to be fired. In the interim, we radioed the various artillery coordinating elements to determine if they had been contacted by any Sidewinder gunships that were enroute to Xuan Loc. Both Bien Hoa and Xuan Loc arty told us they had no contact with any gunships headed our way. Our base operations in Long Binh reported Sidewinder 19 was at our heliport. I contacted him directly and asked that he check with his operations to see if anyone had been tasked as our support. We never received confirmation either way.

Switching back to the tactical frequency, B-50 advised gunships were five minutes out. Rob Spitzer, who was flying co-pilot, and I were looking towards Long Binh. We couldn't see any rotating beacons or navigation lights of any helicopters coming our direction—much less anyone within five minutes of our location. That would mean they were over Xuan Loc—which they weren't. We had now spent approximately ten minutes of flight time trying to contact the ground unit and another 10 minutes trying to locate the elusive gunship cover. B-50 advised that B-100 had two critically injured soldiers that needed to be evacuated. He asked that we go ahead and come in without the gunship escort. Otherwise, the wounded may die.

"Dustoff 40, B-100—we have two strobe lights on at this time and a flare is coming up."

"Roger, B-100, flare is in sight. Be there in two minutes."

Quickly switching back to our Dustoff control frequency of FM 45.70, I told Operations that we were going to fly the night hoist without gunship cover. They probably should notify the commander, as he would want to revoke my AC orders for violating his policies. Probably a little dramatic over the radio, but then again, it seemed my AC orders were issued on one of those "magic write and erase" pads that we used to have as kids. Violate the commander's policy(s), he in turn lifts the plastic and carbon type sheet, and you have a clear piece of plastic to write on again. Poof! The AC orders are once again history.

Back to the real drama—frequency change back to FM 44.45. Rob was flying the helicopter. We had four to hoist so I let him fly the first sequence of two and then I planned to fly the last two. We approached from north to south on short final, using a high overhead circling descent so that we could keep the strobe lights in sight. Enemy contact—which the ground unit said they didn't encounter, was from the southeast. Navigation lights and rotating beacon were off and on very short final, Rob turned both the landing light and the searchlight on.

"Clear on the right side—plenty of room. Pull forward a little more. Whoa, that's good. We are right over them now," came the intercom calls from the crewchief on hot mike.

"Clear on the left," was the call from the medic on the left side of the helicopter.

"Dustoff 40, B-100, you are 30 feet to the front of our position. You need to come back a little."

"Sir, we are right over them, the penetrator is right on the strobe lights," said the crewchief.

"Anybody on the ground where the penetrator is coming down?"

"Yes, sir. There are two or three folks there."

"B-100, Dustoff 40. My crewchief says our penetrator is on the ground where your strobe light is at and people are there with the penetrator. This is about the best position we could find. If it works for you, let's go for it."

"Dustoff 40, B-100. It will work. We'll move the wounded to that location."

"B-100, Dustoff 40. Your guys small or large?""

Dustoff 40, B-100. About average size."

"Okay, let's try hoisting two at a time. Do not send any gear up with them."
120

"B-100, Roger!"

"B-50, Dustoff 40. If you still have the arty guys on this push, ask them to put illumination right on top of us. The extra light will help us see what we are doing."

"Dustoff 40, Anchor 41. I monitored. Can you adjust the illumination for us?"

"Anchor 41, Dustoff 40. Just lay it right on top of this LZ. The wind will cause it to drift away from us. I'll call you if it needs to be adjusted. For now, shoot on top of us and keep it coming."

"Dustoff 40, Anchor 41. Roger, it's on the way."

"Penetrator on the ground. They are loading two soldiers on it now. Okay we're ready—breaking ground. You okay?" came the hot mike communications from the crewchief.

"We're okay, bring him up," came Rob's response.

"Shit sir, he's hung up in the trees—slide back a bit—tail's clear. Good! There, he's clear. Coming up. Half way up! Near the skids. Clear on the right. Coming on board. We got two. Paul, get the wounded," came the hot mike communications from the crewchief.

"Roger! Clear on the left. I have the wounded guys. This guy doesn't look good. Other guy is okay," replied the medic over hot mike.

"Penetrator going down," said the crewchief.

"Rob, you want me to fly the next two? Sure, you have the controls. I have the controls" as Rob and I exchanged communications and switched duties.

"Penetrator on the ground. They are loading the next two. Ready to break ground, coming up. You okay?" said the crewchief over hot mike.

"It's okay, bring them on up," I replied over hot mike.

"Slide it right. Right! That's good! Hold it there. Damn, they're stuck in the trees. Fuck it! They are coming through. We're okay now," said the crewchief over hot mike.

"Whoa, I almost lost it coming through the trees," I exclaimed to the crewchief. The penetrator with the soldiers on it got hung up in the trees' limbs and we couldn't get them dislodged, so the crewchief "brought them on up" through the tree limbs. That extra pull or weight on the right side of the helicopter almost pulled us off our center of gravity balance nearly causing me to lose control of the helicopter.

"The penetrator is just below the helicopter. At the skids! Clearing the skids. Bringing them onboard now," called the crewchief over hot mike.

"Spitz—check with the ground. That's four guys. Is that all we have?" I asked of Rob.

"Sir, two of these guys have to go back down. They are not wounded. They were sent along to hold the wounded on the penetrator," called the medic over hot mike.

"Sptiz! Spitz! Call the ground guys and find out what the fuck is going on," I said anxiously to Rob over the intercom.

"Ah Shit! Okay, here's what happened. They sent the two guys up to hold the other two on and they want us to hoist them back down," Rob explained.

"Fuck!" came an unidentified comment of frustration over the hot mike.

"Fuck me! Okay, we'll send em back down," I said.

"Penetrator is on the way down, sir," the crewchief called out.

"Okay, leave it down, we'll take the two non-wounded back to Xuan Loc with us," I said.

122

"Spitz…….." I started to say.

"Yeah, I just told them. Only wounded on the penetrator. What the fuck are they thinking?" replied Rob as he read my mind and had already radioed down to the ground unit.

"Shift those non-wounded back into the hell hole," I said over the intercom.

"This one is dead," said the medic.

"Man coming up. Breaking ground. Looking good," were the call outs from the crewchief.

"Thirty-eight pounds of torque," was Rob's call out as he scanned our power instruments.

"Oops! Looks like we just have one man on. I think one man fell off," yelled the crewchief.

"Spitz—check to see if we dropped someone," I asked of Rob. Rob came back that they had just sent one person up on the penetrator.

"Spitz—tell those guys to keep the illumination coming. It's looking good. Also tell them we will take the non-wounded keeps back to the 199th location." "Roger!" came Rob's response.

"Man coming in! Let's move these guys back into the hell hole. Make sure they don't fall out the left side of the helicopter," was the conversation between the medic and the crewchief as they moved the wounded and non-wounded soldiers around inside the helicopter.

"Penetrator going down. Bring it to the left. Good! Hold! Hold! Good, right there. Penetrator on the ground," was the crewchief's directions as we continued to hover over the site. This extraction should be our last one.

"Penetrator coming light! Breaking ground! Okay looks good. I can't see the man coming up!" were the rapid statements coming from the crewchief as we raised the last man up to the helicopter.

"40 lbs of torque—everything is green," Rob called out with an instrument check.

"Good on the left," came the medic's call over the intercom.

We were staying clear of the trees, power was about at its maximum limit and the tail wind that we had was causing us to run out of aft cyclic. The option of turning the nose 180 degree and facing into the wind was not a good option fo us. The nose of the helicopter along with the landing lights would be pointing towards where the enemy was assumed to be. Our landing lights would surely be irresistible targets for the enemy gunners if they were in fact located to the southeast of the landing zone. The crewchief and medic were busting their butts getting the wounded off the ground and then taking care of them in the helicopter.

"Where's the penetrator? I'm running out of aft cyclic. Shift the folks as far back in the helicopter as you can get them," I was saying as the aft control limits were being reached. Any forward shift in weight distribution or increase in wind velocity and I would not be able to hold the hover.

"He's coming up through the trees right now. Hold what you got. Good! Hold it there! Hold it there!" came the tense callouts from the crewchief as I worked to hold the hover spot while nearing our aft cycle control limits.

"Okay! He's at the door—let's go!" said the crewchief.

"Spitz, check to see..............." "We gott'em all. Let's go!" was the exchange over the intercom between Rob and myself.

We began drifting forward as our heavily loaded helicopter began losing the battle with the tail wind that was confronting us as well as the inability to get more people back farther in the helicopter. The helicopter seemed to sense when it was time to leave—everybody was on board, and "it" was getting the hell outta there.

As we lifted free of the landing zone, the crewchief and medic quickly changed focus from extracting the wounded to now treating the wounded. The medic did a quick assessment. One guy was apparently paralyzed from the waist down with head and abdominal wounds. He had a strong handgrip on my medic. Doc was worried that he couldn't do anything for him except hold his hand. We had one other wounded soldier with fragmentation wounds to the shoulder and another one with fragmentation wounds to the legs. Unfortunately, one of the four wounded soldiers died! Listening to the cockpit recordings for this mission, I hope the time we dicked around trying to make radio contact with the ground unit and then locate the ever-elusive gunships didn't cost this guy his life. We also had our two non-wounded soldiers who got a "free ride" up on the penetrator that were now along for the ride—to somewhere.

We cleared our route from Xuan Loc to Long Binh with Xuan Loc and Bien Hoa arty so we could avoid flying through any gun target line or impact points. Wide Minnow directed that we take the soldiers with the back injury and leg injury to Queen Tonic (24th Evac) and the KIA and the soldier with the shoulder injury to 20 Ducks (93d Evac). In radio contact with B-50, we coordinated that we would fly his two non-wounded soldiers back to FSB Mace where they could get linked up with their parent unit.

Back in Long Binh, we dropped our patients at the designated hospitals and refueled. There was no one waiting at Operations to replace me as the aircraft commander. Since I had violated the commander's policy of not flying a hoist mission without gunship cover, I figured it would be an automatic happening. But with just 19 days remaining in country until my tour was complete, he probably felt it wasn't worth the effort. Ironically, I flew seven other hoist missions during that field standby without gunship escort.

The soldier who was apparently paralyzed from the waist down got an early Christmas present. His Life! For the soldier who died, his family members by far received the shittiest present that can ever be imagined.

Area Southeast of Xuan Loc where we flew the Night Non-Secure Hoist Mission on December 19, 1969

Nui Chua Chan mountain. Site of the story "Mission Nightmare". Signal relay site on the mountain was manned by the 313th Signal Company.

Location for the non-secure Night Hoist Mission on December 19, 1969

FSB Mace

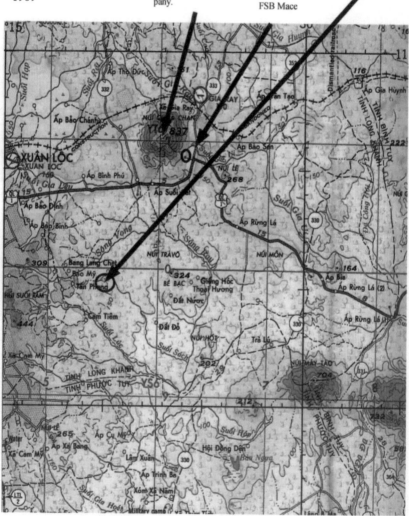

Deceived!

Chapter 14

The day was typical for the Delta—hot, a little hazy with scattered clouds around 3000 feet, and busy. We were flying a field standby out of Tan An and had been there for nearly three days. Tan An was a small military compound located on the edge of the "city limits" of the Tan An village. The military compound had a "bird dog" airstrip, hot refueling and arming points but no aviation units were stationed there. With the South Vietnamese now occupying Dong Tam, the former home of the 9th ID, there were very few US troops between Saigon and Vinh Long. Flying in the Delta was now lonelier—more so if one were to be shot down.

During the early morning, we had flown several missions responding to South Vietnamese troops being injured. Around noon, a call came in for the "extraction of wounded ARVN troops injured by a booby trap—no contact in the area, US Advisors on the ground with the ARVNs." We had several missions on the sheet with this one being the priority. Flight time from Tan An to the pickup site was about 30 minutes to the south. It was my co-pilot's turn to fly, mine to navigate and to plan the next sequenced mission—to pick up a pregnant Vietnamese civilian.

Ten minutes out from the landing zone (LZ), I contacted the ground unit to get an update on the tactical situation, number of wounded and the type of wounds. The "US" Advisor indicated there was no ground contact—injuries were due to a booby trap. They had three injured soldiers all with fragmentation wounds; none were critical. The advisor said he was not located with the unit that had the injured soldiers but was in radio contact with them. Normally, our policy was not to make an extraction where there were no US advisors with the unit. With the advisor being in radio contact with his subordinate unit and no enemy contact, we said that we would make the extraction. If we didn't, it was a safe bet that we would have to return later in the day or at night.

About two miles out from the LZ, we called for the unit to pop smoke and for them to identify its color. The advisor relayed this to his subordinate unit. He radioed back saying, "yellow smoke is out." Smoke was rising directly off the nose of the aircraft and it was a nice yellow plume. I confirmed the color with the advisor and the co-pilot set himself up for a tactical approach.

The LZ was a dry rice paddy bordered on the north by nippa palm trees approximately 75 meters in depth and two hundred meters in length. The soldiers threw the smoke canister mid way out into the dry rice paddy. The winds were calm. The co-pilot setup for a low tactical approach coming in from the southeast to northwest—flying across the one tree line before the intended LZ, then dipping down into the open rice paddy for the landing. The "death zone" for helicopters due to small arms and light automatic weapons fire was from the surface to 1500 feet. In flat open spaces, my preference was to drop down from cruise altitude away from the intended LZ and approach between 50 to 75 feet above the ground depending on the surrounding obstacles. I liked to carry an airspeed of 100 knots while approaching the LZ until on short final approach where we placed the helicopter in a rapid deceleration, with the nose up and slightly out of trim (slipping) if necessary—being careful not to balloon upwards. 'Ballooning' or climbing would expose us to enemy fire at a critical point in our approach to the LZ. Ideally, we would arrive over the intended point of touchdown with zero airspeed and within two feet of the ground.

In most situations where there had been no enemy contact and the area was considered secure, one or two soldiers were generally present in the vicinity of the smoke, guiding the aircraft in—kind of John Wayne style. As we approached this LZ, the co-pilot dropped down rapidly, pulling out at less than 100 feet and traveling "my" requisite 100 knots—approximately a quarter mile from the LZ. There was one tree line in front of us prior to reaching the rice paddy LZ. As we approached the tree line between our helicopter and the landing zone, the co-pilot eased the nose up, bleeding off airspeed, hugging the tops of the trees and acquiring the yellow smoke as the LZ became visible.

The aircraft line of flight was on an angle to the right of the smoke. The co-pilot changed the heading slightly to put us on short approach to the smoke. A first read of the LZ caused us to realize something was wrong—there was no one around the smoke in the "secure LZ," plus the smoke was out in the middle of an open rice paddy. Mental warning lights began to go off—I told the crew that something was wrong and we were going to carry airspeed over the smoke and get out of there if things didn't change—and change real quick. I told the co-pilot that I had the controls and for him to stay on lightly as a back up. The cheeks of my butt were now tight, my gut said things ain't right and my guardian angel riding on the back of my seat was jumping up and down yelling at me to get the hell out of there. Didn't know angels were allowed to cuss—I must have a male for a guardian angel. Just as I made the mental decision to get out of there, the medic said he saw someone waving from the tree line. I glanced over in the direction that he had indicated and sure enough, I saw the soldiers signaling to us.

Today it might be known as multiple tasking. Back then, we were making rapid fire decisions with only seconds to assimilate the information at hand. We came to a hover away from the tree line but in the vicinity of the smoke. Both the co-pilot and I were on the controls.

Working with ARVN troops was different than with US troops-more-flighty and not organized. If they were scared or came under fire when bringing the wounded to the helicopter, it was not uncommon for them to drop the wounded and charge the aircraft to get a "safe ride" out of harm's way. I had one medic who carried a hard rubber mallet to smack heads and fingers of those who tried to grab on to the helicopter at the last minute.

My gut was saying this ain't right, but the visual sensing said it was just a typical screwed up Vietnamese operation. The medic and crewchief were hanging outside the aircraft-eyes wide open looking for anything that was abnormal—even more so now. I started a quick hover towards the soldiers who were waving at us. The faster hover speed was to keep the helicopter flying in case we needed to make a hasty retreat. About halfway between the smoke and the tree line—with the nose of the helicopter pointed towards the tree line—all hell broke loose. We all saw it at the same time!! Small arms and automatic weapons fire trained on the red cross affixed to the nose of our aircraft. It's odd how, when "stuff" happens, the brain can conjure up expletives that one didn't even think were in the vocabulary.

I kicked hard right pedal (rudder for you fixed wing guys), pulled in power and headed out of there. The instant the flank side of the helicopter was exposed to the enemy fire, we could hear bullets whizzing through the open passenger compartment. The crewchief and medic were trying to become as small as possible to avoid being hit. As the tail came around, the enemy fire became more intense and was focused on the cockpit. Of the rounds "passing" through the aircraft, I took three rounds directly in the back of my kevlar-plated seat. Two rounds struck the smoke grenades that were hanging on my seat frame causing them to detonate and dislodge from the seat frame. We were scrambling to get out of there while smoke from the grenades rolling around in the cargo compartment filled the cockpit. It was hard to see and breathe. The crewchief and medic were trying to grab the elusive grenades and toss them out of the helicopter. Underneath the magnesium cargo floor decking are the fuel cells. Smoke grenades burn with an intense heat and we were in danger of the grenades igniting the fuel cells. The rounds that impacted my seat back knocked my guardian angel to the cargo floor. Besides cussing and swearing, he was also trying to get hold of the grenades. Finally, out the door went the grenades and we were clear of the LZ.

The only thing I heard over the radio was--- "Maybe next time GI!"

We gathered our composure the best we could. We rapidly scanned our flight and engine instruments to determine if everything was in the "green". The helicopter was flying—that was good and we were putting distance between us and the a'holes who suckered us into the LZ. Everyone checked out okay—no wounds. Why none of us had been hit escapes the imagination. They had a target lock on us by evidence of the damage to the back of my seat.

As luck would have it, the heading we departed from the LZ placed us on course for the next scheduled patient pickup location. The village was just a few kilometers away and had US advisors on the ground. We figured if we could keep the aircraft flying to that point, we would land, shut the helicopter down and check out the damage. We transmitted a MAYDAY call on frequency 45.70 FM (standard DUSTOFF frequency for that area) and on Guard 243.0 UHF letting people know that we had an emergency in progress. We made quick contact with the advisors at the next pickup point and told them we had been hit and we were coming to their location if all of the parts continued to fly successfully in tight formation with one another.

The flight controls all seemed to be functional but even with that, we carried a higher final approach speed to the village landing pad. Our approach and landing were uneventful. We needed to shut the helicopter down to determine how much damage was done and whether we were still flyable. The advisors were on the ground waiting for us—obviously impatient to get their pregnant female enroute to a hospital. During our post flight, we found holes in my seat back, avionics compartment, and the most critical damage to the tail rotor cables near the 42 degree tail rotor gear box (this gear box changes the drive shaft angle along the tailboom 42 degrees to parallel the vertical stabilizer). The cables that are used to change the pitch in the tail rotor blades run parallel to the drive shaft.

Our helicopter after it was air lifted back to Long Binh. The tailboom was removed and sent to depot maintenance for rebuild of the structural component that was damaged.

The right side tail rotor control cable was severed by more than 50% of its thickness—which isn't all that thick to begin with. A structural member in the tailboom was also severed by gunfire.

There was transmission fluid all over the place but we couldn't find any damage. We weren't going anywhere in this helicopter!

We were all feeling real studly—knowing that once again we cheated death to fly another time. With knees still a little wobbly, we began to remove the radios from the downed helicopter and secure the aircraft so that it could be "hooked" out. Our sister aircraft dispatched from Saigon to come get us informed me that the company commander (a Lieutenant Colonel) said that since there were advisors at this village, the crewchief would be required to stay overnight with the aircraft until it was evac'd the next morning. I had previously told this commander to get screwed when he had challenged my decisions as an aircraft commander—probably a mistake in retrospect. He suspended my aircraft commander orders for three weeks until he realized he was more comfortable with me out of Long Binh flying combat missions from field locations.

I relayed to the inbound aircraft that I was not going to leave a crew member on the ground. This message was relayed back to the commander in Long Binh who came on the radio and said that if I disobeyed his order, I would be court-martialed. Since the commander did not value warrant officers or enlisted men, there was no doubt in my mind that he would carry through with his threat if I challenged his orders. We talked it over as a crew and the crewchief said he would be okay staying with the advisors. We loaded him up with extra ammo and I gave him an order not to stay in or near that aircraft that night---"You stay within an arm's length of the advisors. If they leave, you leave also—screw the aircraft."

We were picked up by the sister aircraft who had orders to drop us off at our field location in Tan An. Here we were thinking about a real cold beer or two and maybe a steak. The commander said he was having a spare aircraft flown down to us. Sure enough, just after we were dropped off at Tan An, another aircraft arrived from Long Binh.

We preflighted the new bird and went to look for a beer and steak. We figured we could drink one beer and not compromise our innate ability to fly. The steak turned out to be meat loaf and mashed potatoes. The "mess daddy" gave us a little extra, so we were happy. As the sun was just emitting

132

its last gasp of light, we were sitting around our radio room, also known as a bunker, when a medical evacuation request came in over the radio. The co-pilot and the remainder of the crew headed out to crank up the helicopter while I got the mission sheet from the radio operator. Something about those ground coordinates seemed awfully familiar. Damn! Right back where we got hit earlier in the day. What the hell was going on out there?

Within three minutes of the mission coming in, we were airborne and heading south to something we were not happy thinking about. When I told my co-pilot where we were going, I thought he was going to jump out of the aircraft. He did not want to go back there in any way, shape, or form. I exclaimed, "Folks, we don't get to vote on this." But his fear and anxiety were so intense that he was nearly incapacitated. We were now a single pilot aircraft. Looking towards the horizon, we could see the illuminated parachute flares floating in the sky. We also noted there was a massive stream of red tracers extending from the sky to the ground. A Spooky (AC-47) gunship was hosing the area big time. When Spooky is called, there is big "stuff" happening and nobody is playing 'paddy cake, paddy cake, baker's man.'

AC-47 Gunship

Our mission sheet showed that we had several soldiers with gunshot wounds. Approaching the area, I contacted our gunship escort that was already on station. First thing I asked them was if they had contact with the ground unit? "Yep—US Advisor!" "Is he really US?" Long pause on the comeback but they said "sure." We made contact with the advisors on the ground, asked them what the numerical difference was between Jack Benny's age and this radio frequency. They got the answer right which was a bit more self assuring. But then again, any respectable NVA soldier probably knew what

133

Jack Benny's age was. The Advisor said his Vietnamese infantry company had made contact with an NVA battalion-sized unit. We had to orbit east of the LZ until the Spooky finished its work. Too long of a delay would certainly place a strain on our fuel if we were going to make multiple trips into the LZ to extract wounded. Spooky finished up and we made our first extraction of wounded soldiers and headed back towards the Dong Tam area to a Vietnamese hospital. A quick turn around placed us back at the LZ with less than one half of our fuel remaining. Even though Spooky tends to destroy anything within its zone of fire, the enemy had re-engaged the friendly unit. As the gunships laid down suppressive fire, we made our second and last extraction and were on our way back towards Dong Tam for the patient drop-off.

Departing the Dong Tam area, we found ourselves VFR on top of a fog layer that topped out at about two thousand feet above the ground. Flying at night in Vietnam on a moonless night was much like flying up the proverbial well digger's asshole—it's totally black everywhere. Of course there were no electronic navigation aids to assist us in finding our way back to our home base. We were down to about 250 pounds of fuel and we typically burned 550 to 600 pounds per hour. At this point, we were 5 minutes into a 15 minute flight back to Tan An.

As William Bendix, the actor, often said, "What a revoltin' development this is." We were flying VFR on top, in the general direction of Tan An, keeping a very close eye on the fuel gauge when the 20 minute amber caution light suddenly illuminated. About 10 minutes of flying left on 20 minutes of fuel. The guardian angel riding on the top edge of my seat was pissing and moaning again. My co-pilot was still ineffective for much more than just sitting there but he was getting less anxious after we flew away from the enemy action.

Flying in the Delta has its pluses as well as its minuses. One major plus was the terrain was flat and nearly at sea level. So I figured a let down through the cloud layer would be reasonably easy. I told the co-pilot to watch the instruments, since the primary instruments for IFR flight are located on the right side of the instrument panel. We found a little "sucker hole" in the clouds through which we made a steeply banked turn and descended at one-thousand feet per minute. We broke out of the overcast at 300 feet and continued down to 200 feet (AGL) to remain clear of the cloud layer. We made radio contact with our base at Tan An and used FM homing to get a directional lock on where "home" was. We arrived at Tan An having flown 15 minutes into a 20 fuel remaining light. We grabbed a full load of fuel from the hot fuel/rearm point and parked the helicopter for the night. Before hitting the sack, for what we hoped would be a few hours of respite, I

This is what Tan An looked like in the monsoon season--approaching west to east. Hot refuel and rearm points are on the left side of the picture beteen the mini canals of water. The medical helipad is to the end and to the left side of the runway.

called back to Long Binh and arranged for a new co-pilot to be flown down in the morning. My guardian angel headed off to have some brewskies with his buds.

Were there lessons learned here for a 20 year old Aircraft Commander? Absolutely!! I think the first lesson was to go with the gut feeling until you have information that proves that feeling incorrect. Your prior experiences and training come to rest in the pit of your gut when things aren't right, it will be your first indication. The second lesson could very well be the number one lesson learned here. Don't listen to incompetent leaders. Do what your mind and heart say are right and blow off the consequences. I still regret leaving the crewchief on the ground. He and the aircraft were evac'd at first light the next morning and they made it back to Long Binh well before I did. But it's the 'what if' that is hard to swallow and put into perspective. The third lesson is to always be cognizant of your surroundings and in critical situations, always question the information at hand. It was obvious the NVA had gained access to our insecure radio network, called in a mission request for a medical evacuation and hatched a plan to entrap a helicopter crew. We were skillful in our ability to make decisions and fly the aircraft but at the same time, we were extremely lucky. One inch here or there would have produced a totally different outcome.

"A Pilot Lives in a World of Perfection, or not at all."

Richard S. Drury ("My Secret War")

Night Ranger Mission

Chapter 15

"Half This Game is 90% Mental." Yogi Berra

With my combat tour completed in January 1970, I returned home, spent a few weeks on leave and then headed to Savannah, Georgia for my next assignment as an instructor pilot. Having flown with my students in the afternoon flight session, I returned to our operations room and found a note to see the branch commander as soon as possible. Lieutenant Colonel (LTC) George Lincoln told me I needed to report to the aviation division commander's office the next morning at 10:00 AM for the presentation of an award. Asking what type of award it was, LTC Lincoln responded that it was a Distinguished Flying Cross for action on October 28, 1969. "Okay, sir, I'll be there." LTC Lincoln asked if I remembered the action. I said, "No sir! Most of the missions we flew were very risky and I couldn't tell you which ones were 'award flights' and which ones were not."

The next morning, I went to the ceremony wondering which mission was chosen for recognition. Here is the citation.

 Award of the Distinguished Flying Cross
CWO 2 Steven D. Vermillion,
United States Army
45th Medical Company(AA),
68th Medical Group, 44th Medical Brigade,
Republic of Vietnam
October 28, 1969

"For heroism, while participating in aerial flight, evidenced by voluntary actions above and beyond the call of duty in the Republic of Vietnam: Chief Warrant Officer Vermillion distinguished himself while commanding a helicopter ambulance during a rescue mission west of Tan Tru. He and his crew had been requested to evacuate four Vietnamese children wounded in a fire fight between enemy elements and a friendly ranger team. When Warrant Officer Vermillion arrived over the conflict area, the ranger team feared an imminent rocket attack and asked that he coordinate helicopter gunships in placing suppressive fire on suspected enemy positions until the wounded children were evacuated. Having directed the gunships in repeated strafing runs on the enemy, Warrant Officer Vermillion then flew his rescue aircraft into the friendly unit's position without the use of landing lights and began the loading of the wounded. Almost immediately after landing, the air ambulance came under intense fire from the enemy force. Warrant Officer Vermillion, nevertheless, calmly maintained his aircraft on the ground until all the children were boarded and then lifted off amid continuing hostile fire. Once the wounded had been delivered to medical facilities and his aircraft had been refueled, Warrant Officer Vermillion flew back to the conflict area and assisted in extracting the besieged ranger team. Chief Warrant Officer Vermillion's outstanding flying ability and devotion to duty were in keeping with the highest traditions of the military service and reflect great credit upon himself, his unit, and the United States Army."

With Paul Harvey's signature comment as a point of departure, "and here is the rest of the story," let me first make a very important point. CWO Vermillion was not flying single pilot on October 28th. There were three other crew members on board, all of whom willingly flew into harm's way to accomplish this mission. WO Rob Spitzer, was the co-pilot, SP5 Hannon was the crewchief, and SP5 Wallace was the medic.

We were once again flying out of my home away from home, Tan An. We had several missions that night which culminated in receiving this mission while we were airborne. It was one of those typical nights in South Vietnam, as black as a well digger's fifth point of contact. There was no moonlight with the only ambient light coming from the small villages dispersed throughout the countryside. Forty miles to the north, the lights of Saigon illuminated the horizon.

138

Our mission involved a nine member Ranger Team that had encountered a Viet Cong force of unknown size.[1] During the fire fight near the village of Tan Tru, four Vietnamese children were wounded and needed immediate medical evacuation. We were told a gunship covering force was enroute to the location. The Rangers were in an open rice paddy with no cover except for the paddy dikes. While enroute to the grid coordinate location, we came up on UHF guard 243.0, made a call in the blind for the Stogey gunships to contact us on FM 45.70. Since every aircraft automatically monitored the Guard frequency, Stogey 41 came up on guard and gave us their internal UHF frequency. The Stogey gunships didn't have an operational FM radio so they asked us to coordinate communications for them with the ground unit. We switched our FM radio back to the ground unit and advised them of Stogey's radio problem. The unit agreed with us that we would then coordinate the gunships for suppressive fire. Stogey 41 advised they were over the area and assigned me an altitude to assume an orbit with them. Four-one's wing-man was blacked out at 500 feet AGL, while he was at 1,500 feet AGL with external navigation lights illuminated.

Working with the ground unit, we coordinated Stogey 41, a UH-1C gunship, to make several rocket runs on the Viet Cong positions while the Rangers attempted to move to a different location. We adjusted the target points as the Rangers provided corrections in direction and distance. The 2.75" aerial rocket was designed to be fired from fast moving F4U Corsairs in WW II. In Vietnam, the Army adapted these rockets for use with helicopters. Although many gunship drivers could shoot a rocket up an elephant's butt, these rockets were still intended to be an area fire weapon. If you were in the "ball park" of the desired location, especially at night, "ballpark" was about as precise as it was going to get.

For a night approach when we had gunship cover, we typically turned off our navigation lights (the red, green and white lights) when we began our approach into the landing zone. When we were approximately 500 feet AGL, we would turn off the red rotating beacon and continue the remainder of the approach blacked out. Ambient light, pilot skill and the tactical situation dictated whether we used a landing light at any time during our approach into an LZ. At times, I would wait until we were about 50 feet

AGL, click the landing light for two seconds for a quick look and then turn it off. Tonight was going to be a non-illuminated approach as we did not want to expose the Ranger team. The Rangers were involved in a mobile battle, so no one was really sure where the bad guys were located. It would be nice for the VC to play their hand so the guns could expend their ordnance for a worthy cause.

Gun drivers are happiest when they are shooting something. Stogey 41 and his wingman hatched a plan they had hoped would cause "Chuck" to play his hand. Three-two relays to us that he wants us to keep our navigation lights on during our approach so his blacked out wingman can trail us into the LZ. "And if they shoot at you, three-three will be there to bust their ass." You could sense the dead silence among my crew members.

"Hey 41, I understand we are your bait, is that a Roger?"

"Don't worry there Dustoff, you are in good hands," came the gun driver's reply.

I briefed the Rangers as to what our plan was and that we were going to be the "bait" for tonight.

The Rangers successfully broke contact and moved to an alternate location. We left the orbit pattern flying away from the LZ to allow Stogey 41's wingman time to slip into trail position with us.

The Rangers had their covered strobe light on to give us a fix on their location. With the strobe light off, we were inbound to the LZ. Our approach path was straight and steady—we had a fully loaded Charlie Model gunship with rockets and mini-guns lurking somewhere behind us ready to hose the bad guys. I told Rob to keep his hand on the exterior light switches that were located on the overhead console. "When I say turn the lights out, you will be late if you don't have the lights off before I finish telling you to turn them off." Back to the Rangers—one more quick flash of the strobe light so we could pinpoint them in the black abyss. Strobe light off!! About three-fourths of the way through the approach, there was no ground fire yet from the VC. Did they know where we were? Would they wait until we got low and slow? I clicked on the mike and checked with our "friend" trailing our approach.

"We be here," came his response.

Once more back to the Rangers, a couple of quick flashes on the strobe—just off the nose about a 100 meters. "Strobe Off!!" We had completed our pre-landing check before we started inbound, everything was still in the green. We had our instrument lights dimmed to a minimum so we wouldn't illuminate ourselves in the cockpit.

"Okay guys, this is going to be hot. Get the kids on board and don't wander away from the aircraft--do not unplug without my permission."

"Roger, sir," was the response over the intercom.

The reflection of the lights gave a glimpse of the ground about 20 seconds prior to touch down.

"Ten feet, five feet, three feet, ground contact, lights out," Rob called out.

I hear the sound of the cargo doors sliding on their tracks to their open position.

"Medic and crewchief are on the ground," was the call over the intercom.

"Stogey 41, Dustoff 40, lights out!"

"Roger, Dustoff! We know where you are."

We weren't on the ground longer than a few heartbeats when the world erupted from the left rear of our helicopter; green tracers coming in our direction, red tracers going back toward where the green tracers came from. The Rangers came on the radio and told us to get out of there. "Get 'em on board; you're burning time," was our response. Man, what an overwhelming urge to "pull pitch" and leave the area. But we may not get a second chance. About the time I switched to the UHF radio to tell Stogey 41 that I thought we found the enemy, the swoosh of the 2.75" rockets trailing a stream of fire impacted to the rear of the aircraft from where the green tracers originated. Trailing behind the rockets was a solid fiery red stream of machine gun tracers impacting the target at several hundred rounds per minute. Thatch hooches exploded and their remnants caught fire illuminating the area around us. With all of the ground fire focused on us at the moment, one quickly realized just how damn vulnerable we were. The Kevelar ® "chicken plate" covered the upper torso and the reasonably armored pilot's seat provided good protection for your sides and back. But in this situation, you wanted to be like a turtle and suck your head, arms and legs back in behind the chicken plate and seat making yourself as small as you possibly could. At six feet, three inches, there was still a lot hanging outside the "tortoise shell."

The second Stogey aircraft rolled in right behind his wing man making a worth while deposit of ordnance for the cause.

"Knock their asses in the dirt" someone said over our intercom.

SP5 Wallace, standing next to the left side of the helicopter, said he was seeing where the tracers were coming from and asked permission to place suppressive fire on the target with his M-16. I gave him permission, as all nine Rangers were located on the right side of the aircraft.

SP5 Hannon left the aircraft several times, wading through knee deep mud, to hasten the loading of the wounded children.

Three minutes on the ground—this is taking too long. With the crewchief receiving the last of the wounded children from the Rangers, I gave a five second warning call to the guns that we were coming out.

"We're up in the back," said the crewchief.

"Coming up, tail to the left."

"Tail's clear right—taking fire from 5 o' clock," called the crewchief.

"Forty pounds of torque, positive airspeed and rate of climb," Rob called over the intercom.

"Stogey 41, Dustoff 40—we're off the ground, blacked out, heading 010 degrees maintaining 50 feet AGL until clear your low orbit Stogey—taking fire from the LZ."

"Roger, Dustoff, we're both lighted now and rolling in on the target."

"Roger, have your lights, our rotating beacon is coming on."

We cleared the LZ and turned inbound to Saigon for the 3d Field Hospital. The medic reported that we had four young Vietnamese children with fragmentation wounds, one with serious chest wounds. Rob radioed Wide Minnow notifying them of the number of patients, their wounds, and our ETA to Saigon. We gave a quick call to the gun drivers giving them a big thanks for keeping the bad guys out of the cockpit. The Rangers were on the move out of the area. The "slick" that was supposed to extract them was not yet on station. I radioed Ranger 22 that we would check on them in 30 minutes after we dropped the kids off in Saigon and grabbed a quick gulp of fuel at Nha Be. Enroute to Saigon, we called ahead to Navy Nha Be and asked them to get their refueling guys ready. We would be there in 15 minutes for a quick hot refuel. Our medic stabilized the kids and both he and the crewchief just held them to keep their fear factor down.

In ten minutes we were on the 3d Field Hospital's hot pad leaving the young kids now in the hands of the excellent docs. The next leg of the mission belonged to Rob to fly so he had the controls and we were quickly airborne heading to Nha Be. The "squids" were waiting for us as we had asked. Their heliport tower controller cleared us direct to hot fuel. The crewchief and medic did a quick walk around with flashlights checking the helicopter for damage. All of the major parts seemed to still be attached, so we were probably okay. With a fresh load of 900 pounds of JP4 on board, we headed back to Tan An for the night. Tan An Dustoff informed us we didn't have any missions pending, so as promised, we came up on the Ranger radio frequency to check on their status. Lo and behold, they were still on the ground.

"Okay, we are available to extract you if you need our help," I told them.

"Our mission is compromised so we're ready to get out of here. We have one slick inbound but that will not be enough to get us outta here. If you are offerin' a ride, we have our thumbs out," came the Ranger response.

"We are about 10 minutes out of your location. Can you tell us where you are in relation to the previous pickup site?"

"East," came the out of breath response from Ranger 22. "We broke contact with the VC after you left and we started heading east to get away from the area. Right now, everything is still quiet."

"Okay, we should be reasonably close to where you are," I radioed.

"Roger, we got your lights, we're at your one o'clock about 3 miles," came the reply. "Hit me with a couple of strobe flashes and then turn it off," I asked. "Roger, got your strobe." We contacted their extraction slick and told him we would be number two into the LZ.

I told Rob to set up for his approach, lights off and without a landing light. "Don't know where "Uncle Chuck" is, so let's not be the bait again."

"Tan An Dustoff, Dustoff 40."

"Four-zero, Tan Dustoff-go ahead." "Roger, Tan An, if you don't have anything for us, we're gonna extract the Ranger team we just worked with. They broke contact—coordinates about the same as last mission. Will call you clear the LZ."

"Roger, Dustoff 40, we'll monitor the tactical FM frequency—keep your head down."

"Roger!"

"Okay guys, the slick is clear of the LZ. We're on final approach to where we saw your strobe flash. If able, hit us with a couple of quick flashes," I radioed to Ranger 22.

"There it is, about twelve thirty and a mile," called Rob.

"Roger, we got your strobe, we'll be there in 30 seconds, lights out, no landing light. Stay cool!"

"Roger," came the Ranger response.

"Everything is green, airspeed 60 kts, 250 feet indicated" I called out to Rob. "Okay we got 40 knots and about 60 feet."

"Visual with the ground out the right side-20 feet," called the crewchief.

"Ground visual on the left," called the medic over the intercom followed by Rob saying "I have the ground."

I called the altitude, "ten feet---five feet---three feet---ground contact," so Rob could concentrate on the final portion of his approach.

"Down on the left, down on the right, outside," came the call from the crew in the back. We saw two soldiers to the front of the helicopter coming our way. Hope these are really the Rangers.

"Got 'em onboard sir, ready in the rear," came the call from the crewchief.

"We're outta here. Coming up," said Rob.

"Everything's green, torque coming up to 40 pounds, positive airspeed and rate of climb. Beacon on—now," I responded.

Since we all wore flight helmets, I didn't have any way to hook the Ranger unit leader into our intercom so he could tell me where he needed to go. I keyed my mike so I could hear him talk and then shouted back to him over the noise of the helicopter. He pointed to a location on our map, and I gave him thumbs up. A quick call to Tan An Dustoff to tell them we were airborne and clear of the LZ enroute to drop the Rangers off at their field headquarters. We settled in for the 15-minute flight to their headquarters area, making contact with their ground radio operator letting them know we were inbound to their location. The ground unit illuminated their "landing" pad with jeep headlights and we made our approach—again with the navigation lights off. Since the area was quasi-secure, we used the landing light on short final so we could avoid any antennas that might be hiding in the dark, just waiting to ding our rotor blades. We shouted our farewells to the Rangers then lifted off, leaving them in the dark void behind us.

We closed back into Tan An after flying for fourteen hours.[2] Feeling butt ugly, tired and hungry, we knew we couldn't sleep for a bit. We missed dinner and had too much caffeine and adrenaline flowing through our bodies. It's three in the morning—maybe the mess daddy is up cooking biscuits or something else that would be reasonably edible.

Walking to the radio bunker, our noses picked up the sweet scent of mess daddy's famous cinnamon rolls being baked. "Yeah, babe! A good day of flying topped off by a little sweetness. Life doesn't get any better than this."

"MISSION NIGHTMARE"¹

A Mission Emblazoning the Epitome
of the DUSTOFF Psyche

Chapter 16

This story is completely true although you may think it is unbelievable. Some people say we never should have attempted the mission, but under the circumstances, we couldn't refuse. Our primary mission was to rescue injured people and we felt we couldn't turn this one down without making an attempt. Read the story, put yourself in the cockpit and make your own decision.

We were asleep on this eventful night when the radio-telephone operator (RTO) sent runners to wake the crew for an urgent night mission. We hurried to the alert shack and discovered we had two U.S. soldiers who had suffered one or more traumatic amputations due to a mortar round detonating in the tube. Their need for evacuation was obviously urgent.

As we proceeded east out of Long Binh, we plotted the landing zone 50 miles east on the top of Nui Chua Chan Mountain (Hill 837). The top of this mountain served as a signal relay site. The 313th Signal Company occupied this mountain top. Although there was no artillery battery co-located, the unit had a security element equipped with a mortar section or platoon. The sides of the mountain were jointly occupied by the NVA and VC forces who used the caves and other terrain features to augment their radio relay as well.¹ Our flying time to the pickup site was approximately 30 minutes. When we were halfway between Long Binh and the "LZ", we could see a cloud layer forming around the mountain top. Elsewhere, the visibility was unlimited, the sky was clear on a moonlight night. In other circumstances, this would have been an enjoyable night for flying. Climbing to 4000 feet MSL, we double-checked our instruments for IFR capability in case the need arose.

Arriving on station, our suspicions were confirmed, the 2,800-foot mountain top was enveloped in what appeared to be a relatively thick cloud layer. We were in contact with the ground unit who advised us they had two critically injured soldiers who needed immediate evacuation. After surveying the situation, we didn't feel there was a reasonably safe way to extract the wounded soldiers. We made the decision to stay on station and watch the weather to see if it would open up long enough for us to slip in and get on the ground. If we could reach the ground safely, we would be able to make an instrument takeoff without much difficulty. We advised the ground unit that we were going to hold off making the extraction until we could get a break in the weather. The RTO shot back over the radio in an almost incoherent voice that we needed to come in and land now to pickup the wounded soldiers. Listening in on our frequency was a doctor located in Xuan Loc who kept telling us that if we didn't make the pickup, the men would surely die.

The ground unit commander came on the radio and said that he could hear us circling overhead. He thought that he could talk us down by using the sound of our helicopter for reference. Dan Voss and I looked at each other and didn't think that was such a hot idea. The ground unit was searching for some form of illumination that they could illuminate the landing pad with. In the meantime, Dan wanted to see if it would be possible to hover up the side of the mountain, underneath the cloud layer. There was a slim chance that we could find a draw or ravine where the cloud layer wasn't right at tree level. Since we were VFR on top of the cloud layer, we flew laterally away from the mountain top until we cleared the edge of cloud layer and were able to descend below the clouds. We then turned back towards the mountain approaching from the south. With the landing light on, we made our approach essentially to the side of the mountain, coming to a hover over the trees but below the cloud layer. Then we began hovering up the side of the mountain at treetop level. We were able to make some progress hovering under the cloud layer before we reached a point where the cloud blended right into the trees.. Now we found ourselves hovering over trees at night, surrounded by cloud –essentially **IFR.** Not a fun place to be by any stretch of the imagination. We had to get away from the mountain so we started an instrument climb with an immediate left turn away from the mountain. Fortunately we broke clear of the clouds without hitting any trees or cumulus "granitus." After a couple of minutes to get our heart rates back to normal, we circled back to the east side of the mountain. With the wind flowing west to east, we thought we might be able to ease up under the easterly lip of the cloud layer and possibly find a clearer route to work our way up to the top of the mountain. Again we made our approach to the side of the mountain coming to hover at tree top level and began hovering up slope towards the mountain top. Once again, we made it less than a 100 meters and encountered the cloud layer right at tree level. What a surprise, eh!

When you bring a helicopter to a hover over 100 foot conifer trees, the limbs constantly move around due to the downward force of air from the helicopter blades. Even though the trees provide some ground cushion effect for the helicopter, higher power requirements are needed to sustain a hover. In the daytime a visual horizon is present to assist the pilots in maintaining a stationary hover over their intended spot. At night, there is no visible horizon—just the tree branches dancing in the illumination provided by the helicopter's landing light. In this situation, the difficulty factor of the task was compounded because the cloud had essentially enveloped us. We made one more attempt to takeoff from the side of the mountain. Again, we were lucky and broke out into the clear, flying away from the mountain. The pucker factor was now to the point where you couldn't squeeze a dime between the cheeks of your collective asses without pre-lubing them with some WD-40. We circled in the clear, climbed back **VFR** on top of the mountain, contacting the ground unit to see if they had found any way to illuminate the landing area. The ground unit radioed back and said they had rounded up a limited number of "Spooky" flares. Spooky flares are a very high intensity flare generally dropped from USAF aircraft. We normally associated them with their AC-47 gunships using them to illuminate the battlefield. We figured they were worth a try and asked the ground unit to place three of them in a triangle and to ignite them. From overhead, we could see the flares on the ground and decided to attempt the approach. We knew there was a tall radio tower lurking somewhere in the cloud. A shallow approach angle increased the depth of the cloud making it more difficult to locate the flares. So using a steep approach angle, we began the descent at 50 knots. A "steep approach" angle is typically considered to be greater than 12 degrees. We were probably at a 20-degree approach so we had to slow our approach speed below 50 knots. The helicopter was shaking and shuddering telling us we were right on the edge of losing effective translational lift. Dan was making the approach from the left seat; I was in the right seat monitoring the primary flight instruments, calling out airspeed, rate of descent, and altitude. Approximately halfway through the approach, the flares went out. Now in total darkness, in the cloud, we made another instrument departure to climb VFR on top. Once we were clear of the cloud, we told the ground unit we thought the cloud layer was about 300 feet thick. We were low on fuel, so we needed to break station and head to Black Horse to hot refuel. Black Horse was a fire support base about 20 miles to the Southwest of our LZ.

Before leaving for Black Horse, we radioed back to our base operations and asked them to dispatch the hoist equipped ship and let them make an attempt at lowering the hoist through the cloud layer. It was certainly a long shot but worth the effort. Flying west from the mountain, we saw that Black Horse and the surrounding area were obscured by a low cloud layer or by ground fog. We called ahead to Black Horse to confirm their weather. The RTO at that location went outside and said he could see the tops of the trees. We came back towards the northeast, about ten miles from Black Horse, where we would be clear of the lower ground cloud layer. We found Highway 1 which we knew connected with the north-south Highway 2 which would pass east of Black Horse by a mile or so. Descending to within 100 feet of the road surface, we held an airspeed between 50 to 60 knots and began our low level journey to Black Horse. We set the landing light to shine directly below us, and aimed the searchlight out in front of us to help locate any wires crossing the roadway. Making the turn onto Highway 2, we found ourselves flying lower and slower trying to stay below the cloud layer. After flying what we thought was about five miles, we made a right turn towards the west. Within a few moments, we saw the dim lights of Blackhorse through the dark abyss. Landing at the small airfield's refueling point, we hot refueled our helicopter and were ready to head back to Hill 837.

We made another instrument takeoff from Blackhorse and began a climb to VFR on top. Breaking clear of the clouds around 1000 feet MSL, we proceeded to climb back to 4000 feet enroute to the mountain top. We found that our hoist-equipped bird had arrived and was working with the ground unit to attempt a hoist extraction. After one sequence of flares, the hoist crew found they couldn't maintain any semblance of a stationary hover over the intended pick up point. The hoist ship crew broke station and it was up to us to try again.

This would be our last attempt at making an approach through the cloud layer as the ground unit only had three flares remaining. Our plan was again to hold a slow airspeed and a higher rate of descent in an attempt to get to the ground before the flares went out. As we entered the top of the cloud, everything was going smoothly. Dan was making the approach from the left seat since the left side of the cockpit provides greater ground visibility. I was monitoring the instruments, once again calling out our airspeed, altitude and rate of descent. We were holding about 40 knots and a 600 to 700 foot per minute rate of descent. We passed the radio tower on the right side, relieved to know that we cleared that obstacle. Now we were about 100 feet above the touch down point and the approach was still okay. Shortly after passing the tower, the medic yelled that we were starting to move backwards and were going to hit the tower. Our airspeed was indicating 35 knots so there must have been a pretty good headwind component flowing over the mountain top. Dan reacted to the medic's warning, by lowering the nose to gain some airspeed and increasing power to control our rate of descent. Just as he made those power changes, we caught a glimpse of the ground before the flares went out. Bam!! Total darkness, somewhere over the landing site at about 50 feet, and out of control.

As Dan attempted to gain control of the aircraft, I watched the instruments as they told a frightening story. The Radio Magnetic Indicator (RMI) had rotated three times, the airspeed indicator was pegged on zero and the RPM audio warning was blaring in our headsets: "5600 RPM" (normal operating RPM is 6600 and controlled within normal ranges by a governor). Along with the attitude indicator alternating plus or minus 10 degrees pitch attitude change, the altimeter showed that we were about 100 feet below the top of the mountain. The crewchief and medic were screaming that there were leaves and sand coming through the open cargo door, the crewchief's toolbox, which wasn't secured, departed the helicopter————then we suddenly found ourselves flying in the clear, free of the cloud and the mountain top. Once we again had a visual reference with our outside environment. Dan quickly got the aircraft back under control. We took a few moments to decide if we were alive and to get our heart rates back in normal range.

At some point during this approach, one of us got a call out on the FM radio as to what was happening. We were brought back to reality by Dustoff Operations calling to see if we needed any assistance. For a moment we really weren't sure that it wasn't St. Peter heralding our arrival at the Pearly Gates. After regaining our composure, we orbited the mountain looking for another way to make the rescue. After 5 hours, we gave it up and returned to Long Binh feeling deflated because we had failed at the rescue attempt. The next morning, the clouds had a momentary break in them that allowed another aircraft from our unit to make the pickup. To our joy, we found out both men were still alive.

Since this mission, I have frequently thought back and tried to analyze the decisions that we made. Dan and I were both rated Aircraft Commanders, so given the situation, we were fairly experienced. At the same time, our zeal could have resulted in catastrophe. Throughout life I have felt that it is necessary to attempt a task in order to find out if it can be accomplished within my limitations. And when a human life is involved, I have always pushed the outer fringes of that envelope.

I am sure it was only a miracle that we survived this experience. Dan did an excellent job of flying the aircraft given the circumstances. I really cannot say how close we actually came to the top of the mountain or exactly what our aircraft was doing for those few long seconds. All of the instruments were working properly during our flight. I suppose the only person who really knows what actually happened is the Being who was flying as our "co-pilot."

"If man does his best, what else is there?"

General George S. Patton

"Third-Up Milk Run Turned Sour"

Chapter 17

The third-up mission flown out of Long Binh tended to be boring and garnered very little flight time for the crews. Sometimes we wouldn't even get to fly. This mission involved the back haul of wounded from combat support hospitals, general patient transfers and the worst case scenario--flying VIPs around. I avoided flying third-up at all costs, but every once in awhile, my turn would come and I would have no other choice than to pony up for these missions. Third-up—the milk run, proved to be exceptionally exciting on September 5, 1969. For some reason, the third-up missions were pretty heavy on this day. Nothing to get your adrenaline elevated but at least our feet were off the ground.

At approximately 1715 hours, an urgent request came over the radio for three Dustoff aircraft to support Company B, 2d Battalion, 3rd Infantry. Company B, located at coordinates YT 269046, was lured into a very sophisticated enemy ambush. Their position was deep inside a heavily forested and vegetated jungle where in midday, the area was not well illuminated. The NVA had constructed a horseshoe shaped complex of bunkers which were very concealed by the jungle foliage. With the exception of firing ports cleared on the front edge of the bunkers, the foliage was undisturbed. The NVA were successful in leaving sufficient "sign" for the US forces to follow. B Company moving in single file, entered the area precisely as the NVA had choreographed. When the majority of the company was inside the kill zone, the trap was sprung. NVA forces first fired upon soldiers about a third of the way back in the column, inflicting casualties and immediate confusion with the initial fusillade of fire. With command and control

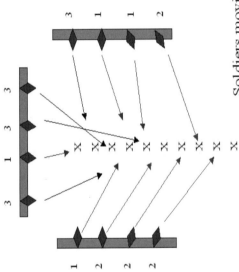

Soldiers moving in a column through the jungle following 'sign.' First volley locations (1), followed by locations (2) and then locations (3).

Concealed bunker line

Firing port

Firing Direction

disrupted, the US force was unable to effectively maneuver and conduct a counterattack. The NVA now concentrated their fire on the remaining soldiers in the kill zone. Essentially, the portion of the unit inside the kill zone were either killed, wounded or pinned down. Company, platoon and squad level leaders were attempting to gain control and extricate themselves from this deadly situation. The element of surprise certainly gave the NVA the momentum advantage in this fight.

Company B incurred six KIA and twenty-two wounded with a large number of those casualties happening very early in the fighting. Medics were overwhelmed with the number of injured and dying soldiers they were faced with. Whether the NVA were mimicking US soldiers calling for help or the calls were actually from the wounded soldiers themselves, the urgency among their peers to rescue them caused more soldiers to be wounded as they were sucked into the kill zone. One can only imagine the intense levels of fear, confusion, anger and determination that existed within Bravo Company as they attempted to regroup.

The second-up crew, the hoist bird, was launched first as it was their turn in the mission cycle to fly. Dustoff 10, CW2 Dave Alderson and his crew, headed out to the site. Operations would not typically launch multiple helicopters to a location, even though the request was for three helicopters, until the full situation could be assessed. WO Dunn and his crew had been alerted and were sitting in their helicopter, ready to go if the situation dictated a need for another Dustoff helicopter.

We were already airborne having been dispatched in our third-up role to transport whole blood to the battalion aide station located in Blackhorse-- approximately five miles south of the ongoing enemy action. Dustoff 10 had made the assessment that another helicopter would be necessary and that with normal sequencing of the helicopters, the first and second-up crews would be able to handle the patient extractions. The exact number of wounded soldiers was not known at the time Dave made his decision--he was working with information known to the ground commander. We did expect that we could be pressed into service for any additional extractions given our close proximity to the ongoing battle. Hey, maybe a little excitement for us.

Before we arrived at Blackhorse, I was able to make radio contact with Dave. He gave us a quick tactical overview of the situation that confronted him. He advised us that he had taken sniper fire from the southwest, northwest and northeast quadrants of the LZ. He described the LZ as being a 150-foot hover hole, large enough for the helicopter to descend and land but at the same time making the helicopter very vulnerable to enemy ground fire. On short final approach to Blackhorse, another urgent mission came into Long Binh Dustoff operations that would require a hoist. After dropping his patients at Long Binh, Alderson was going to be diverted to the new mission location since he was the only helicopter equipped with a hoist. WO Dunn and his crew had been launched and were enroute to the extraction site. We knew we would be headed there after our whole blood drop off at Blackhorse.

Just after we landed at Blackhorse, Fireball 16, the Battalion Commander, landed with a wounded patient that he had extracted from B Company's location. He asked over the radio whether we were enroute to that location and I told him that we were. He instructed me to shut the helicopter down as he had some urgently needed supplies he wanted taken to B Company. He was the battalion commander of the unit in contact, so I gave him a "Roger! Out!" and we shut the helicopter down.

Within a minute or two of our shutdown, Fireball 16 approached me and told me our "medical supplies" were in fact ammunition. As I glanced at the crates nearby, he put his nose in my face and said he didn't want to hear any shit from me about it being in contravention to the Geneva Accords. Sure enough the crates were imprinted with ammunition markings and there was a bunch of it.[1] Bravo Company had been hit hard in the ambush and needed the LAWS and other items of ammunition to fight their way out of the bunker complex. I did an eyeball check with each crewmember and nobody gave me a negative look that indicated they were adverse to hauling ammunition in with us. They understood the situation! With our informal vote taken, I told the crew to load it up. As far as I was concerned they were medical supplies disguised in ammunition boxes--all intended to fool the enemy. Boy, there was a stretch of the imagination.

In the full scheme of things, the enemy waits for unarmed Dustoff crews to

156

arrive on scene and then they shoot the hell out of us. In their "training," the enemy soldiers were taught how to distinguish Dustoff helicopters from other resupply helicopters. They were also instructed that any helicopter was the most vulnerable while landing and taking off. They also knew that Dustoff helicopters were unarmed and could not defend themselves--unless of course we had a gunship escort. The red crosses painted on our cargo doors provided excellent aiming points that would ensure the enemy bullets would hit in our fuel cells and engine compartment.

Maybe it was payback time. If a soldier from B Company was able to use one of the LAWs that we brought into the LZ to shoot up some NVA's ass, it would be partial payment for their shooting down Captain Otha Poole's helicopter on February 5, 1969 killing all four crewmembers. No second thoughts on my part whatsoever.

Our crew, comprised of WO1 Mike Nice, Specialist Four Richard Dean, Specialist Five Earl Deming, and I, departed Blackhorse with our cargo of "medical supplies" enroute to Rattler B-25's location. Coming up on FM frequency 62.35, I listened to WO Dunn's crew as they were in the process of completing their first extraction. We loitered in an orbit area a little south of their location and observed the operation at a distance. After departing the LZ, WO Dunn and I talked about the situation at hand. He said it was difficult to get in and out of area and even though the unit called the LZ secure, he had taken fire during his approach and departure. He said the wind was out of the west but he was able to slip out to the east and still have enough power remaining to clear the surrounding obstacles. He thought the majority of the enemy activity was to the northwest. As a crew, we now had enough information to prepare for our ultimate entry into the landing zone.

We contacted B-25 and told him we were on station and available when he was ready for us.

"Dustoff 40, B-25—the LZ is secure but we have enemy snipers all around the LZ. We have five wounded and two dead for you."

"B-25, Dustoff 40, understand five wounded and LZ is secure. We have a present from Fireball 16 to drop off before we upload with patients."

"Roger Dustoff 40, we are ready for you now."

While I was talking to B-25, WO Nice came up on guard frequency UHF 243.0 in an effort to contact the gunships that were obviously working this area. We didn't have contact with the Command and Control helicopter or the gunships yet as they were heavily involved in the combat action. B-25 did not have a frequency for either the C&C or the gunships. It was obvious from looking at the trees that the gunships had worked over the tree tops, as there were trails of smoke rising from many of them. I concluded much of the sniper fire coming into the LZ was from the enemy soldiers who had climbed up into the upper part of the trees in order to acquire targets in and around the LZ.

"B-25, Dustoff 40—we are going to come in from the Southeast and try to depart that same direction. We'll be with you in just a couple of minutes."

"Roger Dustoff 40."

"Richard, when we get on the ground, I want you to get this ammo off the aircraft as fast as possible and get the wounded loaded. If we can take the KIAs, load them on too. But we want the wounded first."

"Roger!"

"And neither of you guys wander away from the helicopter—stay connected to the intercom cord."

"Roger," came the reply from Earl and Richard.

On very short final to the LZ, B-25 began taking fire and told us to abort the approach. We aborted and made one quick three-hundred and sixty degree turn--setting up for another approach and advised B-25 that we were coming back in for another attempt. Because we had a pretty heavy load of ammunition—oops, medical supplies on board, I wanted to ensure we could take advantage of any head wind coming out of the west so that we didn't run out of power during the descent into the LZ. With all of the bullets flying around in that LZ, I didn't want to spend the night there because I did something stupid. We made this approach again from the Southeast. As we approached the LZ, everything seemed to be calm with no enemy fire being detected. Coming to a hover over the top of the LZ, with the ground 150 feet below us, Earl and Richard slid the cargo doors back to be able to clear the aircraft of any obstacles and in preparation for off-loading the "medical supplies."

"Clear on the left! Clear on the right! Keep on coming down," came the instructions from the crew.

"Forty-two pounds of torque, everything is in the green" was the readout from Mike.

"Looks like the ground is muddy. I am going to hold it light on the skids while you guys off-load this stuff," I told the crew.

"Down on the left! Down on the right! Coming out!" was the callout from Earl and Richard as we touched down on the soft muddy surface of the landing zone.

"The ground guys are coming out to the helicopter," said Earl.

"Get the ammunition off the helicopter now," I told the crew.

"Dustoff 40, B-25—we have movement to our direct front."

B-25, Dustoff 40—which compass direction? Over."

"Dustoff 40, B-25, northwest."

"Roger, B-25, we need your patients—we are off-loading the supplies now."

"Sir, we need to go get the wounded," came the call from Richard.

"Okay," I said. Both Richard and Earl disconnected from their communication cords and proceeded to wade through knee-deep mud towards the ground unit. When they brought back the first group, members of the ground unit were also helping to bring other wounded to the helicopter. I knew that we were at risk of having to leave Richard and Earl in the landing zone if we came under intense ground fire--otherwise our helicopter and our mission would be sacrificed in the landing zone. This was not a two helicopter landing zone, so we could ill afford to be shot down within the confines of this LZ.

"Dustoff 40, B-25—we got heavy movement to our front—get out of here."

"Can't! We haven't loaded all of your wounded and my crew is on the ground with you. We are going to stick it out a bit longer."

Returning to the helicopter with more wounded in tow, Richard and Earl loaded them onboard. Mike gave them the reconnect signal. When Richard reconnected, I asked him what we had left to load. "Two more wounded, plus a couple of KIAs." I told him things were getting ready to turn to shit and we needed to get the fuck out of there. "Get the two wounded. Leave the KIAs," I said to Richard over the intercom. We would be coming out with seven wounded instead of five which, given the hot weather, may put us over our gross weight for the day.

He and Earl waded out through the mud one last time returning with two more wounded soldiers.

"Dustoff 40, B-25—we are taking fire—get out of here now."

"Roger, we are working on it." Richard and Earl had loaded the last two wounded soldiers and quickly scampered aboard the helicopter.

"Coming up" was my alert call to the crew.

We lifted off with seven wounded and left the 2 KIAs for a later time. A very, very quick pause at a three-foot hover showed we were nearly at maximum power. We may not have the power to fly out of this area in which case it would be decision time for us. We had already spent too much time on the ground and each second that ticked off increased our risk as well as that of the ground unit.

"Clear on the left. Clear on the right," was the response from the crew.

"We're taking fire from the right side," called Richard.

Damn, that's the direction I wanted to depart this landing zone. That option seemed to be closing on us.

"Power?"

"Forty-seven pounds" replied Mike.

Our rate of ascent up toward the tops of the trees was beginning to decrease. I told the crew that we might run out of power before we reached the top of the trees but we were not going back down. We would take our chances by flying out of there. We then started taking fire from the northeast. Shit, this enemy is good. They were organized and they might end up taking us out of action.

As we reached the top of the trees, our vertical rate of climb coasted to a stop--much like an elevator slowing as it reaches its intended floor. We were suspended in mid-air at tree top level. Any further increase in power and I would be rewarded with a slight bleed off of the engine and rotor RPM. If that happens, we would be tits-up and would come down vertically in the landing zone in a quasi controlled crash. There was no way we would have the power available to make a 180-degree hovering turn and depart with a tailwind. Enemy small arms fire was now coming at us from all directions. Departing to the west gave a headwind which would require less power. It was our only choice——but that was where those badass NVA were located. I gently eased the cyclic forward and we began to slowly move toward the trees at the edge of our LZ—barely hanging on to the "power curve" and struggling to maintain our 150 foot altitude. The enemy fire intensified! Reaching the edge of the LZ, we were moving forward at about twenty knots of airspeed. Reaching the tree line was a plus in one regard as the airflow off the rotor system gave us an "air cushion" to ride on, so to speak. It gave us a little more power for the helicopter to gain airspeed. The downside was that we were dragging our skids through the tops of the trees because we lacked the power to hover at that altitude while trying at the same time to gain forward airspeed. Small leaves and branches were flying everywhere. I increased our power slightly--no resultant bleed off in RPM--so that we could get the skids out of the trees.

The enemy now clearly had his gun sights trained on us—tree branches and leaves were exploding all around us as the bullets streaked past the helicopter. One round had come through the bottom left of the aircraft, traveled up through the transmission well housing and exited just above the crewchief's head. The rounds coming through the cargo area where the wounded soldiers were created chaos and fear as they were trapped in what could become a deadly volley of enemy fire. The only option was to grit our teeth and hope we made it through the ground fire while continuing to keep our machine airborne. After dragging the helicopter skids through the tree branches, we had gained enough airspeed to "fly." That shudder of the helicopter as it noticeably transitioned from hovering flight to forward flight was a very welcomed sensation. We might live through this after all.

Distance and time allowed us to clear the area and we were able to climb to altitude. Richard and Earl checked the soldiers we had just extracted. No new wounds! All of the instruments were normal and we were still airborne, so we were exceedingly lucky. We continued to Long Binh and the 93rd Evac for our patient drop off--nervously awaiting an impending engine failure due to combat damage. Coming into Long Binh, we were still anticipating disaster but nothing happened. We made our final approach to our small runway and then taxied to the medical pad in front of the 93d Evac. Leaving our patients in the care of the nurses and doctors, we hovered over to our revetment and shut the helicopter down to inspect the damage. Given the amount of fire directed at us, I fully expected to find the helicopter riddled with bullet holes. Fortunately, we only took three rounds—one round passed up through the skid just outside my cockpit door, the other two came through the bottom of the helicopter and exited elsewhere.

Our after action reports which were written shortly after the conclusion of this mission made no mention of our taking ammunition into the LZ. At the time, what our company commander didn't know didn't hurt anyone. I figured if questioned, I could certainly respond that I thought they were medical supplies loaded inside of ammunition crates. After all, the commander didn't expect warrant officers to think for themselves. The commander never asked the question and I never discussed it otherwise. Thirty plus years later, I haven't lost a wink of sleep over the decision to haul the resupply of ammunition into that landing zone.

No score registered for the enemy this time around!! And here I was bitching about being scheduled for third-up missions. This was by far the most exciting "third-up mission" that I had flown during my tour. Now I was ready to return to the hum-drum life of flying hoist missions out in Xuan Loc.

"Flying is Boredom Punctuated by Moments of Stark Terror."

Unknown

Site of "Third-Up Milk Run" Hoist as well as other insecure
hoist missions that we flew in December.

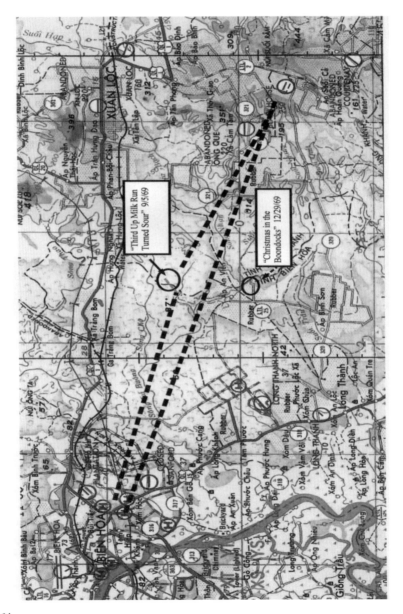

"Very Short Stories"

Chapter 18

These brief "short" stories are not lengthy enough to be chapters by themselves, but each captures a segment of my combat tour. I hope you find these stories interesting, thought provoking and insightful. They are events in my life that were just another part of combat about which people would never know unless they have had similar experiences.

First Flight In-Country

Hot off the flight school production line, I was eagerly looking forward to flying in Vietnam. Did I have the right stuff to fly in this environment? When joining a new unit, you find everyone settled into their ways of doing business. To a certain degree, you are kind of excess baggage for a few days until folks can work you into scheduling, find appropriate secondary responsibilities for you and so forth. For you, it is idle time. You are over the jet lag from traveling around the world. You want to fly but no one will give you the "keys" to the airplane.

On January 15th, my eagerly anticipated day arrived. For my orientation ride, I was scheduled to fly with our platoon leader. Now here is a 20 year old, three months time in grade Warrant Officer going out to fly with the "Major." I didn't approach that flight with anticipation because the Major was nine gazillion pay grades above me. Plus Major Smith didn't have a great reputation for being a strong pilot. And I didn't have any reputation and surely didn't want to tarnish anything by embarrassing myself in front of the boss.

Upon completion of the preflight inspection we were ready to go. We strapped ourselves in and Major Smith demonstrated how to "combat" start the helicopter. I thought helicopters started pretty much the same whether it was in the US or in Vietnam—but I was anxious to learn the "warrior way" of doing things. He completed the pre-start-up checks, turned the fuel on, set the throttle in the flight idle position—not the flight idle detent position that I had learned in flight school. Major Smith, shouted out "Clear—coming hot" and pulled the "trigger" (starter) bringing the turbine engine to life. The spool up of the turbine engine was normal until Major Smith released the "trigger" at 30% N1 (should be held until 40%). With the release of the trigger, you could hear the engine struggle to get through the remainder of the starting sequence. The exhaust gas temperature began to rapidly rise, barely avoiding a hot start on the engine by the time the engine reached 58% N1. When I mentioned to him over the intercom that he used the wrong starting procedures, the silence over my headset was deafening. There's an

This is a picture of our heliport at Lai Khe while on final approach. Our revetments are in the second row near the center of the picture. Our living quarters were located in the left corner of the wood line that bordered the heliport. The 2d Surgical Hospital was located across the open space from our parking revetments.

example of the Warrant Officer mentality working to my disadvantage. Since it was my orientation flight, Major Smith decided I would fly first. I hadn't flown in 90 days and was hoping to take the controls while in flight so that I could get the touch back without having to bring unwarranted attention to my "rustiness." We were parked in a revetment so my first challenge was to bring the helicopter to a hover without making contact with the sides of the revetment and then hover backwards for about 10 feet. I had never hovered in a revetment and in flight school they didn't want you to back up without being able to see behind you. I told him that he might want to get us out of the revetment since I had never done it. His thin lips parted in a sly smile and said "You have the controls-get us out of here." Well, it wasn't smooth, but

166

I didn't dent anything. After our orientation flight, I flew back to our area, parked the helicopter in the revetment and shut it down. When we had our helmets off, Major Smith looked over at me and asked if I thought I was a hot pilot. As I quickly contemplated my answer, I figured either a yes or no answer was going to be wrong. So I said, "Yes, Sir!" He responded by saying, "you are now my assistant maintenance officer. You report to Mister Plume and he will teach you everything you need to know about being a maintenance test pilot." What I assume was meant to be punishment for my feedback on his starting procedures was in fact the best thing Major Smith could have done for me.

Major Smith actually got the last laugh at my expense. Or maybe he was laughing at me all along and I was to dumb to know better. The next day I flew with him again on my first combat mission. Pretty routine field pickup, no enemy contact and no excitement. He showed me some techniques he liked to use to get in and out of landing zones. As he talked me through the process, I was pretty "flight schoolish" in how I flew the aircraft. Smooth and gentle versus any steep banks or rapid changes in altitude as would be necessary in combat flying. After we arrived in the LZ and touched down, I went into my flight school mode and reduced the throttle to 5600 RPM to save fuel while were sitting on the ground waiting for the patients to be loaded. As soon as the RPM started to wind down, the crewchief who was standing outside the aircraft loading the patients quickly came over the intercom questioning; "What the fuck is going on?" Before he could finish with his verbal question, Major Smith was asking the same question but rolling the throttle back to full open. Even the medic got into the conversation. In between trying to answer their simultaneous but individual questions, I think the only thing that came out of my mouth was, "but, this…that's the way I was….." Back in the air, I had no desire to return to Lai Khe in a hurry. I knew everyone in a two-mile radius of our revetment was going to know within ten seconds of our landing that the FNG screwed up. Just the day before I got after Major Smith for not starting the aircraft properly, which he didn't. But now, I cast doubt in the minds of three people as to whether I had any brains at all.

Larry Kipp who was one of our medics relates the story that one of the pilots referred to him as the "Big Dummy" for making a couple of mistakes as a crew member. That name kind of affectionately hung on him for his tour with the fourth platoon. Along with Larry being a superb flight medic and having earned his PhD in "bugology" after leaving the military, he certainly overcame his nickname. I often wonder what my unspoken nickname was or whether I quickly overcame my demonstrated stupidity in order to avoid a nickname being hung on me. "Crow meat is such a fine delicacy!

> "Mistakes are inevitable in aviation, especially when one is
> still learning new things. The trick is to not make the
> mistake that will kill you."
>
> Unknown

"Civil Harassment"

Young pilots seem to have an innate desire to push the edge of the envelope both with their skills and that of the machine they are flying. Fun and excitement for the pilots and the crew may not be viewed by an unwitting group of participants in the same light.

With Long Binh in close proximity to Saigon, we would often transit the Saigon area either to land at the 3d Field Hospital or travel enroute to another location. The Saigon River wound itself around the northern parts of the city limits. A visual air traffic control reporting point for entering Saigon airspace was the "keyhole". The Saigon River's pathway north of the city formed a visual pattern resembling an old fashion keyhole for a lock. Thus, the keyhole was a navigation reporting point that flight crews and air traffic controllers were familiar with.

On a nice sunny day, one could occasionally find a ski boat navigating the waterway with a skier in tow. Now that was like letting a rabbit loose in front a beagle. You just know there is going to be a chase but the rabbit hasn't figured it out yet. The opportunity rarely presented itself that the water  skiing populace and our helicopter were in the same geographic location simultaneously. But when it did and we didn't have a pressing commitment at hand, the chase was on. There were two great ways I found to 'play' with a water skiing Vietnamese. The first method was to drop down from altitude while remaining out of sight from the folks in the boat— preferably behind a curve in the river. Flying just a few feet off the water and approaching at 100 knots, we would come around river's bend approaching from behind the water skier. As we quickly approached, the people riding in the boat would be the first to see us. The closer we got, the more animated they became in trying to signal the skier. It would take less than a minute for us to be flying in "formation" with the skier. One can only imagine the confusion going on in the skier's mind. Typically, the skier would turn his head to see what was about to consume him from behind. The change in balance on his skis would cause the skies to get hung up in the boat's wake and it would be just assholes and elbows from there as the skier sprawled out in the water. A friendly wave to the folks in the boat and we would be on our way. No harm intended!

My other water skier interdiction style was to approach him from the opposite direction of his travel. Here again, it was best to "ambush" him by coming around a corner, a few feet off the water at a 100 knots or so. You could see the nervousness begin to set in with the boat's driver as we rapidly closed in on them. The closer we got to the boat, the nervous gestures changed to those of panic. Pilot and boat driver obtained a visual eye lock on each other. The ultimate game of chicken! Did they know the rules of the game? Did we really care? The skier was now just along for the ride as the boat driver had to decide what he was going to do. If the boat driver didn't flinch and wanted to challenge us, we just climbed a few feet and passed directly overhead—avoiding a collision. I'm sure the rush of the two vehicles passing within just a few feet of each other caused some britches in the boat to become moist. We realized success if the skier was dumped in the water or the boat driver chickened out and turned—which was normally the case.

This was our way of somewhat leveling the playing field. These assholes were enjoying the pleasures of life while we were risking our lives for them on an hourly basis. In Chapter 6, I derided the commander because he thought warrant officers were "cowboys" when they flew the aircraft. Maybe the old guy's assumptions had some merit. I never claimed that we were always on the straight and narrow. But in either case, "Yee! Ha!"

"The Probability of Survival is Equal to the Angle of Arrival."

Unknown

"Bowser Extraction"

In close precedence behind a US soldier for being extracted from the war zone came the scout dog. Within my count of 2200 patients extracted during my tour were two scout dogs. One scout dog had been wounded while the  other dog was accompanying his wounded handler. One mission came to us for the medical evacuation of a scout dog that had been wounded in the genital area by shrapnel from a hand grenade. This extraction was pretty routine. Along with the scout dog came his non-wounded handler who actually cared for the dog while he was with us in the helicopter. The medic tried to examine the dog but was met with a curled lip and a show of big fangs from Bowser. I guess if I had been in Bowser's situation, my reaction would probably have been the same. The medic took this as a hint the dog could manage until we got him to the hospital

In the second instance, the handler had been wounded and his dog was sent along with him since they were trained as a team. Without the handler, the dog was no longer an effective resource on the battlefield. During this particular mission, the soldier was safely in the hands of our medic. Sensing that his handler was safe, the scout dog took up a position between  myself and my co-pilot. With his hind legs braced on the cargo compartment floor, he placed his front paws up on the console very close to our radio controls. His posture conveyed he was in charge—back straight, chin up and eyes alert for any signs of danger. I thought I was working for some sons-a-bitches anyway so having the dog in charge of my chopper was not out of the ordinary for me.

My first encounter with this dog's management style was when I reached down to change a radio frequency. The dog took quick notice of my hand moving towards the radio located on the console near his front paws. With his eyes focused on my gloved hand, he eased his head down towards the radio console. The closer my hand moved to his front paws, the more his lip raised, revealing some nasty looking fangs. Being reasonably observant, I understood who was now in charge of the helicopter and it wasn't me. At this point in time, the dog had not given his permission for me to change radio frequencies. The dog handler was seriously wounded so he wasn't any help to me. Quickly pondering my choices, the first thought that came to me was to use my .38 caliber pistol and lay waste to the dog. But being of sounder mind than that thought conveys, I figured if I just wounded him and not killed him outright, then I would have one really pissed off dog wreaking havoc in the close confines of our helicopter cockpit. So I opted against engaging in a fire fight with the dog.

Even though I felt like I had matured at least thirty years since arriving in country, I had just to reflect back a couple of years when I had a dog of my own. Remembering that dogs determine threats by scent and visual posture, I thought I would take off my nomex flight glove and raise the smoked visor on my flight helmet so the dog could smell my hand and see my eyes. I extended my open hand and looked at the dog with a pleasant smile on my face. He sniffed at my hand and looked up at me. Sniffed some more! With a slight wag of his tail, he raised his head back up and looked out the cockpit windshield. Friends? Probably not friends but the dog seemed to grant his approval for my changing radio frequencies. There was peace in the cockpit for the remainder of the flight. If I hadn't passed the sniff test, my third option was to exercise my "command authority." I would fly the helicopter and my co-pilot would become the coordinator of the radio frequencies. He could deal with the dog.

"Do not Let Yourself be Forced into Doing
Something Before You are Ready."

Wilbur Wright

"Invincible Maintenance Test Pilots"

Within a week of arriving at the 4th Platoon, I was assigned to work with CWO Steve Plume as the platoon's assistant maintenance officer. I'm not sure I knew anything about maintenance but the "good fairy" waved the wand and I was given the title. The "How To" part proved to be a process of assimilating and applying new knowledge over the length of my tour.

When I wasn't flying, I worked with the crewchiefs to learn their skills of how to maintain the helicopter. In a short time, I knew what was a correct procedure from an incorrect procedure. Not only did this part-time job make me more knowledgeable as a pilot, but I became part of a team process that maintained our helicopters at a higher standard than our counterparts. Since we were located in Lai Khe, isolated from easy access to higher levels of maintenance capabilities, we were at times left to our own creativity on how we dealt with the more complicated maintenance problems.

Early one morning, a crewchief notified Steve that his aircraft had a rod end bearing on the pitch change link that was out of tolerance. This pitch change link is a component on the main rotor system and was part of an integral system used to change pitch in the rotor blades while flying. Normally, to tell whether a bearing was out of tolerance, a feeler gauge was required to accurately determine the thousandths of an inch change in movement. This particular rod end bearing didn't really require a measuring device as I could take my hand and move the bearing at least a ½ inch along the longitudinal axis of the retaining bolt. We didn't have a new rod end bearing at our location but we needed to get this aircraft flyable. This is where creativity came into play. Or maybe it would be better to say that, this is where 'stupidity' came into play.

Steve looked at me and asked if I wanted to fly it to Long Binh where we could get it repaired I still had my "I'm a dumbass" sign hung around my neck, so I said, "Yeah, let's go!" Both of us figured that if we took it easy, we could get to Long Binh without any trouble. After all, someone had flown it the night before and the helicopter hadn't fallen out of the sky. We cranked up the helicopter and headed off to Long Binh. At any airspeed, there was a noticeable vertical vibration. As the airspeed approached 80 knots indicated, it felt like we had just dropped a nickel into a grocery store pony ride. The severity of the vertical vibration gave us no choice but to slow down—to 60 knots. And onward we flew at 60 knots with the one-to-one vertical vibration all the way to Long Binh. The forty minute flight to Long Binh left me with a splitting headache. A cold brewsky would have been a nice choice to soothe the throbbing in my head, but we still had to fly the helicopter back to Lai Khe.

After landing at the dustoff heliport, our crewchief found a "real" maintenance officer to examine the rod end bearing. The crusty CWO climbed down from on top the helicopter after examining the rod end bearing and exclaimed, "Where are those dumb asses that flew this helicopter in here?" Steve and I looked at him. He looked at us. He knew the answer to his question. He said, "You guys are a couple of lucky sons a bitches. That's the worst bearing I have ever seen that is still in one piece. You guys damn near killed yourselves." Not much we could do except try not to look dumber than we did. We got the parts necessary to fix the helicopter, tracked the rotor blades and set off on our return flight to Lai Khe. When we got back to Lai Khe, we reported the aircraft was available for mission scheduling.

We didn't whisper a word to anyone about nearly killing ourselves in the process of making the helicopter mission ready.

Jerry Abrams working on "Daisy Mae"-Phase Maintenance.

Much of my maintenance time involved working with the crewchiefs and medics as a third set of hands to complete the regular 25 hour inspections. These inspections happened at least once a week for each helicopter in our platoon. At other times, I was simply the pilot charged with doing an engine run-up to verify that a replaced part functioned properly. If there was an important or major task for me in the area of maintenance, it was tracking rotor blades and ensuring the autorotational RPM was set at the prescribed values.

If a crew is going to spend 10 to 20 hours with a helicopter strapped to their asses, it is really nice to have it fly smoothly. A comparison to which you might relate would be driving a car with tires that are slightly out of balance. Their balance dictates your speed and comfort as well as the handling quality that is provided by the machine. Each rotor blade "flies" on its own separate path or track. The more separation there is between the flight paths, the greater the vertical vibration in the helicopter. Optimally, the flight paths are identical. If the blades are out of balance, then the helicopter incurs a lateral vibration. A helicopter with both a vertical and lateral vibration was the worse to work on. It was not uncommon to have to take a full work day to get the blades flying the "same."

In the center of each rotor blade tip cap is a small protrusion that serves as the rotor blade tie down slot. We typically used red and black grease pencils to color the protrusion on each of the rotor blades a different color. We would then start the helicopter bringing the engine operating RPM to 6600. With the RPM remaining constant, we would pull up on the collective pitch control to where the turbine was producing 20 pounds of torque. At 20 pounds of torque, the helicopter was very light on the skids, almost to the point of lifting off the ground to a sloppy hover. The crewchief would be standing in front of the helicopter at a point where the edge of the tip path crossed over his head. Holding a tracking pole braced on the ground, he would slowly rotate the device until a vertical band lined with masking tape made contact with the blade tips. The grease pencil markings on the blades then would appear on the tape showing the paths of the blades. The objective was then to make adjustments to the rotor head pitch change links or rotor blades themselves to change the flight path of the blades. Sometimes our "guesstimates" of the amount of adjustment to be made was right on. Other times it was more complicated and time consuming. I preferred to track rotor blades at late dusk when the air was smoother. Also by shining the landing light at an upward angle, the edge of the tip path plane was exceptionally easy to see. You could be more precise in your work which saved time and generally produced a better tracking solution.

The other task as a maintenance test pilot was actually test flying the helicopter to see if all the parts worked in harmony with one another. I usually flew the test flights as a single pilot with a crewchief riding in the left seat. After we finished the test segment of the flight, the crewchief would get an opportunity to try his hands at flying the helicopter. This served two purposes. Being able to sit "up front" and drive his own "ride" bolstered his confidence and pride. The second purpose was to give him enough exposure flying the helicopter, that in the event a pilot or both pilots were incapacitated, the crewchief could take over flying duties and get the aircraft safely on the ground. The majority of the crewchiefs got the hang of flying the helicopter with about ten hours of hands-on flying. They could steer in the direction they needed to go and land the helicopter without killing themselves. Remaining calm and confident in their skills was so important in this critical

Richard Dean waiting for a 2nd up mission at Long Binh 1969

situation. We were not shooting for style points—just being able to get it on the ground in one piece was the measure of success.

While performing a test flight with Richard Dean, the crewchief of the Iron Butterfly, we experienced a complete hydraulic failure of the flight controls. We had done repair work on the connectors for two of the hydraulic lines. The ground run up and pressure check showed the lines to be functioning properly. After we finished the ground test, Richard and I took the Iron Butterfly up for a test flight to ensure everything was in working order. We checked the operation of the flight controls with the hydraulic boost turned off and then again with the boost returned to its normal on position. Everything checked out fine. We repeated the test a second time—it checked fine this time around as well. The next test we wanted to perform was checking the rotor RPM during a simulated engine failure. I set the helicopter in a steady state of flight at 90 knots and 3000 feet AGL and then reduced the throttle to flight idle. This placed us in an autorotative descent with a rate of descent at about 1500 feet per minute. I made some steep turns to place more 'load' on the rotor system. With the rotor rpm remaining within its normal parameters during the power off descent, we initiated a power recovery, climbed back to altitude and headed back to Long Binh, satisfied that the Iron Butterfly was "fit as a fiddle." Within a minute or two of making the power recovery and returning back to a normal flight mode, Richard picked up the smell of hydraulic fluid in the cabin area. Looking back to where the inspection panel was located on the transmission housing, we could see red hydraulic fluid running down the outside of the panels. Hmmm! That's not normal.

Yep, a significant leak had sprung forth. Definitely, the "fiddle" wasn't sounding very good. We called back to Long Binh and declared an in-flight emergency. We almost made it back to the heliport with everything still operational. On final approach to the heliport, the Master Caution Light illuminated on the instrument panel signifying we had a problem with an aircraft system. The individual caution light announced we had lost hydraulic pressure. The loud whine of the hydraulic pump combined with the now sluggish control movements confirmed the illuminated indications on the master caution panel. On a comparative basis, so you can understand what we were experiencing, it was like driving an automobile equipped with power steering and having a failure of the power steering pump. You can still drive it but it's not that easy. We made a missed approach at our heliport, completed our in-flight emergency checklist and headed for Sanford AAF located on the northeast edge of the Long Binh compound.

At 80 knots airspeed, the cyclic control (the control located on the floor between the pilot's knees) was easy to move with just the normal control feedback when the hydraulics are turned off. The collective control was easy to move upwards. However, it required two of us pushing down with all of our strength to move the collective through the final part of its downward arc. The normal procedure for handling a hydraulic failure is to make a shallow approach with a running landing, touching down at about 30 knots indicated airspeed. Our heliport required a steep approach to clear wires over the approach end and the surface was rough and uneven—especially for a single pilot. Richard and I were looking for a longer life so we opted to not attempt an approach to our heliport.

Richard changed our UHF radio to preset number two which was the frequency for Sanford tower. We contacted Sanford, declared an emergency, gave the tower controller our location and told him that we needed to make an emergency landing on their nice 3200 foot asphalt runway. The controller gave us clearance to land. I set up for a nice shallow approach and began a gentle reduction of the airspeed so that we would arrive over the runway for a running landing touchdown speed of about 40 knots. It took two of us to apply pressure on the collective control so that we could maintain the shallow approach angle. Just over the end of runway and ready for touchdown, Richard and I could not get the collective to go down any further. My only option then was to reduce engine RPM which also caused a subsequent reduction in rotor rpm. Retarding the throttle from 6600 RPM to 6400 RPM caused a decrease in power (lift) and was sufficient to allow us to touchdown on the runway. With the skids sliding on the runway surface, the weight of the helicopter along with the friction of the skids brought us to a quick stop.

With our helicopter now parked in the middle of the runway, both Richard and I were proud of our reaction to the in-flight emergency. The emergency landing did, however, take us right into the heart of REMF land. In two shakes of a lamb's tail, a captain pulled up next to our helicopter which we had managed to park right in the middle of his fixed wing runway and proceeded to chew my ass for closing his airport. Emergency or no emergency, he had an airport to operate. And now there was a fixed wing aircraft circling overhead with a general on board that would have to divert to another location. Until our helicopter was removed from his runway, the captain could not reopen the airfield for fixed wing traffic.

While we were inspecting our helicopter, we overheard the REMF captain talking with someone on his radio about getting a bulldozer out there to push our helicopter off his runway. Within 20 minutes of our touchdown and before any bulldozer appeared, our company maintenance aircraft arrived on the scene with the equipment necessary to ground tow the helicopter to a different location. Imagine the damage that would have been done to the helicopter if this captain had been successful in getting a bulldozer out to our location.

You know, there really is a God! He looks after dumb animals and REMF officers with single digit IQ's. In both cases, it is necessary for a higher being to guard over them ensuring neither is abused for being ignorant.

> "If You Can't Afford to do Something Right, Then be
> Darn Sure You Can Afford to do it Wrong."
>
> Charlie Nelson

Armored Round Deflector

Flying with Steve Plume in January 1969, one of our missions was in support of the 1st Infantry Division inside the Iron Triangle. The unit was an armor company with a mix of tanks and armored personnel carriers. When we arrived on site, the unit was in contact with an enemy force. We had one litter and two ambulatory patients with gunshot and fragmentation wounds to extract. An armored company can lay down an impressive amount of firepower ranging from 105 MM main gun rounds from the tanks, fifty caliber machines, M-60 machine guns on down to the M-16. Why a dismounted ground element would take on a force with this amount of firepower boggles my mind. But the NVA must have decided they had the upper hand and chose the moment as their option for this particular fight.

With the battle still going on, a medical evacuation helicopter entering the activity is easily detected. The enemy was located in the tree lines and the tanks in the open—not much concealment around for us to stay out of the line of fire. Steve opted to make his approach and land short of a tank at the pickup point. His reasoning was to put the tank between the enemy force and us. Good plan!! The tank had guns—big guns and we didn't. No sooner had we pulled in behind the tank than there was a significant explosion directly in front of our helicopter. The explosion sent pieces of shrapnel through our windshield and instrument panel. One piece hit me in the arm, and my comment over the intercom, was that I was hit. That's all it took for Steve to pull pitch and get the hell out of there. Unfortunately, the crewchief was standing away from the helicopter and missed his "ride" out of the LZ. Also we didn't have the patients on board. The ground unit said the explosion was an enemy rocket propelled grenade (RPG) that had hit the angled portion of the tank's turret that we were "hiding" behind. The slope of the turret caused the round to detonate but not penetrate the turret. The exploding shrapnel then continued in our direction.

As we climbed up and away from the LZ, I pulled my fatigue shirt sleeve up to check for the wound but couldn't find any wound. The skin on my forearm and wrist were red where the shrapnel had hit me. The tank turret, the nose surface of the helicopter, and the instrument panel dissipated the energy of the flying shrapnel to where it didn't have enough oomph to break the skin on my arm. My ego was bruised as my "announcement" of "being hit" resulted in Steve reacting to my callout and lifting out of the LZ. And I hadn't lost a drop of blood.

We quickly circled back and slipped into the LZ, taking up a hiding position behind a different tank. We got our crewchief along with the wounded soldiers on board and then got the hell out of there. Needless to say, the crewchief was not impressed with finding himself as an interim "grunt" while we flew off the first time. And since it was my fault *per se* that we departed so quickly, he took great joy in asking how my 'wounded' arm was until his feelings were finally placated.

"Never Fly in the Cockpit with Someone Braver than You."

Richard Herman, Jr. (Firebreak")

Beaver Patrol

Land Beaver in Vietnam consisted of three general species, French, American and Vietnamese. The French Beaver was infrequently detected as their species were few in number and were elusive to the average GI. French Beaver could sometimes be seen sunning themselves in the compounds of their rubber tree plantations. The French plantations were posted as no-fly areas and were off-limits to American helicopters. But if they wanted to file a "complaint" they had to know who we were and our unit identification. A formidable task even for the cunning French plantation owners. Whenever we passed known French Beaver habitat, all eyes were searching for the elusive prey. If found sun bathing in the nude, we would swoop down for a quick look and be on our way satisfied with the pleasures of the visual sighting.

American Beaver was also a pretty limited species as well. Generally it inhabited military hospitals and American Red Cross facilities. American Beaver commonly referred to as "round eyes" was a delicacy seemingly reserved for the doctors and the commissioned officers. Every once in a while, a warrant officer would be fortunate enough to capture one of these select critters. But that was the exception more so than the norm. Warrant Officers spent too much time in the field to be able to set an effective trap for this species. The hooch next door to ours was occupied by a married commissioned officer. When we were back from the field and able to sleep in our own beds, the thin plywood walls would allow us less fortunate souls to occasionally hear the soft moaning and cooing of a round eye beaver that he successfully captured for the night. Heaven forbid such delicacies would be reserved for only a select few.

Vietnamese Beaver was by far the dominant species in the area. One of our married Warrant Officers captured the company's resident beaver who adorned the Officer's Club by day. His encounter with this particular Beaver produced an off-spring which was hatched in our combat surgical hospital. The company commander, however, deemed the officer to be too prolific in his hunting so he was quickly dispatched to the 1st Cavalry Division as a reward. After his departure, one of the commissioned officers provided her comfort at night. It was not appropriate to return her to the wild as now she was domesticated. I always wondered which of the married officers returned to the states with her.

There was a variety of the Vietnamese species that was easily detected at night in the company area. For some reason they were easier to capture but it also required a monetary payment. Responding to a knock on the door followed by a soft whisper of: "GI, boom, boom—500 piasters" [one piaster approximated one US penny] could result in the short term capture of one of these nocturnal Land Beavers.

On one occasion, a crewmember in another aviation company captured a Vietnamese nocturnal Land Beaver that was infected with a foreign antibody. The antibody created great havoc for him. Out of desperation to rid himself of this infestation, he traded one of our medics a door-mounted mini-gun for sufficient penicillin to effect a cure. Great trade for us until the Criminal Investigation Division (CID) came looking for the missing mini-gun.

In time of war, why do the daughters of the occupied land become the whores of those sent to ensure their freedom? And if a wife cannot trust her officer husband to forgo his hunting privileges in her absence, how can soldiers within the unit trust him in combat?

"God gave men both a penis and a brain, but
unfortunately not enough blood supply to
run both at the same time."

Robin Williams

SECTION

REMF Tales

REMF Mentality

Christmas in the Boondocks

Here Today--Gone Tomorrow

The Six Hundred Dollar Television

REMF Mentality

Chapter 19

I think it is important to highlight a mission where the headquarters placed greater importance on the well-being of the aircraft than on the survival of the soldiers who were being extracted. An aircraft commander had the responsibility of ensuring the safety of his crew and completing the extraction of the wounded soldiers. Between the two requirements, there was a very fine line separating the risk factors for both entities. I did my best to always adhere to the premise of "No Compromise, No Rationalization, and No Hesitation—just fly the mission." Our mission was to extract wounded soldiers who we knew needed critical life saving medical care. If we were injured in the process, that was the risk of the job. If the aircraft got damaged, it could be repaired or replaced.

We were flying a field standby out of Xuan Loc about 25 nautical miles east of Long Binh. A call came that reported members of the 199th Light Infantry Brigade had been engaged by the enemy and had taken several casualties. They were asking for extraction by hoist because there was no LZ available. The unit was attempting to withdraw and break contact from the enemy. The infantry company was essentially fighting a disorganized delaying action through a large coffee tree plantation, running from one delaying position to the next attempting to break contact. Scouts and gunships were applying counter pressure from above on the enemy. We arrived over the area, assessed the situation and decided not to use a hoist. Coming to a ten-foot hover, lowering the jungle penetrator, having them strap a wounded soldier on it and then "reel" him back into the helicopter would take too much time and place the ground unit at greater risk. Our plan was to find a location slightly ahead of the delaying ground force, and use the helicopter to make as much of a LZ as possible. The coffee trees were about ten feet or so in height and looked pretty flexible. I came to a hover over a "likely candidate" we chose to become our improvised LZ and essentially lowered the helicopter down on top of it. The tree wasn't going to support the entire weight of the helicopter without splintering and quite possibly impaling the bottom of the helicopter. We were able to get within about 3 feet of the ground before the tree branches gave way under the weight of the helicopter. With the medic holding onto the back of the crewchief's flak vest, the crewchief was able to lean down far enough to grab onto the soldiers and pull them into the helicopter. We extracted their four wounded in the time that it would have taken to hoist one. We were on our way to the hospital and the ground unit was again on the move to another delaying position. The gunships continued to hammer the pursuing enemy until the VC decided to end the chase and return another day to fight again.

On short final to our heliport which was co-located with the 93d Evac, the tower controller told us we had what appeared to be tree branches sticking out of the bottom of the aircraft. Now where do you expect they came from? After dropping the wounded off at the hospital, we parked the helicopter so the damage could be assessed. Peering under the helicopter, all of the reports of tree branches sticking out of the bottom of the helicopter were true. There were enough branches riding with us that we may have been able to start our own mini-coffee plantation. While the maintenance folks started the necessary repairs, I walked up to my hooch to check the mail and to get an ice cold Coke. With the cold drink in my hand plus one for the road, I headed back to the helicopter. And who did I find 'supervising' the repair--none other than the infamous Major Domo. As I approached him, his demeanor turned to anger and he questioned me as to why we had damaged the helicopter. Giving him my report, his body language and facial expression told me he wasn't interested in what I had to offer. He asked me if I was aware of the regulation pertaining to the requirements that a ground unit had to meet before a medical evacuation could occur. I said, "Yes Sir, I have read the regulation but it didn't fit this situation." He said that I had broken the ADF housing which was made of fiberglass and punctured some other holes in the bottom of the aircraft. "You are going to pay for the damage," he said. With my typical anti-REMF tone of voice, I told him to send me the bill. With that, he started off on another tangent by chewing my ass because we had left our weapons in the helicopter while we checked our mail and got something to drink. "Don't you know the rules for securing your weapons?" he asked. My flippant response was, "Sir, I didn't think you or anyone else working on the helicopter would steal 'em. I guessed wrong, didn't I, sir!"

I hope you remember that Major Domo was the "instructor" that I had heard early in my tour quoting AR 40-10 to the ground unit over the radio on how they would set up the LZ or he wasn't going to land. The holes in the skin of the helicopter could be fixed another day. The ADF fiberglass housing was "trashed" and a new one was ordered. In the meantime, a little "hundred mile an hour tape" ("duck tape" for you civilian folks) fixed our problems and we were back on our way to the field standby location to resume our missions.

> "In theory, there is no difference between theory and practice.
> But in practice, there is."
>
> Jan L.A. van de Snepscheut

Nellie Fox

Pee Wee Reese

Christmas in the Boondocks

Chapter 20

Chapter 6 was my analysis, in part, of our unit's leadership climate during the last half of my combat tour. Not only did that type of environment affect me personally and professionally, it affected the organization as a whole. And from reading this chapter (you didn't skip it, did you?), you can see that I had little respect for the style of leadership and the negative impact that it had on the unit's soldiers and its mission.

Young kids often latch on to a sports hero as their idol or role model. As a young kid, I, too, selected baseball players that I wanted to emulate on the field of play. Since I played short stop and second base for the majority of my baseball "career," I tried to emulate Nellie Fox and Pee Wee Reese. Both were leaders in their sport--both on an off the field. Ironically, Pee Wee Reese died on my birthday in 1999. For my role as a leader in the military, I selected commanders and non-commissioned officers who were excellent leaders. I have worked to analyze and assimilate the best of their talents. Poor leaders served equally as role models. I witnessed their style and its ramifications on the people and the functionality within the organization. I committed myself to not assimilating their negative attributes.

Later in life, my leadership development focused more on the theories of teachers and scholars like Stephen Covey, Eric Allenbaugh, Frosty Westering and Pat Bettin—to name a few. Each teacher has his own approach and style for conveying the "lessons." But yet their teachings are similar in that they focus on human interaction, self-awareness and determining what is important. I pride myself in the fact that I continue to apply these new teachings to my personal and professional lives. I don't always get it right the first time, but with practice, I find myself improving more as time goes on.

But what has this diatribe on leadership have to do with "Christmas in the Boondocks?" Ineffective leadership created the scenario for this story. My crew flew a great deal over the holiday period, completing several very hazardous missions resulting in lives saved. We were glad to have been there over the holidays but at the same time, a day off would have been nice. This story follows squarely on the heels of "Busted" in Chapter 8. It also bangs on my issue with the leadership climate that existed in the organization.

With the command group opting to play REMF Roulette to determine when I would be able to again fly after having exceeded the thirty consecutive day flying hour maximum limit, I had departed on R&R to Australia. Seven days away from the unit in a non-flying status brought my flight hours back into a range where I could fly unimpeded until my tour was slated to end in January. Time off provided me with the physical and emotional rest that I also needed. I was itching to strap a Huey on my butt and to go forth and smite the enemy one more time. Our assistant platoon leader scheduled my crew for field standby duty at Xuan Loc for the period of December 17, 1969 to December 26, 1969. The crew scheduling plan called for a rotation of crews in the field location over one of the holiday periods—but not both. It was obvious that my crew was chosen to be in Xuan Loc for Christmas.

Our crew was experienced and we were flying the more intense missions in the Xuan Loc area which was fine by me even though the grease penciled numbers on my cockpit door window showed that I only had a few days left in country. At worse case, we anticipated being back in Long Binh then for New Year's Eve. Vietnam didn't embody the spirit of Christmas. No neon lights beckoning shoppers. Carolers going from door to door singing songs of joy were non-existent. There were no corner lots selling fresh, green Christmas trees. And the friendly Salvation Army bell ringers were no where to be seen. Only "Uncle Charles" concealed in the depths of the jungle foliage waiting for unwary soldiers to walk into their lair. So being in the field wasn't a major drawback--at least there was a proababilty that we would be flying. New Year's Eve was easier to celebrate as there was always plenty of cold brewskies in our mini-officers' club. With one of the holidays being designated as down time for us, my crew was satisfied with there being a sense of fair play in crew scheduling.

We packed our stuff for a week long stay. We had enough lubricants and support materials to complete two 25 hour inspections on the helicopter if the need arose. There was the usual political bantering going on about a cease-fire over the holidays. Whether it would come to fruition or not was yet to be determined. We packed for the worse case scenario.

After our arrival in Xuan Loc on the seventeenth, we averaged eight hours per day of flying. Christmas Eve found us flying 5.1 hours—reasonably light but yet fairly heavy for that particular day of the year. As we wrapped up the daylight flying, we hoped for peace and quiet on Christmas Day. And for the most part it was. We flew mainly priority extractions without being fired upon. Those that we evac'd on Christmas Day were due to illness or other injuries not related to direct action with the enemy. Rising on the morning of December 26th, we were eagerly awaiting the arrival of our replacement crew. We preflighted our helicopter for our return to Long Binh. Around 10:00 AM, our replacement crew had not arrived. We were getting anxious about the delay of the replacement crew's arrival. The later their arrival, the later in the day we would have to work cleaning the helicopter and performing our preventative maintenance checks. Not only did we have the maintenance to perform, but after a couple of weeks in the field, the helicopter needed to 'hit' the wash racks so the dirt, blood and grime could be washed off.

I told the crew to go ahead and load our stuff in the helicopter. We would take off and once we were airborne, we would be able to communicate with our base operations to find out what was going on. Climbing to 1500 feet, I contacted base operations over our FM frequency. The RTO didn't know anything about our replacement crew. Hum! This wasn't lookin' good for the home team. I asked them to locate our platoon leader and find out what the hell was going on. We set up a high orbit over Xuan Loc while we waited for our answer. We waited!! And we waited a little longer!! Finally, the radio crackled to life with their response. I'm sure glad we wore seat belts and shoulder harnesses in the helicopter. When the RTO's message came over the radio informing us the Assistant Platoon Leader's decision was for us to remain in the field until after New Year's Day, I came unglued. Had I not been strapped in, I am sure I would have shot right up through the overhead "green house" window. I was down to approximately ten days before I was scheduled to go home—and I was really looking forward to being able to stop putting my ass on the line every day in hopes that I would make it home in the upright position.

My radio transmission back to base operations was more in the form of feedback for the Assistant Platoon Leader. I had a one way conversation with my "mike boom" with which I explained the full meaning of the word REMF and how the platoon leader and his assistant fit all of the criteria. After I finished my feedback session, we descended very quickly from altitude and landed back at Xuan Loc. It would be an understatement to say I was pissed about what had transpired. The rest of the crew was pissed as well, but as we walked back to our operations hooch, they gave me a wide berth. When someone is having a major hissy-fit and at the same time carrying a weapon, giving them a wide berth and room to cool down is always a wise choice. By the time I got back to the operations building in Xuan Loc, I was cooled down emotionally. We swallowed our bitter pill and resolved ourselves to just move on. Five or six more days in the field didn't make a rat's ass difference in the full scheme of things. Each time after that when we found ourselves flying a hot mission, we "thanked" our platoon leadership over the intercom.

On December 29th, we supported a company about 20 miles east of Long Binh—although we were flying out of Xuan Loc at the time. Shows the priority that we were given over the holidays. We flew in support of this unit for a good portion of the day, making five trips into the LZ to hoist wounded soldiers. The soldiers were considered urgent and there was no gunship cover available for us. Even though the company policy was to not fly a hoist mission without an escort, we continued our general rule of thumb by figuring out the best decision based on our knowledge in the cockpit. At this point in time, I was about eight days from leaving country, so even though there was risk involved, we were not taking unnecessary risks. After all, the wounded soldiers were why we existed. They risked their lives in the jungles and rice paddies. It was only fitting that we laid ours on the line for them.

In the next six days, we flew 43.2 hours. One day found us flying 11.1 hours. Our time was well spent and I hope that those we evacuated during that window survived and appreciated our efforts on their behalf. On New Year's Eve, there was a Vietnamese band playing in the small enlisted men's club close to our operation building. We wandered over to the small club to listen to the band thumping out good old rock and roll songs. Our crewchief and medic were allowed in the club as you would expect, but the officers had to remain outside. There was a kind of half door next to the bandstand where we were able to see into the club and enjoy the music. I allowed the crewchief and medic to each have a brewskie to celebrate the start of the New Year. While we were standing outside the club enjoying the music, a Brigadier General from the 199th Infantry joined us and chatted for a few minutes. We had worked with his troops for the past couple of weeks and he was familiar with my call sign. He was appreciative of our efforts especially over the holidays.

The one plus for us, unlike our counterparts in the jungle, was that we didn't spend Christmas or New Year's out in the elements wondering if "Chuck" was going to deliver an unwanted Christmas present.

The next morning, our replacement crew arrived. We packed our stuff and hit the airborne highway back to Long Binh. While were expecting to be relieved the day after Christmas, one must always anticipate Murphy's Law or the imposition of poor leadership. Given the time of the season, either the platoon leader or his assistant should have been on field standby along with their aircrews. Even though I was pissed at the time, leaving me in the field was fine, but they should have been respectful of my crew and brought them back for New Year's. When ample flight crews are available, which there were at that time, fair is fair in mission scheduling.

Our assistant platoon leader was the "rater" for my performance evaluation encompassing the last 59 days of my tour prior to my departure from Vietnam. I received my final evaluation in the mail after I had returned to the states. I had to chuckle when I opened up the mail to find the evaluation neatly folded in the envelope. Both the rater and the endorser (platoon leader) found it necessary to down grade me from an "A" to a "B" for 'Tact'[1] on this performance evaluation. Although it was a downgrade from what I expected, it could have been worse given the amount of "feedback" that I provided to them. Being introverted, I tend to hold my emotions in check until the "BS Gauge" reads in the red. I haven't changed much from 1969. I *still* tend to speak my mind when the gauge reads "red." I never had a chance to fly with either the platoon leader or his assistant. I don't think they liked "wild and wooly." They preferred "warm and cozy." I always wondered if they ever got up the courage to venture out and fly from a field standby location.

You may have drawn the opinion that because we were left in the field for both holidays, that my story is just merely whining about a situation that was of no major consequence. If so, my response would be that this story along with several others in this book focus on leadership and how to care for your "horse." This air ambulance company was replete in examples of poor leadership--but yet, the folks that comprised the crews that I flew with always rose to the challenge and remained focused on the mission. Why? Was it pride in the mission? Would we have continued trying to uphold the Kelly legacy even if the leaders were not there? I'll let you ponder those thoughts while I finish up this chapter.

During our Christmas holiday season in the boondocks, my crew lived up to Major Kelly's expectations. On December 17th, we picked up an aircraft that had been flown for about six hours since completing its one hundred-hour phase maintenance inspection. Between December 17, 1969 and January 1, 1970, our crew flew 93.9 hours. When we returned to Long Binh at the completion of our standby on January 1, 1970, the aircraft was ready for its next one hundred hour maintenance inspection.

It was a great beginning for a New Year!!

> "The Essence of Leadership--was, and is, that Every Leader from
> Flight Commander to Group Commander Should Know and
> Fly His Airplanes."
>
> Air Vice Marshal, J.E. "Johnnie" Johnson, RAF

Here Today—Gone Tomorrow

Chapter 21

In June 1969, our platoon received a new helicopter as a replacement for one damaged beyond local repair. To this day, I remember the smell of its newness. The instruments were brand new and all of the "holes" in the instrument panel were filled with operational components. The radio console had new radios and I am sure all of them worked. And the skin of the helicopter did not appear to have an overactive case of acne from patched bullet holes. Platoon members would come by the helicopter, touch, smell and rub up against it much like a cat does with a bag of cat-nip.

Before we had time to flow the new machine into our combat schedule, Major "Domo" scheduled a "check ride" for another company officer and

had tasked us to provide the new helicopter for their training flight. With disdain, I watched them fly off in our new helicopter.

I used a pseudonym for the Major in order to protect the identity of the guilty until proven otherwise innocent for flying with their "head in the up and locked position." Domo is the same Major referred to earlier transmitting his requirements to a beleaguered ground unit on how they were suppose to prepare the landing zone in order for him to land. Likewise, he is also the "star" of the story on REMF mentality. Every organization has one or two of these folks running around creating havoc. In this case, he had the rank and the authority to make life difficult. I can only assume that Domo was a certified instructor pilot. *Where* he obtained his training and how *recent* that training had been would have made a difference in his capabilities as an instructor. When my combat tour was complete, I returned to the states and went through the flight instructor's course to teach contact maneuvers—which also consisted of what we termed "emergency procedures" training. Even though I was "certified" at the end of the qualification course, I only became comfortable performing all of the emergency touch down procedures after training a couple of student classes. In Vietnam, instructor pilot training was conducted at Vung Tau. I don't know if this training was up to par with stateside qualification courses nor how "confident" the graduates were in performing emergency type procedures.

In any case, Domo decided to give the check ride at an old dirt airstrip outside the security perimeter of Long Binh. A helicopter with a skid type landing gear found on the UH-1 does not slide as well on dirt as it does on a hard surface. The softer the dirt, the more opportunity there is for one or both of the skids to sink into the soft dirt and/or for the tail stinger not to stop the downward motion of the tail boom, thereby allowing the tail rotor blades to make contact with the runway surface. Whether it was a hot dogging contest between two pilots or an actual check ride, I will never know. I never saw the accident report for this flight nor was it ever briefed at any of our pilot meetings.

Domo, early in the check ride sequence, decided to demonstrate the low level autorotation. A low level autorotation is performed to simulate an engine failure at low altitude and cruise airspeed—80 knots. To perform a low level autorotation in a training/check ride situation, the instructor descends to 50 feet AGL on final approach; maintains 80 knots airspeed with constant power—no descent or climb during the final approach portion. When the runway can be safely reached, the instructor rolls the engine throttle to the flight idle detent, which reduces the engine power to an "idle." At the same time, the nose is raised to decelerate or slow the airspeed while maintaining the 50 feet of altitude. The helicopter eventually slows to the point where the helicopter's pitch attitude is lowered into a landing attitude. At approximately 10-15 feet above the ground, the pilot applies a rapid upward movement of the collective to about half its arc of travel. The application of collective control increases the angle of attack in the rotor blades, further slowing the helicopter's vertical and forward speed, and the helicopter descends toward the ground. The collective and cyclic control input are then used to arrive at the point of touch down on the runway with no vertical or forward motion in the helicopter as it touches down on the runway surface. A little forward momentum is preferred to let the helicopter slide about half its length—this eliminates touching down with zero airspeed and having a hard landing. The primary caution during this maneuver is the close proximity of the ground in relation to the end of the tail where the tail rotor is located. A high nose pitched angle causes the tail to be much lower to the ground. It is possible through inattention or by flying the maneuver incorrectly, that the tail stinger followed by the tail rotor could make contact with the ground. Sorry for having to include the explanation of a low level autorotation but without it, you might not understand what happened during Domo's maneuver.

Somewhere in the flight sequence, Domo rolled the throttle off, entered the low level autorotation and held the nose in a higher than normal position or applied more nose up pitch at the conclusion of the maneuver. He promptly managed to bury the tail "stinger" in the soft dirt surface during the maneuver's required nose up, tail down rapid deceleration sequence. When the tail stinger failed to stop the downward motion of the tail boom, the tail rotor contacted the runway's surface, causing it to fail. Without the tail rotor, the pilot lost directional control, spun the helicopter and crashed. Neither Domo nor the other pilot was injured. While still in the helicopter, they were unable to stop the fuel flow to the engine using the conventional fuel, throttle and battery switches/controls. Somehow, the unabated fuel flow created a fire that could not be extinguished. Helicopters tend to burn quickly as a majority of the components are made from magnesium. In a short amount of time, the new helicopter was rendered down to a barely recognizable heap of melted parts.

Maintenance was dispatched with a forklift and a five ton truck to retrieve the remains of our new baby. Unfortunately, the maintenance crew got the forklift mired in the soft dirt and couldn't get it out. Says alot about the condition of the dirt runway which was being used by Domo for his most difficult training manuevers.

The company commander made the decision to provide a security force to prevent the "bad guys" from destroying the forklift. Another great idea generated by our superb leadership. Because the helicopter belonged to our platoon, I was flown out to the site along with a small security force, to

guard the remains of the aircraft until it could be recovered. Walking up and down the airstrip, it was clear as to what happened. The surface was too soft to begin with. I wonder if they ever landed first to inspect the the "runway" to determine if they could safely complete the power off, touch down type emergency maneuvers they were planning to do. I could only stand there in

amazement. What had been a brand new helicotper hours ago could now fit into the back of a 5-Ton Truck. My only words were---"how could they do this to us?" Our other helicopters were patched, taped and wired together. This one hadn't even tasted combat!

We stayed with the downed helicopter—ten people with M-16's and a .38 caliber pistol to guard the forklift. Time marched on with no follow on maintenance recovery team in site to retrieve the mired equipment. Surely the commander wasn't intending to leave the ten of us out there overnight to guard that thing? We had no cover or concealment, not all that much ammunition and we probably weren't the best "infantry" group of people to have in a fire fight. Oh! We didn't even have a radio to get help if we needed it. Little did I know the decision had been made to wait until daylight the next day to send out a recovery team.

At last light, I managed to get the attention of a LOACH pilot flying by our location. He came back and landed to find out what the hell we were doing out there. He said an ARVN infantry unit was going to sweep through there that night. He contacted Dustoff Operations and let them know of the situation. Finally someone made a decision to fly two helicopters out to our location and extract us. I think if the ARVN sweep hadn't been planned to come through that area, the company commander would have left us there all night.

The next morning, the forklift was still there—all in one piece. A recovery team retrieved the forklift and the remains of the helicopter. Here today! Gone Tomorrow! Arrogance and ineptness in its finest hour-the death of a new helicopter that came well before its time.

> "There is more stupidity than hydrogen in the
> universe, and it has a longer shelf life."
>
> Frank Zappa

The Six Hundred Dollar Television

Chapter 22

"Some cause happiness wherever they go; others, whenever they go."
Oscar Wilde

The Company provided three aircraft on mission standby each day. The "first-up" and "second-up" crews rotated combat missions throughout the daylight hours. The first-up crew was the primary crew for night time unless a backup was required. The exception to rotating missions came when the mission required the use of a hoist. The second-up helicopter was the only one equipped each day with a hoist and was dispatched for any mission needing that type of equipment. A third aircraft was available primarily for hospital-to-hospital patient transfer. Occasionally, when airborne with an empty and non-committed aircraft, the third-up crew could "scarf" a tactical mission by being closer to the location than any crew on standby—thereby saving time. It also gave us the opportunity to get the pulse rate elevated with a quick "sip" of adrenaline. If both first and second-up aircraft were committed and away from Long Binh, the third-up crew became the next crew to be committed for tactical operations.

The third-up assignment was basically a "milk-run" mission, if you might. Generally not much flight time accumulated during the day. Every once in a while, we got to fly an entertainment troupe around. Good-looking women always brightened the day. The drawback, though, was we didn't have rear view mirrors in the helicopter cockpits and it was impolite to turn around and stare. We had to rely on the crewchief and medic to give their verbal picture over the intercom on the finer aspects of our passengers. Based on the verbal description we got over the intercom, there were times I wish I could have traded positions with one of the 'guys in the back.'

One of the rare times I found myself flying the third-up standby, we had patient transfers at the 36th Evac in Vung Tau to be flown to the 93d Evac in Long Binh. It was a nice day for flying and we had a couple of non-medical "Space-A" (space available) people on board who needed transport from Long Binh to Vung Tau. If we had the room in the helicopter, we would accommodate Space-As who were trying to get some place for R&R, or for other personal reasons. But patients always had the priority and others were truly a Space-A arrangement.

We are on short final to the 36th Evac in Vung Tau. The four medical landing pads can be seen on this side of the hospital.

Upon landing at the 36th Evac medical heli-pad, the crewchief and medic opened the side cargo doors and awaited the patients who were going to be transferred on our flight. Along with the patients and the accompanying medical staff came other standby personnel hoping to grab a space on board the helicopter. On this particular flight, we had a litter patient and two ambulatory patients. The one litter patient consumes the space across the width of the helicopter. This eliminated our ability to use the fold down passenger seats. The two ambulatory patients could be seated in the "hell hole" seats (two seat spaces per side of the helicopter) leaving us with room for two Space As needing a ride back to Long Binh. We had more Space-As than we obviously had space for so the ground personnel were trying to determine who the two lucky people were going to be that would get on board. One obnoxious and over zealous person was trying to push his way on board the helicopter. Complicating his problem was the "box" that he had with him. This box looked to be about three feet square on all sides. With the litter patient on the floor, this box wasn't going to fit anywhere in the helicopter that was not already occupied with people or equipment.

This passenger was insistent upon his being allowed to get on board with his "package." I keyed the intercom and told the crewchief to move the guy and his package away from the helicopter and put two people on-board so that we could leave. The crewchief escorted this guy away from the helicopter, loaded two other passengers on board and we departed. When we were airborne, the crewchief commented that this guy told him we would be back shortly to pick him up as he was going to call the general and tell him we wouldn't let him on board the helicopter. Whatever! I didn't plan on bumping a patient or a passenger so that his box could go for a ride. I asked the crewchief if he knew what was in the box. "TV," came the crewchief's response. "A TV?" "There is only one channel and that's AFVN and who the hell has time to watch TV?" I commented over the intercom.

Arriving back at Long Binh and while dropping off our patients and passengers at the 93d Evac, our FM radio crackled to life with a call from Operations. The RTO asked if we had some Specialist 5 on board with his package. We said that we didn't. He had been bumped in Vung Tau to make room for hospital transfer patients and other passengers. "Standby" came his response. A minute or so later, the RTO came back on the radio and said the Commander had directed us to return to Vung Tau to pickup this guy along with his television.

We went to the hot refuel point, grabbed a fresh load of JP-4 and headed back to Vung Tau. Turns out that this Specialist 5 was some general's gopher. He was dispatched to Vung Tau to pickup a television set that had just arrived at the PX. After we arrived in Vung Tau and retrieved our passenger along with the general's newly acquired television, we headed back to Long Binh. When we were airborne, I glanced back and made eye contact with this asshole and expressed my displeasure through my scowling look. He just gave a sly shit-eating grin knowing he had one-up'd us. Our brief "conversation" with each other was quickly concluded and we settled in for the flight back to Long Binh. Above and beyond whatever the general had paid for the television, the total transport costs for the helicopter's maintenance and fuel was probably around $600. Our labor was free!

REMFS!! Ya gotta love 'em!

SECTION

Closure

Uncommon Heroes

Value Added?

The Aftermath

Those That Gave All

Uncommon Heroes

Chapter 23

The warriors listed herein are the ones I was most involved with during my combat tour and who truly had a positive impact on my life. They came from all walks of life, formed cohesive teams and flew against all odds.

Enlisted Crewmembers

The enlisted crew members gave of themselves twenty-four hours a day, seven days a week. Without them, our mission would not have been successful.

Richard Dean	Larry Kipp	Terry Ackroid
Drexel Johnson	Jose Vergera	Paul Lakey
Alan Morris	Steve Huntley	Richard Mathews
Bill Stalfort	David Ross	Mike O'Brien
Mike Logan	Chet Crump	John Sabanosh
Danny Hilton	Wayne Davidson	Bill Mostek
Tom Cash	Stephen Hannon	Bob Richards
Del Williams	Jerry Abram	Mike Casper
Dave Billeter	Bruce McCartney	Jake Bailado
Earl Deming	Rick Blackwell	

Officers and Warrant Officers

Each of these guys piloted their helicopter into harm's way each and every day to rescue the wounded. They challenged their skills, their fears, the enemy, the weather and the terrain. They never ran from the enemy. They truly have the right stuff and they don't need no stinkin' badges to prove it.

Charles Kelly	Tony Alvarado
John Temperelli	John Smith
Si Simmons	Dan Weaver
Randall Radigan	Robert Spitzer
Steve Plume	Basil Smith
T.C. Greer	William Dunn
Gerard Cataldo	John Murray
Gary Calhoun	Mike Novosel
Gary Mock	John Mitchel
Tom Hall	David Jones
Tom Wills	Jerry Kinsey
Tom Barfoot	Barry O'Connor
Michael Nice	Dan Voss
Jerry Forester	Robert Bixby

"Success is peace of mind in knowing
you did your best."

John Wooden

Value Added?

Chapter 24

Value in this instance is truly in the eye of the beholder. Bean counters may view the question from a return on investment (ROI) position. What did it cost us to save a life? A tactical ground commander may determine value based on the number of aircraft available or not available to him for airmobile assaults. Last but not least, the person who was lifted out of the jaws of death by a Dustoff crew will have a totally different perspective on whether or not Dustoff was valuable.

One of my themes in this book used the cavalryman's adage of caring for his most valuable resource—his horse. For this analogy, the horse equates to the soldier fighting the war on a daily basis. Peter Dorland and James Nanney state that between 850,000 and 900,000 allied military personnel and Vietnamese civilians were evacuated by helicopter air ambulance.[1] My research shows that 214 Dustoff crew members lost their lives during the Vietnam War. Although the death of one soldier is priceless, the ratio for crew members lost to the number of sick, injured or wounded that were evacuated was 1 crewmember for every 4206 soldiers evacuated. Having known several of the Dustoff crew members who were killed, this ratio is still quite acceptable despite the crew member losses.

One of the more valuable aspects of Dustoff was found in the morale of the ground soldiers in combat. They knew that if they were wounded, they had a very high probability of making it back to medical facilities where their life or limb could be saved. Therefore, there was less hesitancy among the soldiers to commit themselves to fighting the enemy. Although this is an intangible value to a certain degree, statistics show the percentage of deaths among those soldiers admitted to a hospital facility during WW II was 4.5% and in Vietnam it was 2.6%. Even though the Vietnam percentage is lower, the percentage is actually somewhat inflated given the circumstances found in the two wars. The helicopter with its ability to reach a critically wounded soldier within the *golden hour* contributed to hopelessly injured soldiers dying in the hospital rather than dying on the battlefield as they would have done in WW II. Even though the 2.6% died at the hospital, they were still given the best opportunity available to support their chances for survival.[2]

There is also the premise that the allocation of dedicated resources for medical evacuation limited the ability of other tactical aviation units to perform their mission. Early in the war when helicopters, especially the turbine powered UH-1 models, were scarce resources, an argument could be made as to who was the winner and who was the bill payer as far as the ability to employ the resources was concerned. On an average, Dustoff units experienced an aircraft availability rate of 75%. There were times, though, due to combat damage or for other reasons, a unit was at a zero percentage of flyable organic aircraft. In dire straights like that, other Dustoff units would cross level crews and aircraft to ensure there was no degradation in mission capability. Did it stretch resources? Yes! Was a new helicopter within the supply system ever diverted from a tactical aviation unit to backfill a Dustoff unit? Probably! Did it occur often? In my estimation the answer would be no. Was the trade-off worth it? In my opinion, it was.

Paddy Griffith, one of Great Britain's most noted military historians specializing in battlefield tactics, wrote an article in *Vietnam* entitled "Reevaluating the Role of Dustoff." One of the assessments that he makes is for every hour of flight time incurred, nine hours of maintenance were also required thereby reducing the overall availability of the aircraft for combat operations at any given time to around 10%. His hypothesis then boils down to there being very few excess aircraft that could be dedicated to medical evacuation due to this low availability rate.

Mr. Griffith also takes the question of value down another different avenue. He looks at the difference between the hospital death rate of 2.6% in Vietnam and the 4.5% in World War II and concludes the 1.9% increase in survivability actually became a future liability to our nation. The liability comes in the form of long term disability payments, medical care and other related costs that would be paid out to the survivors. Additionally, he states that the actual costs incurred during combat operations are also higher. He validates his argument in part by claiming there would be the need for expanded medical care in the rear echelons both for the treatment of the patients as well as the long term and convalescent care for the increased number of survivors.

Senior ground commanders had to take the value of a human life and weigh it against the ongoing tactical operations. Some concluded that Dustoff impeded offensive tactical momentum on a non-linear battlefield thereby forcing the commander to decide between medically evacuating his wounded or continuing his offensive operations. In a company level operation, the commander may have two platoons committed with one platoon held in reserve to serve as a blocking element or a reinforcing element to exploit a tactical advantage. To extract wounded soldiers during the battle, typically necessitates the commander to commit his reserve platoon as a security force to facilitate the medical evacuation mission. When he commits that reserve platoon, he loses offensive momentum and at best must revert into a defensive posture. In a linear battlefield with an organic medical capability via land, the wounded are initially treated at the company aid station while battalion level resources come forward to evacuate the wounded. A Dustoff crew would then evacuate from the battalion aid station versus the front line. In Vietnam, the battlefield was not linear and for the most part there was no ground evacuation capability present within the ground maneuver units. To bring a Dustoff helicopter into the foray of battle required the commitment of ground assets to provide security for not only the wounded but for the helicopter. In a linear battlefield, the ground unit commander should not be impeded in regards to his tactical momentum. Medical assets are available at the company, battalion, and brigade levels to effect the evacuation of wounded. For future non-linear battles, the commander will have to make the hard, cold determination regarding his priorities. That's why he gets paid the big bucks.

In Vietnam, Dustoff proved its value by reducing the *golden hour* of evacuation from three hours to just under an hour after a soldier was wounded. A life saved is a life saved and no price can be placed on that life. Long term health care, etc., for those soldiers who participated in a war is the cost of doing business for the government who elects to choose war over other available options. If "bean counters" or politicians have a problem with this philosophy, they should do a cost analysis before launching military tactical operations. Failure to do so means they assume the liability for their actions.

For the future, I envision Dustoff will continue to be an effective combat component. Future pilots and crew members will redefine "wild and wooly" to fit their role and style of combat flying. **What won't change is the value of the human life that is "Dusted Off" from the battlefield.**

> "Not everything that can be counted counts, and not everything that counts can be counted."
>
> Albert Einstein

The Aftermath!

Chapter 25

January 1970 arrived and when all was said and done, it was time for me to go home. Had the command climate been the same or better than when I first arrived in the unit, I would have gladly extended for another six months. But you know, the command group never asked any of us to extend. Staying alert to avoid the death traps that we encountered while flying was stressful enough without having to contend with a company commander that we couldn't trust. I was marching to a different drumbeat—the one Major Kelly set as the tenor for how Dustoff should operate. Albeit, I was just one cog on the wheel and my role was to be a follower, the drummer was taking us down a path with which I totally disagreed. I have found through experience that when you are out of step and you cannot change the drummer, it is time to pull pitch and head off in search of a better band. One in which the beat is in sync with your inner spirit.

The sixth day of January was my departure date from the unit, a quick stop at the 90th Replacement Battalion and then home. My last day of flying was the first of January giving me five days to wind down, gather up my belongings, out-process through the company and brigade, and give away or sell those tangible things like the air conditioner and refrigerator. The air conditioner had seen its better days so it went for free. For some reason, the government frowned upon us selling their real estate, so we willed our hootch to a couple of homeless new guys. For a plywood structure, it was pretty comfortable—not that I would want to live like that again.

As the Freedom Bird lifted off from Saigon, there was no special joy for me. I felt like I had left good friends behind and had abandoned the new pilots who would likely suffer from the lack of experience within the unit. Seated next to Tom Barfoot, we settled back in our seats for what was going to be a long trip home. My mind pondered the previous twelve months searching for the answer as to whether I lived up to the standards of what Major Kelly set forth for Dustoff Pilots. If we meet in heaven, I will ask him the question. Our first stopover was Japan. We had to remain on the ground for eight hours in order for an airline crew to have enough crew rest time in order to become legal to fly the remainder of the trip home. We all sat in the terminal, impatient to get under way but glad to have at least made the journey this far toward home.

Arriving in San Francisco on January 8th was sensory overload. One day you are flying combat missions and trying to stay alive. Seemingly the next day you are thrust into a sea of strange people. We were still wearing our jungle fatigues when we got to the terminal as there was no out-processing for us in Oakland. People stared at you because you wore a "combat" uniform and apparently represented something they despised. Bald headed guys in white robes, singing and chanting to a weird drumbeat, crossed our path in the San Francisco airline terminal. As one of them saw my uniform and turned towards me, a menacing stare from my tired eyes and pursed lips served notice to him that I wasn't in the mood to be screwed with. We slipped into the nearest restroom and changed into our summer light weight uniforms and headed to the airline ticketing counters to find a way home.

Waiting next in line at the ticket counter, some guy along with his wife and her white poodle stepped in front of me as if I were invisible. They never glanced at me, spoke to me, or acknowledged that I existed. She told the ticket agent they were in a hurry. He helped them first. Not like I had any place important to go. It was more prudent to brush the incident aside and not acknowledge the man and his wife in any manner. Saying anything would have made me the instant loser in the verbal debate. With money in hand, I bought a ticket to Los Angeles. Being late at night, my parents reluctantly agreed to make the drive from Santa Paula to the Los Angeles International airport. My home life growing up was not a "Leave it to Beaver" environment. Home for me was a place to visit on occasion, but not hang out there. I stayed a few days and then drove my new car up to Oregon to visit friends and a girl friend in Portland. I no longer fit in with the kids with whom I to high school. Our life experiences were now totally different. I felt that I had lived a lifetime and they were just beginning their jobs working in the local lumber mills or finishing college. Anxious to get on with the rest of my life, I remained at home in Santa Paula for a short period of time before heading east to Savannah, Georgia where I was slated to become an instructor pilot.

After a day or so at Hunter Army Airfield in Savannah, I ran across Tommy [Rodman] Kershner who had been in my basic training unit at Fort Polk and my flight class at Fort Wolters, Texas. We decided to rent an apartment and hung out together for nearly a year enjoying the bachelors' life. Flying, drinking beer, water skiing, drinking more beer and then water skiing some more seemed to consume our life's activities. Through hometown friends of Tommy's, who were stationed with the Navy at Charleston, S.C, I met and then married my wife, Lori. As I complete this writing, we have been married for 32 years. For some illogical reason, I elected to accept a direct commission in May 1970 and continued serving in the Army for a total of 26 years before retiring in 1993. I did have the privilege of commanding an armor company when the military was at its peak of racial unrest. This was a true learning experience for me and I am better for having met that leadership challenge. The military did consume a great amount of time—long hours and frequent deployments to the field. Lori maintained the home and raised our children so that our values were imparted to them.

In 26 years and serving at nearly all levels in the military, I saw the best and the worst in leadership. My career flourished and I was the happiest with commanders who shared a similar philosophy to that of Charles Kelly, "No Compromise! No Rationalization! No Hesitation! Complete the Mission!" Career regression occurred when I served with commanders who were indecisive.

I received a near fatal performance evaluation in 1981 when I declined to falsify an aircraft status report by changing my air cavalry troop's aircraft status from amber to green. I served as the commander of an Air Cavalry Troop in 1980 and 1981. The Army had transitioned to the new AH-1S Cobra, but we still had the old G models. I think our Squadron was at the bottom of the new equipment distribution list. National Guard units were receiving the S models while we still had the Gs. Army budgets were such that we were not allocated sufficient ammunition to conduct an aerial gunnery qualification exercise each year. And at times during my twenty-four month command tour, we encountered spot shortages of aviation jet fuel (JP-4) leaving our aircraft grounded or allowing us to only fly enough to meet flight proficiency minimums. Likewise, we often lacked the funding for spare parts. Our G models had previously been used as test platforms for a variety of weapons and gee whizz black boxes. Electrical wiring harnesses in these 'birds' were a convoluted patchwork of splices, electricians tape and soldering. We would get a system operational and it would last until the first time it rained--do not pass Go and do not collect a "flyable" helicopter.

The next scheduled aerial gunnery qualification would be the first one where money, fuel and ammunition would allow us to qualify all of our Cobra pilots. With a three-month lead time prior to the scheduled aerial gunnery exercise, we performed a very thorough inspection of the gun turrets and rocket pods to ensure there was ample time to prepare the weapons system for the upcoming aerial gunnery exercise. Prior to the weapons system preparation, I informed the commander of my intentions. The majority of my AH-1s were considered to be in a non-mission capable status due to the weapon's systems deficiencies—albeit the aircraft were still flyable. Our AH-1 availability, or lack thereof, brought the entire Squadron into an "Amber" status for the monthly unit readiness report. Obviously, the Squadron Commander was displeased that he would have to report an amber status to the division command group as the division would probably be rated in an Amber Status for attack helicopters when their report was forwarded to higher headquarters. I might add here that the other two air troops who had AH-1s were confronted with the same maintenance problems for their weapon's systems. The difference was their weapon systems deficiencies were not accurately reflected on the readiness report.

The progression line started with me and ended at the Army level. The Squadron Commander directed me to change my report and to not reflect the weapon's systems as being down. After all, we could cannibalize from the "fleet" to make the aircraft fully mission capable if we needed to. My report was accurate, we intended to repair the weapon's systems and they would be fully mission capable within the following 30 days. I was not going to change the report. The Squadron Commander had the authority to override my decisions and I told him that he could change the report if he felt I was wrong and if changes were needed in the report. He, in turn, explained to me that he was not going to change the report--I would be the one to make any changes. And if I didn't change the status report, he would reflect it in my command performance evaluation. Damn my warrant officer mentality! You *know* that I just couldn't resist daring him to write in my evaluation that I refused to falsify an aircraft status report thereby justifying a lower mark on my evaluation.

The evaluation, on the surface, was fine. It contained nice words and was complimentary of what I had accomplished as a troop commander for twenty-four months. The damage done was through what was not written—recommendation for promotion ahead of contemporaries, selection for higher levels of command, advanced schooling, etc. If nothing else, I maintained my standards and had the opportunity to spend some additional time as a Major.

While in Vietnam, we supported the 9th Infantry Division until they departed Vietnam in July 1969. The 3d Brigade of the 9th Infantry Division was headquartered at Tan An—where I spent a great deal of field standby time. Twenty years later, I served as Colonel Beau Bergeron's S-3 and XO when he commanded the 3d Brigade, 9th Infantry Division (MTZ) at Fort Lewis, Washington. History over time may prove the following statement incorrect, but I believe I am the first and only Aviation branched officer to have served as both the S3 and XO of a motorized infantry brigade.

In 1989, my gold oak leaf was converted to an oak leaf of silver. I worked with great leaders during my tenure at Fort Lewis from 1985 until 1989. Major General Roger Bean, supported by Colonel A.J. "Beau" Bergeron, facilitated my final promotion in the military. To both of them, I owe personal gratitude for their continued support and perseverance against an unforgiving bureaucratic process.

Serving as the Professor of Military Science at the University of Washington was my last tour prior to leaving active military service. These four years were very rewarding. Along with my instructor cadre, we had the opportunity to prepare the next generation of leaders for their roles in the military. When the Clinton Administration took office, the Commander-in-Chief through his personal actions implied that lying, cheating, stealing and condoning those that do were acceptable leadership standards. They surely didn't fit my level of acceptability as a professional military officer. So I made the choice to move on with my life.

In every circumstance, a person is always given a choice on how to influence the outcome. Clinton didn't impress me as being a leader and I refused to allow such a person in his role as Commander in Chief to order me into combat for some half assed reason. So, if you can't change the drummer, find a different band. Retirement from active duty officially came on the last day of June 1993. While still on terminal leave from the military, I went to work for state government in a middle management capacity. I stayed with the Washington State Department of Revenue managing their timber excise tax program for ten years. The military was bureaucratic but the organization has always been able to remain focused on a mission until it was accomplished. And not everything is fair, but life as a whole is not always fair. State government, or at least my experience within it, allows itself to become mired down until minimal progress is achieved. Poor leadership abounds throughout. Lots of smoke and mirrors used to portray that change is occurring. Efficiency is the spoken mantra, but very little changes over time. Political appointees do not seem to have a grasp on what leadership is all about. Different band, less palatable music!

Still searching for the right drummer! In 2003, I changed career paths again and returned to the military world as a senior military analyst. What will the band hold for me this round? One can always hope for the winning lotto ticket.

> "Be more concerned with your character than with your reputation. Your character is what you really are while your reputation is merely what others think you are."
>
> John Wooden

Dustoff Crewmembers Who Made the Ultimate Sacrifice
Chapter 26

These soldiers, one and all, made the ultimate sacrifice so that others might live. They knew the risks, accepted the challenges, faced adversity and flew the missions. They are the true heroes of Dustoff.

Thomas Adams
Russel Ahrens
Ronald Allgood
John Alling, Jr.
Orin Allred
Robert Alverson
Rodney Arnold
Steven Arnold
Orval Baldwin
William Ballinger
Stephen Beals
Gary Bowdler
Robert Bradley
Paul Brass
Clifford Bratcher
John Bregler
James Brooks, Jr.
Joseph Brown
Harry Brown
Michael Brummer
Robert Burlingham
Edward Bush
Gerald Caton
William Cheney
Thomas Chiminello
John Chrin
Ralph Cinotti
Timothy Cole, Jr.
James Conway
Donald Cook
Robert Cottman
Charles Covey
Daniel Cox

Michael Darrah
Sylvester Davis
Ray Delgado
Billy Denley
Louis DiBarri
Robert Dieffenbach
Robert Donaldson
Gary Doolittle
Ronald Doolittle
James Doran
Gary Dubach
Zettie Dunlin
Dennis Easley
Gary Englehardt
Guy Ephland
William Esposito
Joseph Feeney
Dennis Ferrell
Robert Fillmore
James Fortenberry
Joel Fowler
Reinis Fox
Randall Freeman
Joe Fulghum
David Funes
Alfred Gaidis
Lawrence Gallego
Kent Gandy
Charles Gay
Harold Gay
Hugo Gaytan
Dennis Gilliland
Francis Glazebrook

Dalton Goff
Bruce Graham
Ronald Lester
Willie Green
Johnny Gregg
Dennis Groth
Wade Groth
Allan Gunn
Gregory Habets
Terrance Handley
William Hawkins
William Henderson
Victory Hernandez
Ramiro Herrera, Jr.
Clifford Herrin
Theodore High, IV
John Hill
Robert Hill, Jr.
William Hix, Jr.
Ferman Hodges
Joseph Hoggat
William Holland
Robert Horst
Rudolph Jackymack
Robert Jones
David Johnson
Gary Johnson
Guy Johnson
Phillip Johnson
Steve Johnson
Charles Kane, Jr.
CharlesKelly
Michael Kelly

John Keltner
Jeffery Kuersten
Kurt Kuhns
Douglas Kyser
Kenneth Lamborn
Larry Lance
Lawrence Lano
John Larget
Brent Law
Robert Layman, Jr.
Jerry Lee
John Levulis
William Lewis, Jr.
Jack Lichte, Jr.
Randall Love
Chester Luc
Christopher Lucci
Charles Lumm
David Muclurg
Douglas MacNeil
William Malenfant
James Margro
Donald Marlow
Ronald Martin
Gilivado Martinez
Thomas Martinez
Alan Mate
Calvin McGilton
James McNish
Guy Mearns, Jr.
David Median
James Megehee
Anthony Mensen
George Miner
Billy Morris
John Murphy
John Nesovanovic
Roland Nielsen
Kenneth Nokes

Edward O'Brien
William Parker
Ricky Pate
Billy Pedings
Hugh Pettit
Harry Phillips, Jr.
Michael Poll
Otha Poole
Robert Porea
Larry Powell
Thomas Pursel
Forrest Rains, Jr.
John Rauen
Dennis Reese
Karl Reineccus
George Rice
Jeffery Richardson
James Richardson
Charles Rideout
Richard Rochacz
Don Rock
Jerry Roe
Robert Rose
Carlos Rucker
Kenneth Rucker
Marion Runion
Stephen Saluga III
Richard Sanders
Kenneth Schlie
Phillip Schmitz
Howard Schnabolk
Anton Schnobrich
Ronald Schulz
StephenSchumacher
Arvid Silverberg
Wayne Simmons
Teddy Sininger
Robert Sloopye
Charles Smith

John Smith
John Souther
Robert Speer
Thomas Stanush
Roy Stillwell
Douglas Stover
John Supple
Hubert Sutton
Loran Sweat, Jr.
Gary Taylor
Gary Thatcher
John Trasher
Lewis Trask
Ronald Trogdon
Johnathan Vars
David Wainwright
James Walters
Frederick Walters
Richard Walton
Thomas Weiss
David Wencl
Gregory White
Jeffery White
James Wieler
Leroy Williams
Morris Williams
Jesse Wisdom
Jack Wolfe
Donald Wood
Donald Woodruff
Dwight Woolf
Kirk Wooley
James Zeimet
Alan Zimmerman

The names of the crewmembers listed herein have been cross referenced with the data bases in the VHPA directory, Dustoff Association, Virtual Wall, 498th Medical Detachment web page, the casualty listing contained in *Rescue Under Fire* and Si Simmons' web page. Since there is no known formal record maintained with the names of Dustoff crew members who lost their lives in Vietnam, those who are developing data bases are making changes as new information is gained. I hope that our research has added to that ongoing effort.

"The grave yards are full of indispensable men."

Charles de Gaulle

 # APPENDIX

The UH-1
"Huey Helicopter"

On February 23, 1955, Bell Helicopter was awarded the contract for the development of a new US Army medical evacuation helicopter. Three prototypes were ordered. The prototype was designated the XH-40 or Bell Model 204 and first flew on October 22, 1956.

The Model 204 was Bell's first production turbine powered helicopter. The Lycoming T-53-L-1 turboshaft engine rated at 700 horsepower was incorporated into the Model 204. Bell used its traditional main and tail rotor configuration consisting of two bladed rotors and a stabilizer bar on the main rotor. Bell continued with its tradition of using a skid type landing gear in lieu of a wheeled landing gear. To assist maintaining the helicopter level in forward flight, a horizontal tail plane or stabilizer was added to the tail boom.

The three XH-40 prototypes were followed by the production of six "YH-40" test helicopters. The YH-40 helicopter was stretched one foot in length and equipped with a T-53-L-1A engine derated to 770 horsepower. The YH-40 was capable of carrying a pilot and co-pilot along with six passengers or two stretchers and a medical attendant. The Army took delivery of the first of nine pre-production, newly renamed HU-1 Iroquois helicopters on June 30, 1959.

An additional 183 HU-1A's were ordered including 14 configured with dual controls and arranged for instrument training. The HU-1A delivery was completed in 1961 with medevac versions of the "A" model deployed in Alaska, Europe and Korea.

Bell YH-40 in
Flight

Performance improvements requested by the Army were incorporated into the HU-1B. The "B" model first delivered in March 1961 was modified with a lengthened fuselage allowing for an increased payload capacity. The "B" model could be configured with two pilots and seven passengers or in a medical evacuation configuration which allowed for three stretchers, two sitting casualties and one medical attendant. In its cargo configuration, the "B" model was capable of carrying 3000 pounds of internal cargo. The later production series of "B" models had the new T-53-L-11 engine which produced 1,100 horsepower.

In 1962, the helicopters were redesignated in the new tri-service designation plan as UH instead of HU thereby becoming known as the UH-1. The UH-1B became recognized as the early workhorse in Vietnam by filling three roles—troop transport, medical evacuation and gunship. In the gunship role, it was initially fitted with the M-6E armament system which was comprised of two M-60 machine guns mounted on each side of the helicopter along with the four round rocket pods. The machine guns were mounted on a flexible mounting system allowing them to be aimed through a sighting device in the cockpit. Within certain limits, the machine guns could be flexed vertically and laterally to engage targets not directly aligned with the helicopter's flight path. In the transport configuration, the "B" model was equipped with two externally mounted M-60 machine guns operated by independent gunners seated on each side of the helicopter. The transport version of the helicopter was termed the "slick," a nickname resulting from the smooth appearance of the helicopter when not equipped with external armament stores.

UH-1 B Model Cockpit. in the Gunship Version

The desire for improved performance and increased capabilities are unique to nearly everything man has invented and produced. The helicopter was no exception. Once the helicopter was viewed as a potent offensive weapon, the military asked for new and improved versions beyond the capabilities of the "B" model. Bell Helicopter was in the process of developing the AH-1G Cobra as a pure attack helicopter. As an interim solution to meet the need for greater offensive capability, Bell developed and produced 750 "C" model gunships. The horsepower rating of the engine was increased along with a larger fuel capacity. The new "540" rotor system destined for the AH-1 was adapted for the "C" model. The rotor system's increased performance capabilities provided a more lethal weapons platform with which to support ground combat operations.

While the UH-1Bs were rolling off of the assembly line, Bell Helicopter engineers were designing the "B" model's successor—the UH-1D. The "D" model was again a stretched version of the "B". The "D" model came with an 1,100 horsepower turboshaft engine which provided a greater payload capability. The first "D" model flew in August 1961 and entered service in August 1963. The Army ultimately purchased 2,008 "D" models. Four years later, the "H" model entered the Army inventory. The Army purchased 3,573 UH-1Hs. The newer version was used primarily in a mission support role—troop transport, medical evacuation, etc. With its increased engine horsepower and lifting capability, the "H" was an optimal helicopter for the hot temperatures and high density altitude conditions the pilots faced on a daily basis.

Author hovering out of a parking revetment in Long Binh 1969. The helicopter is Hover Lover-crewed by Bill Mostek.

Although I flew the "B" and "D" models in advanced flight training, I only flew "H" models in combat. Even as a novice pilot at the time, the difference in performance between the airframes was easily recognized. Later in my aviation career, the use of aircraft performance charts in pre-mission planning became mandatory. The computation of weight and balance, hover charts, fuel consumption, etc., to include the infamous "go-no-go" hover check made just prior to departure were all used to determine whether the mission could be flown. In Vietnam, we never used performance charts. Not that performance charts are unimportant, we didn't have time to use them. If we had computed the helicopter's performance based on the charts, the majority of the missions I flew would have been well outside the helicopter's prescribed performance limitations. "Cause the performance charts said it wasn't safe" was not a viable excuse for not flying the mission.

The Huey was abused time and time again but it never failed me. Even when we flew Flower Power into the ground at night, which turned out to be its last flight, the helicopter brought its precious cargo back safely to our field aid station. In my opinion, Bell Helicopter provided the Army's young aircrews with a superb product which undoubtedly saved many lives because of its

229

excellent capabilities. The UH-1 series will be officially retired from active and reserve military duty in 2004.

The following data reflects some of the operational capabilities of the UH-1H

Engine	T-53-L-12 Turboshaft, 1,400 HP @ 6600 RPM
Fuselage Length	41 feet, 5 inches
Maximum Length w/rotors turning	57 feet, 0.67 inches
Rotor Diameter	48 feet, 3.2 inches
Height	14 feet, 8.2 inches
Empty Weight	5,210 pounds
Maximum Loaded Weight	9,500 pounds
Maximum Speed	124 knots
Service Ceiling	12,600 feet
Range	280 Nautical Miles
Fuel	209 Gallons/1359 lbs of JP-4

UH-1 Dimensions

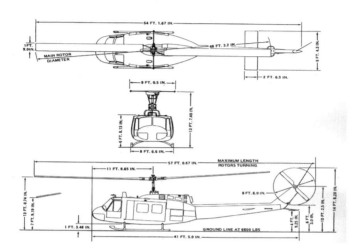

UH-1 Cockpit

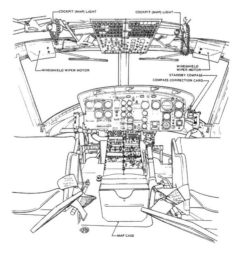

Note that the pilot/copilot seats are shown
in a reclined position in order to better show the cockpit layout.

UH-1 H Model Cockpit
Pedestal, Collective and Cyclic
Controls Diagram.

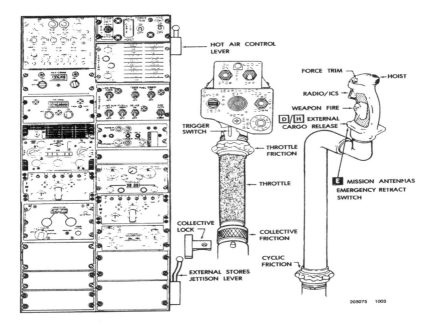

HOT AIR CONTROL LEVER

FORCE TRIM — HOIST

RADIO/ICS

WEAPON FIRE

D/H EXTERNAL CARGO RELEASE

TRIGGER SWITCH

THROTTLE FRICTION

THROTTLE

E MISSION ANTENNAS EMERGENCY RETRACT SWITCH

COLLECTIVE LOCK

COLLECTIVE FRICTION

CYCLIC FRICTION

EXTERNAL STORES JETTISON LEVER

205075   1003

Hoist Information

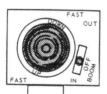

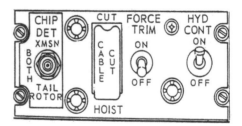

The picture at the top of the page shows the hand held hoist operating control (the diagram shown immediately to the left of this narrative).

The extended hoist arm contained an electrically operated device to sever the hoist cable. The panel above shows the cable cut switch that was located on the radio/control pedestal located between the two pilots. The switch had a flip up red protective cover which we had safety wired in the closed position (down as shown in the diagram above) with a very light tensil weight safety wire to prevent accidental activation of the cable cut switch.

Hoist Information-Continued

We encoountered several hoist failures while I was flying as a Dustoff Pilot. The heat build up in the electric hoist motor and the time interval between hoist lifts may have been a strong contributing factor to these failures.

256 FOOT CABLE

WEIGHT	CYCLES	NOTES
Lower 250 lbs. Raise 250 lbs. Lower 0 lbs. Raise 250 lbs.	8	1, 2, and 3
Lower 0 lbs. Raise 400 lbs.	4	1, 3, and 4
Lower 400 lbs. Raise 0 lbs.	4	1 and 3
Lower 0 lbs. Raise 600 lbs.	3	1 and 3
Lower 600 lbs. Raise 0 lbs.	3	1 and 3

NOTES:

1. One cycle equals one complete lowering and raising of the 250 foot usable cable.

2. Equivalent to lowering a medical attendant and raising nine patients with the attendant.

3. Thirty-second rest period at the end of each raise or lower cycle. A 2.5 hour rest period at completion of listed cycles.

4. Thirty-second rest period at the end of each raise. A 2.5 hour rest period at the end of four cycles.

The Overseas Weekly
Pacific Edition
Saturday, October 4, 1969

COMMANDER DEMORALIZES HELICOPTER COMPANY
By Richard Boyle

Long Binh, South Vietnam—Calling the pilots who daily risk their lives to save wounded GIs "scum" and "punks," a new honcho has demoralized one of the best dustoff companies in 'Nam.

The name-calling was just one of the accusations of over one dozen officers and enlisted men of the 45th Helicopter Ambulance Co at Long Binh against their CO, LTC XXXX. We are tired of being talked to like dirt and treated like dogs," said a warrant officer who has flown hundreds of mercy missions.

According to one WO, XXXX told pilots in front of three GIs, "punks, that's all they send over here." Another time it was charged, he said, "why don't some of you goddamn warrants clean up this place?"

XXXX admitted using the word "scum" in front of the men. Saying he used it "generally," XXXX sneered, "what would YOU call them?" Adding that many of the warrant officers use the latrine "to crap and then not flush it." XXXX continued, "if the one who made the allegation (of the word scum) is guilty, yes, I did say it and I did mean it." He didn't, however, recall saying "punks."

The light bird admitted saying to one warrant officer before an IG inspection "I may go down, but I'll take a damn bunch of you warrants with me." Explaining his statement, XXXX said, "as commanding officer, I am responsible for everything they do. Should I be relieved, it would be reflected in their efficiency reports."

Another warrant officer reported the colonel told him warrant officers are like seagulls, because they "squawk, eat and shit."

On other occasions, the men revealed, the colonel made statements such as, "warrant officers are supposed to be seen and not heard" and "warrant officers aren't supposed to think."

No Apology

XXXX fired back, saying, "I told them to do something and they stood me down. Stood toe-to-toe and told me (he emphasized the word me) where I had made a mistake." That's when he said they should be seen and not heard the colonel recalled.

XXXX strongly denied he has anything against warrant officers. One WO said he was once derided by the commanding officer because he didn't have a college education.

"When I leave here, I am leaving with an Army Commendation Medal or Legion of Merit," XXXX also reportedly told the same pilot.

Although the pilots object to the constant verbal abuse, "What really hurts," said one of the WOs, "Is the way he screws over the EM."

After one shakedown inspection, related a chopper crew chief, "my room was pilfered. My bags had been gone through and some personal things were gone."

Another Spec 5 said four prescription bottles given to him by a doctor were taken from his room. "The colonel thinks everybody is a dope addict," said the GI. Neither man was present during the searches.

After finding what he thought might be marijuana seeds behind a barrel, the colonel said he was concerned with the drug problem. "I don't know if it was grass but it sure as hell looked like it," he added. One way to fight the drug problem, he noted, was to keep the men busy. "Idle hands are the devil's workshop, you know."

Although they made repeated requests, several of the dustoff crewmen said, they couldn't get the supplies needed to treat their patients. Pointing out that they consider their patients first, one air medic stated, "I don't care where I get them (medical supplies) as long as I can get them."

One of the most badly needed items not available through regular supply channels were cutter sets, which the medics managed to scrounge. During one of XXXX's raids of the men's quarters all the cutter sets were confiscated. A cutter set is a device used in a blood transfusion.

No Equipment

"We still haven't got them back," said one Spec 5. "The last time we flew I felt we didn't have enough equipment." Another medic said a Vietnamese died on his chopper because "they took away my ambu bag [that] gives artificial respiration.

"What they had," XXXX answered, "was in violation of USARV regulations. Contraband misappropriation of property." Some of the contraband, XXXX stated, included "syringes, needles and penicillin."

One of the major reasons the men haven't been able to get the supplies, they said, is because the colonel hoards the equipment.

A senior NCO charged that stored equipment, never used, "was rotting." About "$10,000 has already gone down the drain," because the equipment no longer was usable, he noted.

The real reason XXXX seized the medical equipment, said the men, is that he has an obsession with neatness in their personal living quarters.

Taking this writer on a half hour inspection of the billets to point out what was wrong and right, XXXX appeared to favor the sterile, barracks like quarters to the more personally decorated and fixed up hootches.

Despite harassment from their CO, many warrants have tried to help their crewmen.

Once, when the warrants went to their CO to try to get club reefers, a sort of small refrigerator, for their men, XXXX snarled, according to one WO: "What do you want, the EM to live as good as you?" "After he said that," said the pilot, "my mind went blank....just what could I say?"

Speeding Ambulance

The case of WO Steve Vermillion, called by his fellow officers as one of the best pilots in 'Nam, once exceeded the 145 mph red line to get a dying GI back to a hospital. To set an example, XXXX punished the pilot by taking away his aircraft commander's orders for one month.

The other pilots said they sometimes broke rules, pushed the choppers almost to the breaking point, took unnecessary chances, went where no one would have faulted them for refusing just to save the lives of the men on the ground. Their colonel, said the pilots, is more concerned with impressing his superiors with a good maintenance record and spotless barracks than saving lives. After one mission, some said, they were chewed out because their chopper was muddy.

The final straw, pilots said, came when one of the air medics, groggy after flying 36 hours in two days and who suffered a leg wound was told by the CO, "You need a shave."

Reckless Stunt

"I raise cain about flight safety," chortled XXXX in defense of his punishment for Vermillion.

Yet, according to a copilot who flew with XXXX, the colonel pulled a needless stunt which might have killed 13 persons. Flying a med-evac chopper on one of his regular trips to the seacoast resort of Vung Tau with a bevy of attractive round-eyed nurses and brass, the colonel did a highly dangerous "autorotation" maneuver.

The move simulates a power failure procedure and should never be used for fun and games. Under the best of conditions, it is an extremely hairy maneuver, but with 13 persons aboard, point out veteran pilots, it is almost suicidal.

In his defense, the colonel said: "Autorotation is a perfectly safe maneuver." XXXX is also a stickler about allowing non-pilots to sit in the left seat of the chopper and has punished pilots for committing that error.

Yet at least seven members of his unit have stated they have seen him fly with his round eyed, red-haired girl friend to Cu Chi and other places where he let her sit in the left seat. "Just about every weekend he would fly her down there to spend the night and fly her back," said one witness.

Misuse of Choppers

Misuse of choppers that should be reserved for saving lives is one of the biggest gripes of the men of the 45th Bn. Recently, they said, XXXX took a chopper off the hot spot –the pad for emergencies-to taxi another colonel. XXXX, however, is proud of his taxi service saying: "Any time they want to go somewhere for business or pleasure, we are ready." Red Cross girls, nurses, majors, and colonels are given med-evac rides, he noted, because they would otherwise be forced to take the convoy to Saigon.

"There is always an aircraft to fly a nurse, but not enough for the missions," said one pilot.

The colonel may be winning points with the big brass, but his men are fed up.

"We are so damn nervous with all this petty "s—t," said a warrant officer who has just decided not to extend although he was considering it. "If you're mad, you can't do a good job and that is going to cost somebody's life."

Many said they tried to go to XXXX to discuss their problems, but he insulted them. XXXX, they added, has a blacklist and carries a personal vendetta against some of the men.

XXXX told one pilot who is married to an Army nurse in 'Nam, that he was going to make sure the warrant would not see his wife. His sin was missing one pilots' meeting. For weeks the pilot has been restricted to base, other jocks reported. "He wants nothing but yes men around," said a pilot. "If a man disagrees, he tries to ship him out to a unit where he is likely to get zapped."

One way XXXX gets back, they charge, is by forcing the troops to stand early formation, although many have been flying most of the night before.

Despite the statements of men who said they saw him fly with a girl in the left seat of his chopper, XXXX denied it. But he said the same couldn't be said for the former commander. Several times XXXX criticized the unit's former CO in front of the men.

Names of the pilots and enlisted men of the 45th are not used because they feared reprisals from their CO. A shroud of fear has settled over the base. The men interviewed came into a hootch, some one at a time, told their stories and quickly left. Each man was warned by one of the warrant officers of the risks they were taking, but still they talked.

Colonel Backs Him

Notified of the warrant officer and EM charges against XXXX, Col Douglas Lindsey, straight talking deputy commander of the 44th Med Brigade, said the chopper honcho "was wrong" if he called his men "scum" and "punks."

Lindsey launched an investigation into the complaints against the light bird, whose helicopter ambulance outfit comes under command of the medical brigade.

After looking into the matter, Lindsey said XXXX made a "rapid speed descent" but not in fact, an autorotation, as charged by the officer's copilot.

The copilot told *OW* he saw XXXX "roll the throttle off" and saw the aircraft go into "flight idle" which he said is a power-off autorotation. A veteran chopper jockey said a "rapid speed descent" probably was a "power-on autorotation" maneuver. Although it is somewhat safer than a power-off autorotation it still causes sometimes severe engine damage because it brings torque below minimum.

No Hanky-Panky

Lindsey backed his under fire subordinate on several counts, saying he doesn't believe there's any "hanky-panky" going on between brass and round-eyes. "The fact that these women are nurses doesn't mean there are fun and games going on," said the full bull.

He backed up XXXX's punishment of the warrant officer who exceeded the chopper speed limit to get a critically wounded GI back to a hospital. "The best thing for the patients," pointed out the brigade Number Two man, "is to stick to the speed limits."

Lindsey also said he doesn't believe there has been misuse of med-evac choppers by brass and nurses or that XXXX is more concerned with "impressing the brass" than saving lives.

Some of the pilots charge otherwise.

[The above article has been retyped verbatim in order to fit the format for this book. The commander's name is redacted (XXXX) so that his name is protected]

DEPARTMENT OF THE ARMY
Headquarters, 4th Battalion 12th Infantry
199th Infantry Brigade (Sep)(Lt)
APO San Francisco 96279

AVBHC-SC   31 December 1969

CW2 Steve Vermillion
45th Medical Company (AA)
APO San Francisco 96491

Dear Mr. Vermillion:

I would like to take this opportunity to extend to you my personal thanks and those of the officers and men of Company A for the "Dust Off" you performed north east of Dinh Quan on 28 December 1969. Company A had been in contact off and on for two days and had sustained one wounded who was DOA and one other wounded who died before you arrived on station.

The effect that a KIA has on the morale of a unit cannot be over stated. Moreover, it becomes even more critical if he cannot be extracted prior to darkness or if the unit has to carry him a great distance to a PZ. I'm sure that you understand this thoroughly or you would have not agreed to do the extraction.

I fully realize that this could have been detrimental to your career and you would have been completely within your rights to refuse. Had you chosen to do so I would not have blamed you. However, your actions speak highly of you as an individual and a soldier.

I hope that someday I'll have the opportunity to meet and thank you in person for your unselfish devotion to duty. You will forever have my gratitude and that of the officers and men of the 4th Battalion 12th Infantry.

With warm personal regards.

                                    Sincerely,
                                       /S/
                                    Robert H. Clark
                                    LTC, Infantry
                                    Commanding

-STATEMENT-

On or about 1530, 29 December 1969, my unit had been engaged with approximately a company sized enemy force dug in bunkers at YT 258998. During the days' contact, my company had taken 9 W.I.A. Two of the personnel were badly wounded, and, without immediate medical attention, were in danger of dying.

At about 1540 hours, Dustoff 40 came on station. At that time I explained to "40" that due to the man's condition, I felt that we were unable to pull him back any further; also that I had no gunship support to cover the dustoff. I also informed "40" that we were only 250 meters from the enemy forces and that they had machine guns and automatic rifles.

Dustoff 40, completely disregarding his own personal safety, came in without hesitation. He hovered above the tree tops and dropped the rigid litter. His aircraft, with no air support, was openly exposed to close enemy positions for over 15 minutes.

There is no doubt in my mind that without the actions of the dustoff, two of my men would have died. It must also be noted that on 5 different occasions, Dustoff 40 came to within 300 meters of heavily fortified positions to dustoff my personnel.

/S/
Michale L. Lanning
1LT   INF
Commanding

Consecutive Flying Days

Dates 1969	Days of Continual Flying	Hours
10/1	1	1.8
22	2	6
23	3	9.7
24	4	4.4
25	5	7.8
26	6	5.8
27	7	5.8
28	8	12.8
29	9	1.3
30	10	10.9
31	11	7.5
11/1	12	14.3
2	13	1.4
3	14	5
4	15	3.8
5	16	2.7
6	17	3.3
7	18	6.9
8	19	4.5
9	20	1.6
10	21	10.2
11	22	5.3
12	23	3.4
13	24	3.6
14	25	2.5
15	26	2.6
16	27	7.9
17	28	7.3
18	29	14.2
19	30	6.7
20	31	8.4
21	32	7.3
22	33	15.5
23	34	0.3
		212.5

REMF ROULETTE

Date	# of Days											
26-Oct	1	5.8										
27	2	5.8	5.8									
28	3	12.8	12.8	12.8								
29	4	1.3	1.3	1.3	1.3							
30	5	10.9	10.9	10.9	10.9	10.9						
31	6	7.5	7.5	7.5	7.5	7.5	7.5					
1-Nov	7	14.3	14.3	14.3	14.3	14.3	14.3	14.3				
2	8	1.4	1.4	1.4	1.4	1.4	1.4	1.4	1.4			
3	9	5.0	5.0	5.0	5.0	5.0	5.0	5.0	5.0	5.0		
4	10	3.8	3.8	3.8	3.8	3.8	3.8	3.8	3.8	3.8	3.8	
5	11	2.7	2.7	2.7	2.7	2.7	2.7	2.7	2.7	2.7	2.7	2.7
6	12	3.3	3.3	3.3	3.3	3.3	3.3	3.3	3.3	3.3	3.3	3.3
7	13	6.9	6.9	6.9	6.9	6.9	6.9	6.9	6.9	6.9	6.9	6.9
8	14	4.5	4.5	4.5	4.5	4.5	4.5	4.5	4.5	4.5	4.5	4.5
9	15	1.6	1.6	1.6	1.6	1.6	1.6	1.6	1.6	1.6	1.6	1.6
10	16	10.2	10.2	10.2	10.2	10.2	10.2	10.2	10.2	10.2	10.2	10.2
11	17	5.3	5.3	5.3	5.3	5.3	5.3	5.3	5.3	5.3	5.3	5.3
12	18	3.4	3.4	3.4	3.4	3.4	3.4	3.4	3.4	3.4	3.4	3.4
13	19	3.6	3.6	3.6	3.6	3.6	3.6	3.6	3.6	3.6	3.6	3.6
14	20	2.5	2.5	2.5	2.5	2.5	2.5	2.5	2.5	2.5	2.5	2.5
15	21	2.6	2.6	2.6	2.6	2.6	2.6	2.6	2.6	2.6	2.6	2.6
16	22	7.9	7.9	7.9	7.9	7.9	7.9	7.9	7.9	7.9	7.9	7.9
17	23	7.3	7.3	7.3	7.3	7.3	7.3	7.3	7.3	7.3	7.3	7.3
18	24	14.2	14.2	14.2	14.2	14.2	14.2	14.2	14.2	14.2	14.2	14.2
19	25	6.7	6.7	6.7	6.7	6.7	6.7	6.7	6.7	6.7	6.7	6.7
20	26	8.4	8.4	8.4	8.4	8.4	8.4	8.4	8.4	8.4	8.4	8.4
21	27	7.3	7.3	7.3	7.3	7.3	7.3	7.3	7.3	7.3	7.3	7.3
22	28	15.5	15.5	15.5	15.5	15.5	15.5	15.5	15.5	15.5	15.5	15.5
23	29	0.3	0.3	0.3	0.3	0.3	0.3	0.3	0.3	0.3	0.3	0.3
24	30	0.0	0.0	0.0	0.0	0.0	0.0	0.0	0.0	0.0	0.0	0.0
25	30	182.8	0.0	0.0	0.0	0.0	0.0	0.0	0.0	0.0	0.0	0.0
26	30		177.0	0.0	0.0	0.0	0.0	0.0	0.0	0.0	0.0	0.0
27	30			171.2	0.0	0.0	0.0	0.0	0.0	0.0	0.0	0.0
28	30				158.4	0.0	0.0	0.0	0.0	0.0	0.0	0.0
29	30					157.1	0.0	0.0	0.0	0.0	0.0	0.0
30	30						146.2	0.0	0.0	0.0	0.0	0.0
1-Dec	30							138.7	0.0	0.0	0.0	0.0
2	30								124.4	0.0	0.0	0.0
3	30									123.0	0.0	0.0
4	30										118.0	0.0
5	30											114.2

■ DAYS FLOWN
▒ DAYS GROUNDED
▓ AVAILABLE TO FLY

243

HOME OF LONG BINH DUST OFF

NO LZ TOO TIGHT

NO HOIST TOO DIFFICULT

IV FLT. PLT.
45ᵀᴴ MED. CO. (AA)

4th Platoon, 45th Med Co (AA) 1968

Back Row Left to Right: Mike Casper, CWO Randy Radigan, WO Gary Mock, Major Basil Smith, WO Jones, WO John Murray, SGT Buholtz, and SP5 Bob Richards

Kneeling Front Row Left to Right: Rick Blackwell, Drexel Johnson, Joe Vergara, Lewis, Russell, Helms, and Johnny Withrow

Not Shown: LT Dan Weaver, WO Marler, SP4 Tom Cash and SP5 Larry Kipp who were on field standby at Quan Loi

Three of DUSTOFF's Heroes

Major General Patrick Brady

CWO Mike Novosel

WO Louis Rocco

Note the Polished Cyclic and Collective Controls. The metal was magnesium and by using emery cloth and Brasso, the surface would appear to be chromed. This is the cockpit of the Iron Butterfly

Drexel Johson (Crewchief) and Bob Richards(Medic) with their helicopter at Tan An

The Author with Magnet Ass (No I didn't cause the damage)

Richard Dean with his helicopter-Iron Butterfly

Patient pickup at the 24th Evac in Long Binh

Long final approach to the 3rd Field Hospital in Saigon. The helipad is in the center of the triangular shaped field.

Helicopter sitting on the Number 1 "Hot Spot"

Visitng UH-1C Gunship from the Robin Hoods

Gunships taking off from Tan An after rearming and refueling

Author pointing out an exit point for a bullet that entered elsewhere in the helicopter

Kneeling left to right, Jake Bailado and Allan Morris
Standing left to right, the author and Bill Mostek

Chris Noel and Allan Morris at 3d Field Hospital in Saigon
One of the benefits of having the Saigon Field Standby duty

The photographs on this page and the following page are in mission sequence.
Smoke is Out marking the LZ

US Advisor standing and guiding our helicopter in. It is reasonable to think
the Landing Zone is secure

US Advisor working with his ARVN soldiers to load the wounded. Note how young this Advisor appears. And we thought we were the kids.

Dustoff Helicopter just touching down at the 93rd Evac in Long Binh

Bob Bixby in front of the entrance to the Tan An Dustoff Operations 'Bunker'

Helicopter named the Body Snatcher. As of this writing, we have been unable to identify the crew chief or medic for this helicopter

255

Mike Casper with his monkey Jo-Jo. Mike is on the left, Jo-Jo is on the right. Note the choice of drink for Jo-Jo.

John Murray on the left and Dan Weaver on the right taken at Lai Khe

Larry Kipp-Dustoff Medic

Tom Cash-Dustoff Crewchief

Mike Casper on the left, and Randy Radigan on the right.

The 45th Dustoff Heliport taken while airborne over our short active
runway.

CW2 Steve PLume--Tan An--1969

The Unsung Heroes--our POL Hot Refueling Guys at Long Binh.
They were always there--24 hours a day to refuel the helicopters.

An Air America C-7 Caribou at Tan An --1969

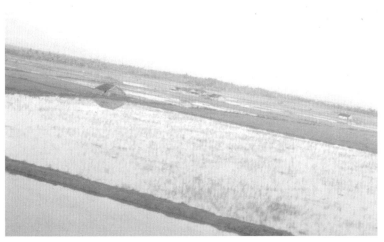

The "Delta" during the rainy season. Note the water in the rice paddys and the border of the paddy--the 'rice' dike. The thatched hut is the farmer's home.

Dong Tam--the home of the 9th Infantry Division Headquarters

Fire Support Base about 20 miles north-northeast of Long Binh

Personal Data

Birth Year: 1948
Enlistment Date: November 17, 1967
Age in Vietnam: 20 and 21 years

Flight School Class: 68-29, 1ˢᵗ WOC, Fort Wolters
Hunter AAF, GA: 68-17
Appointment Dates: WO November 4, 1968
                   Aviator November 5, 1968
Commissioned Date: May 17, 1970 from CW2 to 1LT.

Vietnam Tour Dates: January 7, 1969 to January 7, 1970
First / Last Flight in Country: January 15, 1969 and January 1, 1970

Hours Flown: 1127 Missions Flown: 1450
Patients Airlifted: 2210 Hoist Missions: 26

Pay and Allowances September 1969 as a WO1:
Basic Pay:	$ 378.90
Hazard Pay:	$ 65.00
Flight Pay:	$ 100.00
Subsistence:	$ 47.00
Total Monthly Salary:	$ 591.78
Annual Salary:	$7,101.36

Combat Awards: Silver Star, Distinguished Flying Cross, Air Medal 29 OLC, 1/V Device, Vietnam Service Medal (4), Vietnam Campaign Medal, and Vietnamese Cross of Gallantry w/Palm.

Non-Combat Awards: Legion of Merit, Meritorious Service Medal (2 OCL), Army Commendation Medal (5 OLC), Army Achievement Medal, Humanitarian Service Medal, Armed Forces Reserve Medal, Army Service Ribbon, Overseas Ribbon, National Defense Service Medal w/Bronze Star and Master Aviator Badge.

Retirement Date: June 30, 1993

Glossary

AC	Aircraft Commander
ADF	Automatic Direction Finder—navigation equipment
AGL	Above ground level
ARTY	Abbreviation for artillery
ARVN	Army of Republic of Viet Nam—South Vietnamese Soldier
Autorotation	Maneuver or capability of the helicopter to glide to a power off landing
B-52	USAF Heavy bomber. Strikes were called Arch Lights
Bean Bag Light	Landing zone light consisting of a 12" x 12" canvas bag with weights and a colored light.
"Charles"	Slang for Viet Cong. Chuck or Uncle Charlie.
Cherry	Taking fire for the first time. Loss of virginity.
Chicken Plate	Kevlar chest plate worn by helicopter crew members (body armor)
Collective	Flight control basically used to climb or descend
CWO	Chief Warrant Officer
Cyclic	Flight control located between the pilot's knees and changes the lateral flight path of the helicopter.
DEROS	Date that the soldier is scheduled to return from overseas
DME	Electronic equipment that measures distance of the aircraft's position away from the navigation aide.
ETA	Estimated time of arrival.
ETE	Estimated time enroute
Fire Fly	Generally a UH-1 equipped with a xeon search light mounted in the cargo door entrance used to illuminate ground target areas.
FM	Frequency modulated radio—primary air to ground unit radio communications.
FNG	Fucking New Guy—new arrival in country.
FSB	Fire Support Base
Green	All flight instruments in the correct operational range
Guard	Frequency 243.0 UHF and 121.5 VHF used for in flight emergencies
Gunships	Armed helicopters
Gun Target Line	Generally the line of fire from an artillery unit to the target
Hoist	Device to extract wounded soldiers from a site where no landing can be made.

Hot Fuel	Refueling the helicopter while it is still running
Hot Mike	Open mike over the helicopter's intercom system
IFR	Weather below visual flight minimums—flight by instruments only
ITO	Takeoff from the ground by using internal flight instruments only
JP4	Name for the jet fuel used for helicopter turbine engines—essentially a kerosene based fuel.
Knots	Measure of airspeed—nautical miles per hour.
Loach	Scout / observation helicopter. In Vietnam an OH-6 and later an OH-58
LZ	Landing zone where at least one helicopter can reach the ground with equipment or personnel.
Mayday	Radio call announcing that a flight crew is in trouble and may ultimately crash.
Main Rotor	Primary aerodynamic wing that rotates on a helicopter thereby providing lift and the ability to fly.
OV-10	Twin turboprop two passenger observation airplane used by Air Force and Marines primarily to control close air support missions.
Penetrator	Device attached to the hoist cable that wounded soldiers can ride to be extracted from the jungle.
Peter Pilot	Co-pilot
Pop Smoke	Means activate smoke grenade canister so the color could be identified and the location marked.
REMF	Rear Echelon Mother Fucker-someone who didn't participate in direct combat operations
RPG	Rocket Propelled Grenade
RTO	Radio Telephone Operator
Slick	Troop Transport helicopter—normally a UH-1
Spooky	Air Force cargo plane converted to a gunship—mini guns, cannons etc.
Strobe Light	Hand held light that flashes with a high intensity normally used to mark the landing zone
Tail rotor	Smaller rotor blade system located on the tail boom of the helicopter to provide yaw control.
Tits Up	Slang for meaning, broken, not operational
UHF	Ultra high radio frequency—air to air or air to ground communications
VHF	Very high radio frequency—air to air or air to ground communications
VFR	Means the height of the clouds are at least 1000 feet above the ground and the horizontal visibility is 3 miles or greater.

Bibliography

Allenbaugh, Eric *Deliberate Success.* New Jersey: Career Press, 2002

Allenbaugh, Eric *Wake-Up Calls.* New York: Simon & Schuster, 1994

Burkett, B.G. & Whitley, Glenna *Stolen Valor.* Texas: Verity Press, Inc., 1998

Cook, John L. *Rescue Under Fire. The Story of Dust Off in Vietnam.* Pennsylvania: Schiffer Military/Aviation History, 1998

Covey, Stephen R. *The 7 Habits of Highly Effective People.* New York: Simon & Schuster, 1989

Dorland, Peter and Nanney, James. *Dustoff: Army Aeromedical Evacuation in Vietnam.* Washington, D.C. Center of Military History United States Army, 1982

Frieberg, Kevin & Jackie *Nuts!* New York: Broadway Books, 1998

Glasser, Ronald J. M.D., *365 Days.* New York: George Braziller, Inc., 1991

Hardaway, Robert M. *Care of the Wounded in Vietnam.* Kansas, Sunflower University Press, 1998

Hendrix, John-Michael *To Have and To Hold.* Washington: WinePress Publishing, 1998

Holley, Charles. *Aero Scouts.* New York: Pocket Books, 1992

Jorgenson, Kregg P.J. *Acceptable Loss.* New York: Ivy Books, 1991

Kelly, Michael P. *Where We Were in Vietnam.* Oregon: Hellgate Press, 2002

Mills, Hugh L. Jr. *Low Level Hell.* New York: Dell Publishing, 1992

Novosel, Michael J. *Dustoff: the Memoir of an Army Aviator.* California: Presidio Press, 1999

Westering, Frosty *Make the Big Time Where You Are!* Washington: Big Five Productions, 1990

Westover, John G. *Combat Support in Korea.* Washington D.C. Center of Military History, United States Army, 1990

Other Media Sources
History Channel, *Suicide Missions, Vol 4. Combat Medics.* A&E, 1998
45th Medical Company (AA) 3d Quarter Newsletter 1969

Griffith, Paddy. *Reevaluating the Role of Dustoff* Leesburg: Vietnam, June 2001

1st Battalion, 28th Infantry Daily Logs from FSB Oran, Feb 1-4, 1969, Declassified 7/24/01

IV Corps Advisory Group Directive 40-1, Medical Service Aeromedical Evacuation, October 9, 1967

Neel, Spurgeon. MG (MD). March 1974 Aviation Digest, , Fort Rucker, Alabama, Page 6

Simmons, Si web page at: http://psysim.www7.50megs.com/html/dustoff.htm 2002

Vermillion, Steven D. Captain 1972. Aviation Digest, Fort Rucker, Alabama, page 2.

Wilson, Wayne March 21, 2002, DFC Society Presentation, Boeing Museum of Flight, Seattle, WA

Endnotes

Chapter 1

[1] Video, Suicide Missions, Vol 4: Combat Medics (P-1-C55E16) History Channel, 1998 A&E

[2] John Dennison's website: http:// www.1stcavmedic.com/medic_history.htm

[3] Video, Suicide Missions, Vol 4: Combat Medics (P-1-C55E16) History Channel, 1998 A&E

[4] Ibid

[5] John G. Westover, 1990. Combat Support in Korea, p 111. CMH Publication 22-1, Center of Military History, United States Army, Washington, D.C. Viewable on the web at: http:// www.army.mil/cmh-pg/book/korea/22-1-5.htm

[6] Ibid. p 112

[7] Peter G. Dorland and James S. Nanney, 1982. Dust Off: Army Aeromedical Evacuation in Vietnam. Center of Military History United States Army Washington, DC, 1982, page 24. Viewable on the web at: http://www.ehistory.com/vietnam/books/dustoff/index.cfm

[8] Ibid, page 25

[9] Ibid, page 25

[10] Ibid, page 27

[11] Ibid, page 28

[12] John L. Cook, 1998. Rescue Under Fire: The Story of Dust Off in Vietnam, Schiffer Military / Aviation History, Atglen, Pennsylvania, page 53

[13] Ibid, page 54

[14] Ibid, page 70

[15] Op. Cit. Dorland and Nanney, page.40

[16] Op. Cit. Cook, page 71

[17] Personal communication from Armond "Si" Simmons December 2002

[18] Wayne Wilson, March 21, 2002, DFC Society Presentation, Boeing Museum of Flight, Seattle, WA

[19] Op. Cit., Cook, page 65

[20] Op. Cit., Cook, page 69

[21] Op. Cit., Dorland and Nanney, page 55

[22] Loc. Cit

[23] Jim Truscott, email message, dated July 9, 2002

[24] Op., Cit., Dorland and Nanney, page 121

[25] Loc. Cit

[26] Steve Huntley, personal communication dated October 17, 2002

Chapter 2

[1] John L.Cook, 1998. Rescue Under Fire: The Story of Dust Off in Vietnam, Schiffer Military/Aviation History, Atglen, Pennsylvania.

[2] Peter G. Dorland and James S. Nanney, 1982. Dust Off: Army Aeromedical Evacuation in Vietnam. Center of Military History United States Army Washington, D.C., 1982 Viewable on the web at: http://www.ehistory.com/vietnam/books/dustoff/index.cfm

[3] Ibid, pages 29 and 30
[4] Op., Cit., Cook, pages 44 and 45
[5] Si Simmons web page at: http://psysim.www7.50megs.com/html/dustoff.htm

Chapter 3
[1] John L.Cook, 1998. Rescue Under Fire: The Story of Dust Off in Vietnam, Schiffer Military/Aviation History, Atglen, Pennsylvania.
[2] Ibid., Cook pages 90 and 91
[3] Peter G. Dorland and James S. Nanney, 1982. Dust Off: Army Aeromedical Evacuation in Vietnam. Center of Military History United States Army Washington, D.C., 1982 pages 75,76 and 77. Viewable on the web at: http://www.ehistory.com/vietnam/books/dustoff/index.cfm

Chapter 4, 5 None

Chapter 6
[1] John L.Cook, 1998. Rescue Under Fire: The Story of Dust Off in Vietnam, Schiffer Military/Aviation History, Atglen, Pennsylvania. page 69
[2] Stephen R. Covey, Four Roles of Leadership-Class Guide, Pages 8 and 9
[3] Op., Cit., Cook, page 36
[4] Op., Cit., Covey, page 9
[5] Ibid, Page 10
[6] Op., Cit., Cook, Page 54
[7] 45th Medical Company (AA) Newsletter-3d Quarter 1969 (Author's Personal copy)
[8] Overseas Weekly, October 4, 1969—see Appendix
[9] Overseas Weekly, October 4, 1969
[10] Michael P. Kelley, 2002. Where Were We in Vietnam, Hellgate Press, Central Point, Oregon page F-67

Chapter 7
[1] Department of the Army (DA) Form 759-1 [
[2] John L. Cook, 1998, Rescue Under Fire: The Story of Dust Off in Vietnam, Schiffer Military / Aviation History, Atglen, Pennsylvania. page 104
[3] Ibid
[4] Ibid

Chapter 8
[1] DA Form 759-1, October/November 1969

Chapter 9
[1] Stephen R. Covey, 1989. The 7 Habits of Highly Effective People, Simon and Schuster, New York, New York.
[2] Ibid, page 35
[3] Ibid, page 35
[4] US Army Regulation 670-1
[5] Kevin and Jackie Frieberg,1998. NUTS! Broadway Books, New York, New York. page 283

Chapter 10
[1] Michael P. Kelley, 2002. Where Were We in Vietnam, Hellgate Press, Central Point, Oregon, page 378
[2] Duty Logs from FSB Oran, February 1-4, Declassified
[3] DA Form 759-1 for February 1969
[4] Op. Cit

Chapter 11
[1] DA Form 759 dated November 1968

Chapter 12, 13, 14, None

Chapter 15
[1] General Orders 1083
[2] After Action Statement written in 1969
[3] DA Form 759-1, October 28, 1969

Chapter 16
[1] Captain Steven D. Vermillion, 1972. Aviation Digest, Fort Rucker, Alabama, page 2.
[2] Michael P. Kelley, 2002. Where Were We in Vietnam, Hellgate Press, Central Point, Oregon, page 5-367

Chapter 17
[1] After Action report submitted by the ground unit commander
[2] Aircraft Commander's non-submitted after action report.

Chapter 18, 19 None

Chapter 20
[1] See Appendix-Officer Efficiency Report for further explanation.
[2] Field standby locations included Quan Loi, Dau Tieng, Xuan Loc, Tan An and Saigon.

Chapter 21, 22 and 23 None

Chapter 24

[1] Peter G. Dorland and James S. Nanney, 1982. Dust Off: Army Aeromedical Evacuation in Vietnam. Center of Military History United States Army Washington, DC. pages 116 and 117

[2] Loc Cit

Chapter 25 and 26 None

INDEX

D

E

F

G

H

O

OH-13 5, 6
OH-23 5, 6, 29
Oran, Fire Support Base 71, 72, 73, 74, 75, 76, 77, 78, 79
Overseas Weekly 46, 48, 57

P

Paddy Control 83
Paris Approach Control 83, 84
Patton, George S. 16, 152
Penetrator, Jungle 95, 97, 105, 106, 110, 111, 112, 113, 120, 121, 122, 123, 125, 187
Pilot Rock 27
Plume, Steve 44, 50, 53, 66, 71, 74, 76, 77, 173, 174, 188
Poole, Otha 95, 157
Price, Arlie 14, 43

Q

QSY 107

R

Radigan, Randy 41
Rangers 139, 140, 141, 142, 143, 144, 145, 146, 147
Rebel 51 75
Rebel 61 75
Reese, Pee Wee 190, 191
REMF 57, 59, 178, 179, 187, 192, 194, 197, 199, 205
Rocket Propelled Grenade 95, 96, 119
Roler, Warren 14

S

Schwarzkopf, Norman 39
Scout Dogs 171, 172
Sidewinder 118, 119
Simmons, Si 12, 18
Smith, Basil 40, 41, 165, 166
SOI 18
Southwest Airlines 64
Spencer, Lloyd 10, 16, 17, 18, 19
Spitzer, Rob 118, 119, 120, 121, 122, 123, 124, 138, 143
Spooky 75, 133, 134, 149
Stilwell, Brigadier General 9, 12, 13
Stogey 139, 140, 141, 142, 143,
Surfer's Paradise 61
Syrus, Publilius 32

Closing Comments

Looks like we have both reached the end point of this book. I hope that you enjoyed reading what I have written as much as I enjoyed presenting the stories. A side benefit of this project was being able to reconnect with people that I have not seen or heard from in over 30 years. My draft stories were shared in their early stages with various crew members. Ironically, guys like Mike Casper were able to put names and faces into a couple of the stories—since he was one of the "Guys in the Back" on those particular missions. Mike, Larry, Richard and "Willie" helped ground truth the stories.

This book is divided into five sections. Each section represents one of the five officer ranks that I held. The military ranks align by pay grade. Therefore the first section with a Second Lieutenant bar is a pay grade 0-1 and is accompanied by a Warrant Officer 1 bar indicating a pay grade of W-1. Besides time as a private and specialist fifth class (rank assigned as a Warrant Officer Candidate), I held the rank of WO1, CW2, 1LT, CPT, MAJ and LTC (pay grade 0-5). The twenty six chapters coincide with the number of years I served on active military duty.

If you would like to send your thoughts and or comments about what I have written, I would enjoy reading your feedback. My email addresses are: wearetsunami@msn.com and dustoff40@msn.com. Or you can reach me through Wild 'N Woolly Publishing--their address is shown on the copyright page.

Cherish life on earth and live it to the fullest possible extent! And remember to properly care for your horse!

Give the Gift of "DUSTOFF"

to a
Friend, Colleague, Fellow Veteran or to a Library

☐ YES, I want _____copies of DUSTOFF at $24.95 per copy plus $5.00 for postage.

☐ YES, I would like to have Steve speak or give a seminar to my company, association, school, or organization. Please send me information.

☐ A cockpit voice recording of the actual hoist mission from Chapter 13 is available on CD for $7.00

☐ A 45th Medical Company (AA) jacket combat patch is also available for $7.00

Residents living in the State of Washington need to include 8.8% sales tax.

Name:_____

Organization_____

Address_____

City/State/Zip_____

Phone_____Email_____

Please make your check payable and mail to:
Wild 'N Woolly Publishing
PO Box 731452
Puyallup, Washington 98373

www.dustoff40.com   Call (253) 906-2938